CHOTA NAGPORE

CHOTA NAGPORE

A LITTLE-KNOWN PROVINCE OF THE EMPIRE

BY

F. B. BRADLEY-BIRT, I.C.S., F.R.G.S.

AUTHOR OF
'THF STORY OF AN INDIAN UPLAND' 'THE ROMANCE OF AN EASTERN CAPITAL' 'THROUGH PERSIA FROM THE GOLF TO THE CASPIAN' FTC.

WITH AN INTRODUCTION
BY THE
RIGHT HON. THE EARL OF NORTHBROOK, G.C.S.I.

SOMETIME VICEROY OF INDIA

ISBN: 978-93-5128-975-3(HB)

First Published in 1910
Indian Reprint in 2017

Published by

Kalpaz Publications
C-30, Satyawati Nagar,
Delhi – 110052
E-mail: kalpaz@hotmail.com
Website: kalpazpublications.com
Ph.: +91-9212142040

TO

SIR WILLIAM WILSON HUNTER

IN GRATEFUL MEMORY

PREFACE

TO

SECOND EDITION

The many changes that have taken place in Chota Nagpore during the last seven years have necessitated considerable alterations in revising and bringing the first edition up to date. The railway now runs direct to Ranchi, bringing many changes in its wake, not only to the town itself, which seven years ago was seventy-five miles away from a railway station, but to all the surrounding district, while yet other schemes for the further extension of the line are afoot. The Gobindpur Sub-division has not been lost to Chota Nagpore, the orders for its transfer from the Province having been cancelled, though its headquarters have since been moved to Dhanbaid, and it is now known as the Dhanbaid Sub-division. Apart from the necessary alterations that these changes have entailed, many additions have been made to the book which it is hoped will add to its interest and completeness.

Owing to a mistake, the dedication was

omitted from the first edition. The second edition gives me the opportunity of inscribing it to the memory of one whom I shall always regard with gratitude as my first guide into the fascinating realm of 'Indian Affairs.'

MAGISTRATE'S HOUSE, KHULNA, BENGAL,
August 27, 1910.

PREFACE

TO

FIRST EDITION

THESE pages, written during a two-and-a-half years' residence among the scenes and peoples described, attempt to give nothing more than a glimpse of Chota Nagpore, which, with its varied interests and numerous races, might well form the study of a lifetime. The only object of these lines as preface is to enable me to offer my sincere thanks to all those who have given me their help. I am indebted to so many friends that it is impossible to mention them all by name here, but they will know that I am none the less grateful for their valued assistance.

GOBINDPUR, MANBHUM, CHOTA NAGPORE,
March 3, 1903.

INTRODUCTION

I COMPLY very willingly with the request of Mr. Bradley-Birt that I should write a few lines of introduction to his 'Chota Nagpore.' Independently of the literary merits of the work and the interest of the subject, the description he has given of an outlying part of Bengal will serve the useful purpose of putting picturesquely forward the contrasts which form a striking feature of our Indian Empire.

Those who know India well do not need to be told that, whatever progress education may have made among certain classes, the masses of the people remain much the same century after century. This, however, is hardly sufficiently appreciated at home, and so the difficulties of Indian administration are often underrated. Everyone who reads Mr. Bradley-Birt's graphic account of the tribes of Chota Nagpore, together with his amusing description of the 'crowning of a Raja,' and compares them with the chapter on the extension of the coal-fields, will have the contrast between primitive customs and Western civilisation exhibited to him in a shape which he is not likely to forget.

Mr. Bradley-Birt mentions that I was the only Viceroy who had an opportunity of visiting Ranchi. He has reminded me of a very pleasant episode of my life in India. It occurred in 1874, when the Government of India were kept at Calcutta during the hot weather for the purpose of assisting the Lieutenant-Governor of Bengal in grappling with a severe famine in Behar. At that time no Famine Code, which was of so much use to Lord Curzon in his successful treatment of the far more extensive famine of two years ago, existed, and every detail had to be worked out—a heavy task upon us all. In October, when all business was at a standstill in consequence of the Hindu holidays, I went for a short time to Hazaribagh as a welcome change from the moist heat of Calcutta, and took the opportunity of making a trip to Ranchi. I travelled much in the same style as has been described by Mr. Bradley-Birt, crossing the hills in a *palki*, the bearers crooning all night long their '*Hay, Tookum, Tookum—Tookum—Tookum, Tookum, Tookum, Hay.*' The villagers turned out as I passed, in the fashion of the country, with flags, drums, and dancing.

All I saw convinced me of the merits of the Commissioner, Colonel Dalton, and of his popularity. He and Sir Henry Ramsay in Kumaon were two of the few remaining soldier-civilians who performed such remarkable services as Indian administrators ; and these outlying districts give, perhaps, a stronger impression than the better-known Provinces of the benefits derived from British rule by the people of India.

The rainy season prevented me from seeing as much of the country as I wished, but one recollection remains fresh in my mind. I visited at Ranchi two large churches, in which the native Christians from the neighbourhood were accustomed to collect upon the great festivals of the year. One was built by the Society for the Propagation of the Gospel, the other by a German Lutheran Mission, both societies having excellent schools ; and I was delighted to find that the two bodies worked together with the greatest cordiality. I trust that this continues to the present day. The aboriginal tribes of India afford a promising field for missions, for among them converts to Christianity are not looked down upon : it must not be supposed that the work of these missions is superficial, I saw at the German college natives of the country preparing for the ministry who could read the New Testament in Greek, and sketch out the heads of a sermon from a given text with considerable success.

Mr. Bradley-Birt's volume suggests many topics upon which I am tempted to write, but I am very sensitive that, seven and twenty years having passed since I left India, my opinions must be somewhat obsolete; and I leave the volume to speak for itself, with my hearty recommendation to everyone who feels an interest in India.

NORTHBROOK.

May 1903.

CONTENTS

CHAPTER		PAGE
I.	SOME LEGENDS AND A LITTLE HISTORY	1
II.	MANY RACES AND SOME QUAINT CUSTOMS	26
III.	OLD CHUTIA NAGPUR	57
IV.	THE LAND OF THE HOS	84
V.	LIFE IN A SANTAL VILLAGE	113
VI.	THE SACRED HILL OF PARASNATH	138
VII.	THE GATEWAY OF CHOTA NAGPORE	159
VIII.	PALAMAU	205
IX.	A TRAMP ON THE GRAND TRUNK ROAD	229
X.	THE GARDEN OF A THOUSAND TREES	253
XI.	SOME MEMORIES OF THE MUTINY	272
XII.	THE CROWNING OF A RAJA	297
APPENDIX		321
INDEX		323

ILLUSTRATIONS

A PRIEST ABOUT TO SACRIFICE . . . *Frontispiece*

A MUNDA YOUTH . . . . *To face p.* 13

A GHASI FROM BARABHUM (MANBHUM) . . „ 14

THE SUBARNAREKHA RIVER, SINGBHUM. . „ 26

A GROUP OF MUNDAS . . . . „ 37

A GROUP OF MUNDA CHILDREN . . . . . „ 40

AN UMBRELLA CONSTRUCTED SOLELY OF LEAVES . . . . „ 45

RANCHI KHERRIAS . . . . „ 48

HOOK SWINGING AT THE CHURUK PUJA . „ 54

CHUTIA TEMPLE . . . . „ 57

THE TEMPLE OF JAGANNATH, NEAR RANCHI . „ 66

SMALL TEMPLE AT THE FOOT OF JAGANNATH „ 68

SOME FOLLOWERS OF THE PROPHET BIRSA BEING ESCORTED TO JAIL BY THE POLICE „ 78

A HO FAMILY (THREE GENERATIONS) . . „ 84

THE MAIN STREET, CHAIBASA . . . . . . „ 96

A SNAKE-CHARMER AT THE 'MELA' . . . „ 99

HO MEMORIAL STONES . . . . „ 104

THE HO METHOD OF SNARING A TIGER . „ 108

THE MANJHI THAN . . . . „ 118

GIRLS AND MUSICIANS AT A SANTAL DANCE . „ 130

SANTAL WOMEN CARRYING PITCHERS FROM THE WELL . . . . *To face p.* 137
A DOOLI . . . . „ 140
A MANBHUM KHERRIA GIRL . . . . . . „ 160
THE SAHEB BANDH, PURULIA . . . . . „ 170
WOMEN ON THEIR WAY TO ASSAM TEA GARDENS . . . . „ 175
A REPRESENTATION OF VISVA KARMA, THE HINDU VULCAN . . . . „ 179
GROUP OF COOLIES' CHILDREN . . . . . „ 190
GLIMPSE OF THE JHERRIA COAL-FIELDS . „ 190
A GROUP OF LOCAL RAJAS IN THE GOBINPUR SUB-DIVISION . . . . „ 202
A BARBER AT WORK BY THE WAYSIDE . . „ 233
THE POTTER'S WHEEL . . . . „ 233
A TEMPLE AT PANDRA . . . . „ 236
TRAVELLING ON THE GRAND TRUNK ROAD. RIDING A NATIVE TAT (PONY) . . . . „ 240
TRAVELLING ON THE GRAND TRUNK ROAD ON FOOT . . . . „ 248
PRISONERS AT WORK BEATING OUT ALOE FIBRE . . . . „ 259
A BANGHI-WALA . . . . „ 266
A SUGAR MILL . . . . „ 268
A GROUP OF TEMPLES AT ICHAK . . . „ 270
THE PRESENT RAJA OF SERAIKELA . . „ 289
THE THAKUR BARI, WHERE THE FAMILY GOD RESIDES . . . . „ 299
TWO OF THE RAJA'S GUESTS . . . . . „ 308
THE CROWNING OF A RAJA . . . . . . „ 318

MAP OF CHOTA NAGPORE . . . . *At end*

CHOTA NAGPORE:

A LITTLE-KNOWN PROVINCE OF THE EMPIRE

CHAPTER I

SOME LEGENDS AND A LITTLE HISTORY

CHOTA NAGPORE is one of the out-of-the-way places of India. The globe-trotter, busy on the beaten track, goes home again probably in ignorance of its very existence, or with but a hazy notion of having heard the name. It lies right between the two great highways of steel that join Calcutta and Bombay, but left untouched by either, the whole central plateau of Chota Nagpore proper was without a single line of rail until four years ago. It has never become famous or forced itself into history, and, holding out no gaudy advertisement to attract the passer-by, it escapes, in the land of great sights and historic memories, the notice that it well deserves.

Yet, to those who know it, Chota Nagpore has a charm all its own. Right away in the south-west corner of Bengal, bordering the Central

Provinces, it is totally distinct from the Presidency to which it belongs. Bengal is the land of the plains: Chota Nagpore is one long undulating sweep of hills throughout. Its centre is a vast plateau, averaging something like two thousand feet in height, and descending in its outlying districts to the plains below, with ridges running out here and there beyond its borders into Bengal itself. There are hills everywhere, grouped in range after range or rising abruptly a thousand feet and more out of the surrounding level, thrown up like watch-towers over the land. Many of them present a formation curious and fantastic, rocks lying piled one upon another in apparently endless confusion or towering on the summits of the hills, precipitous and inaccessible, forming weird and irregular outlines. All are covered more or less with thick tree jungle, showing bare patches of black rock beneath, while on the lower and more undulating slopes grow vast tree forests that stretch over the land for miles around.

The whole forms one of the most charming series of views imaginable. The far-off hills in the background, in exquisite tints of blue or purple as the light falls; the nearer hills picturesquely shaped and luxuriant in every shade of green, with their bold escarpments in black or grey; and the plains below furnishing their quota of colour in the tender green of the early rice, the brilliant yellow of the *sirguja*, or the gold of the fields at harvest,—present a panorama of perfect charm and beauty.

One of its chief attractions is its almost endless variety. Here a hill tract of jungle, wild as if never trodden by the foot of man, makes a striking contrast to a smiling stretch of cultivation, where the rich red soil bears evidence of the tender care of many generations. Close by a picturesque bit reminds one strangely of far-off Dartmoor, where some tiny stream runs over the rocky channel it has made and the branching trees meet overhead, while just beyond the familiar bullock-cart or *sagar*, laden with bamboos, is winding its way along the rough uneven track between the palms that leads to the mud-built village—a picture that could be nothing else but Indian. Far away from the stir of life, in the absolute seclusion of the Tundi jungle, it is hard to imagine that less than twenty miles away lies the Jherria coal-field with its ceaseless activity and many enterprises, while Parasnath, the home of the gods, with its stream of wealthy pilgrims from the busiest cities of India and its multitude of glittering temples, furnishes a scarcely less striking contrast to the mud-built Santal villages beneath its shadow, whose gods, invisible and vague, need no shelter but the sacred grove.

Save only in the mining districts, and on the outskirts of the province along the lines of rail, the primitiveness that forms not the least of the charms of Chota Nagpore is still undisturbed. It is about as near as one can get to-day to the real India, and little or nothing has changed in the daily round of existence since the multitude of races that peopled it first settled here centuries ago. Custom handed down through countless generations has prescribed the manner of their lives, and greater contact with the outside world has not yet been of sufficient duration to counteract the influence of ages and work a radical change. With them, still, tradition is everything, giving them their only grasp and knowledge of life.

But a great change, that has little affected the rigid customs and habits of the people, has been steadily at work in the conditions of Chota Nagpore itself. A hundred years ago it was an unknown land, covered with vast impenetrable jungles where no white man had ever been, and only exaggerated rumours told of the wild and lawless tribes that peopled it, their jealousy of outside interference, and their determination to defend to the uttermost the country they had made their own. Rough tracks through the forest served as roads, and the jungles, filled with game and fruit, provided subsistence for a people who demanded little of life and avoided the necessity of all but the scantiest cultivation. Men strove only to become great warriors and mighty hunters in those days, and the women were content with the one ambition of the women of their race—to become the mothers of sons strong and skilful with the bow.

Then quickly, with the extension of British influence, there came a change. The Grand Trunk Road, with startling rapidity to the native mind, cut its way through the jungles of Manbhum and Hazaribagh, opening out the wildest district to the civilising influence of trade and commerce. So dense was the jungle through which it passed that at first the traveller went with his life in his hand. Tigers carried off men and cattle in broad daylight, and rendered some of the halting stages so unsafe at night that they had to be removed to more open spaces further on along the road. Dacoities, too, were an every-day occurrence, and deeds of robbery and violence went undetected and unpunished. But nothing availed to stop the flow of traffic that poured down the newly opened road, connecting Calcutta with the great cities of the north. Stimulated by the improved means of communication, large annual fairs were started in the various centres of Chota Nagpore, and traders from all quarters of Northern India penetrated into this new and hitherto unopened mart. The keen-eyed Hindu merchants from the north were quick to gauge the simple character of the primitive peoples in possession. Here was a land that lay at their feet, and a steady influx of foreigners began.

Ingratiating themselves with the semi-Hinduised local chiefs, they secured large grants of the coveted soil, ousting the aborigines from the holdings they had so long possessed. But the newcomers had underrated the risk. The Kols and Oraons they so much despised were dangerous foes when pushed too far. Outrivalled in craft and cunning, they were irresistible when once the arrows of war, like the fiery cross, had passed among them, rousing the whole country-side to arms. Fire and sword struck terror into the hearts of zemindars and interlopers, and taught the British Government that special cases need special laws, and that a backward people at the mercy of unscrupulous adventurers called for timely assistance and protection. The exactions of the foreigners ceased, and those who remained settled down peaceably beside the earlier possessors of the soil, while Chota Nagpore became and has since remained a non-regulation province of Bengal.

But the greatest change of all has come within the last fifty years. The enormous strides that civilisation made everywhere during the latter half of the nineteenth century could not fail to affect Chota Nagpore, just opened, as it was, to outside influence. Railways spreading like a network over the face of India quickly robbed the Grand Trunk Road of its importance. The crowd of traders with their caravans that thronged it from end to end in the days of its prosperity disappeared as if by magic, deserting it with only a passing wonder at the marvellous speed of the iron horse.

Entering Chota Nagpore on three different sides, the railway has slowly crept towards the central plateau, eventually to bring the same change over the face of Old Chutia Nagpur as over the outlying districts where it has already worked its way. Vast stretches of jungle have disappeared, swept clean off the surface of the land or represented only by a puny growth of saplings that will take a century to rival the magnificent trees that were there before them. Timber gained a sudden market value with the coming of the railway; and the clearings in the forest provided new lands for the more extensive cultivation that the increase in the population necessitated, mile after mile of paddy-fields now appearing where once the country was impenetrable with its thick undergrowth and mighty trees.

The big game, for which the land was famous, startled at the noise of the pick and the shriek of the engine, have fled from their old haunts or fallen a prey to the *shikaris* of all sorts who poured into Chota Nagpore as it grew more accessible. The tiger has long since ceased to molest the few travellers that still frequent the Grand Trunk Road, and even the bears that swarmed in the dense shrub jungle have grown more wary and retreated into the deeper seclusion of the caves on the rocky slopes of the hills. The days of the old annual fairs are over, their *raison d'être* gone now that the railway deposits daily at their gates all the supplies that the people can desire. Dacoities have grown rarer with the strengthening of authority and the disappearance of the jungle, and the old fighting days have passed never to return. The long arm of the British law reaches everywhere, even to the smallest village in the most remote recesses of the jungle, and the people go in fear and awe of this all-knowing power that not the smallest incident escapes. Yet only to a certain point and no further does the law go. On the inner lives of the people it has wrought no change. Careful to observe the most minute customs and prejudices of the conquered race, the law has left each man free to go his way, so long only as he does not molest his neighbour or transgress the fundamental principles of British right and justice. Where necessary it speaks with no uncertain voice, but never descending to vexatious interference or petty restrictions, it has laid thereby the foundations of the greatness and power of British rule. The daily round of native thought and action has gone on untouched, and the festivals, the worship, the marrying and giving in marriage, and every inner detail of domestic life, have never lost the continuity of many centuries of custom and tradition.

All that concerns the beginning of these aboriginal tribes is shrouded in doubt and uncertainty. Chota Nagpore is a land without a written history, and records are few of all that occurred more than a hundred years ago. Legends only have passed down from generation to generation, gathering additions as they went, and obvious fables have been invented to account for the causes of those things that baffle the limited native intelligence and defy authentic explanation. It is a land of mystery, witchcraft, and spirits, mostly evil and malign, that cause the ignorant, shrinking native to pass his whole life in fear and dread and unceasing attempts at propitiation.

Each race has its own story of its origin, most of them mixed up with the doings of the gods of their mythology. The Nagbansis, of whom the Maharaja of Chota Nagpore is the head, tell a typical fable of the founder of their race. They take their name, so runs the legend, from Pundarika Nag, the great serpent who transformed himself into human shape and married Parvati, the daughter of a Brahmin at Benares. The wedded happiness of this couple was complete, save for one thing. Pundarika was human to look upon, except for the double tongue which he had been unable to shake off with the rest of the serpent form, and one day, in spite of his efforts to conceal it, his wife discovered the defect, and, with true wifely curiosity, wanted to know the reason of the strange phenomenon. Pundarika, fearing to sink in her estimation if the truth were known, took her on a pilgrimage to the great temple of Jagannath at Puri to divert her thoughts. But on returning through Chota Nagpore, then known as Jharkhand, the Forest Tract, Parvati's inquisitiveness was to be put off no longer and forced the truth from Pundarika. The latter was so overcome with shame after he had told her, that he jumped into a pool of water close by and disappeared from sight, never to return in human form. Parvati was inconsolable at his loss, and leaving her newborn child, sacrificed herself in a paroxysm of grief on the funeral pyre.

The unfortunate infant, thus deserted, was not long left alone. A Brahmin, passing by, carrying his idol, the image of the Sun, and stopping to drink at the pool in which Pundarika had disappeared, saw the child lying on the bank with a great hooded snake on guard over it. About to run away in fear, the Brahmin stooped to pick up his idol, but found that he could not lift it. As he struggled to move it, the snake spoke. It was Pundarika, returned to his original form to watch over his deserted offspring. Relating his history to the Brahmin, he confided to him the care of the child. He prophesied that the infant would one day become the Raja of the country where they then were, and further directed that he should be always known as the 'Snake-crowned.' From this child the Nagbansi family claim descent, and it is said that, in commemoration of their mythological ancestry, its members still wear their turbans so wound round their heads as to present the appearance of a serpent with the head protruding in front. The crest of the family is a cobra with a human face under its expanded hood. The serpent in the legend, of course, represents the Devil, and to be able to claim relationship with him is considered 'a very ancient and honourable connection.'

Later on in their history, the Nagbansi Rajas fell under the long arm of the Musulman Emperors, and in the annals of their conquerors appear the first authentic accounts concerning them. Kokrah, as Chota Nagpore seems to have been called in their time, excited the cupidity of the Emperors by reason of the report of the diamonds to be found in its rivers. Stones of the value of a lakh of rupees (100,000 rupees) are said to have been found there; and when Ibrahim Khan, the Governor of Behar and younger brother of the famous Empress Nur Jahan, had subdued Durgan Sal, the forty-fifth Maharaja, in 1616 A.D., eighty-four crores of rupees' worth of jewels were refused for his ransom. It was a splendid ransom for an 'unknown petty rajah,' as the Emperor Jehangir contemptuously styles him in his diary.

Durgan Sal was imprisoned for twelve years, and it was only owing to his being a connoisseur in diamonds that he eventually obtained his release. The Emperor had two diamonds brought before him concerning the purity of which the jewellers disagreed, and, remembering Durgan Sal, he sent for him to ask his advice. The Chota Nagpore Raja at once saw the flaw in one of them, and, on the jewellers still disputing his judgment, offered to prove by ocular demonstration that he was right. Having obtained the Emperor's permission, he tied the diamonds to the horns of two fighting rams, which immediately on being released rushed with full force at one another. The diamond containing the flaw split at the shock of the first concussion, while the other remained intact until the end of the fight. The Emperor, delighted at the ingenuity of the Raja, at once released him and restored his lands. Durgan Sal, thinking this an opportune time to ask for further favours, prayed that his former rank might be given back to him and that he might be allowed to remain seated in the presence of the Emperor. This honour was accorded to him, and only a nominal annual tribute was to be paid in future by the Rajas of Kokrah.

The aboriginal races have nothing but the vaguest traditions to account for their presence in the land. The Mundas, probably the oldest of the settlers now remaining in Chota Nagpore, know

A MUNDA YOUTH.

little of the manner in which they took possession or whence they came, but they recount a curious story of the creation of their race. Sing Bonga, the Sun, to whom they ascribe the chief place in their mythology, created a boy and a girl whose family in course of time numbered twelve of either sex. When they had all come to an age to shift for themselves, Sing Bonga divided them into pairs and placed food of all kinds before them. On their choice depended the fate of their descendants. Those who took vegetables only became the ancestors of the highest caste of all, the Brahmins ; while the Santals, the lowest of all castes, spring from those who chose pigs. The Kols declare that they are descended from those who took bullock's flesh, and to the sustaining powers of the food of their choice the Larka or Fighting Kols attribute their strength and fine physique. When these latter, at the beginning of last century, first met English troops, they were quickly impressed with their wonderful fighting powers, and, finding that they too ate bullock's flesh, they paid them the greatest compliment in their power and assigned them the same pair of ancestors as themselves. But by the time that eleven pairs had chosen their share of the food provided, there was nothing left for the unfortunate twelfth couple, and they had to beg food from the others who had fared better. From this unlucky pair spring the Ghasis, who do no work, but support themselves on the charity and leavings of others. They are great musicians, however, and no wedding or funeral ceremony is complete without its band of Ghasis with their drums, kettledrums, horns, and pipes.

It is interesting to compare the Santal version of the distribution of the human race with this one given by the Mundas. Their divergence shows the wide distinction of thought between the two peoples and the intense dislike of the Santals for the Brahmins. It was much later in the history of the human race, according to the Santal legend, that the distribution took place. Marang Buru, the Great Spirit, wishing to divide the people into tribes and spread them over the earth, made a great feast. Everything that was good to eat was provided—beef, goat's flesh, fish, rice, and vegetables. The people were assembled some way off, and Marang Buru told them that at a given signal they must run to the place where the feast was spread and choose what they liked best. Now the Santals ran more swiftly than all the others and arrived first at the place of the feast. Looking round, they saw that the beef was the biggest and the best of the dishes provided, so they promptly took it and went off into the jungle to enjoy it. The Musulmans arrived next, and they chose the goat's flesh. Then came the Bhuiyas, who took the fish as the most substantial part of the food that was left.

A GHASI FROM BARABHUM (MANEHUM).

Last of all—and this is the point of the story—the Brahmins arrived on the scene. For them nothing remained but the rice and vegetables, with which they had perforce to be content. This version of the story makes them play a very different part from that assigned to them in the Munda account. The animosity of the Santals against the Brahmins is intense, though it is hard adequately to explain the cause. They even carry it so far as to refuse to eat food cooked by a Brahmin. During the famine of 1866, the highest caste had been naturally chosen to prepare the food provided by the Relief Committees, which were at first ignorant of this prejudice on the part of the Santals. Before it had been discovered, many of these unfortunate people proved themselves so tenacious of immemorial custom and bound down by hereditary animosity that, in the face of starvation, they preferred to die rather than eat food from the hands of the people they so much hated.

The majority of the zemindars of Chota Nagpore probably originally belonged to the same race as their people; but few of them are willing to acknowledge it, and all without exception have become Hinduised, claiming, like the Nagbansis, to be of Rajput descent. It is in the endeavour to substantiate this claim that many of the legends accounting for their origin have been invented. The story of the beginning of the Nagbansi race is only one of many, and a fertile imagination or the necessity of a pedigree has woven a romance round the unknown ancestry of every local potentate. The Rajas of Barabhum have a curious legend of the manner in which their estate came into the possession of their family. The two sons of the Raja of Kirat quarrelled with their father, and, leaving him, took up their residence at the court of Vikramaditaya. There, the younger brother was sawn into two pieces—the reason of this outrage, with typical Eastern vagueness, being left unexplained—and his blood placed as a mark upon his elder brother's forehead by Vikram. The latter then gave the elder brother two umbrellas and told him that all the land he could ride round in a day and a night should be his. The circuit he accomplished is said to be the estate of Barabhum; and the story must be true, the legend concludes, because the prints of his horse's hoofs are still visible on the southern slopes of the hills.

Concerning the first arrival of the British there is almost as much vagueness as about the earlier history of Chota Nagpore. Many of the records of the first years of the British occupation were destroyed during the Mutiny, and tradition has surrounded it with many an embellishment that cannot be vouched for. The famous compact of 1765 brought us first into touch with Chota Nagpore, which was included in Behar, when the dewani of that province, Bengal and Orissa, were ceded by the Nawab. It was not, however, until seven years later that the first recorded British entry into Chota Nagpore took place.

A curious story survives of the first meeting of a British representative with the Raja of Chota Nagpore. In 1772 Captain Camac with a small force entered the district and met the Raja Dripnath Sahi at the Satbarwa forts. The Raja acknowledged himself a vassal, and agreed to pay twelve thousand rupees tribute and furnish help against the Mahrattas. But Captain Camac, the story runs, having done his part for the Company, was seized with a desire to acquire something for himself. The Raja's turban was ablaze with diamonds, and a happy thought occurred to the British leader. The exchange of turbans, he explained, was always the sign of lasting friendship and good will, which had just been sworn on both sides. The unfortunate Raja was not in a position to decline, so the exchange was made and the first agreement cemented—much to the advantage of the British Raj and its representative.

When first seriously taken in hand about the year 1780, a district was formed and known as the Ramgarh Hill Tract. The magisterial courts were held alternately at Sherghati, now in the Gaya district, and at Chatra, thirty-five miles north-west of the present headquarters station of Hazaribagh. At the latter place was stationed the local force of native infantry, the Ramgarh Battalion, under its own European commander. At first there was only one officer, who performed the duties of judge, magistrate, and collector, and all appeals lay from him direct to the Governor-General. It was a huge district under his control, including all Hazaribagh and Palamau with parts of Gaya, Monghyr, and Manbhum, while Chota Nagpore proper owned a vague allegiance under its own chiefs. A letter written by Captain Roughsedge, commanding the Ramgarh Battalion, to Mr. C. T. Sealy, magistrate of Ramgarh, in May 1809, gives a vivid picture of the state of the district in those early days, and of the difficulty of enforcing law and order. 'Scarcely an individual in the whole country,' he writes, 'has remained unchargeable with some act of arbitrary violence, the origin of which is to be found in the notion, only now destroyed, of peculiar privileges and exemptions from the usual course of justice.' To prevent lawlessness, and at the same time to enable persons living in outlying districts to obtain speedy justice, he proposed the establishment of eight Thanas, which he strongly advocated should be placed under the control of one of the principal inhabitants of the locality, selected by the Raja and approved by the magistrate. He further strongly deprecated the introduction of 'hired and irresponsible strangers' as police officers, who, being out of touch with local custom and sentiment, would have little chance of success among the peculiarly exclusive and clannish people of Chota Nagpore. Though all Captain Roughsedge's ideas were not carried into effect, the main principle on which he insisted, that special laws were necessary to meet the special case of the people of Chota Nagpore, was never lost sight of by Government.

For some time after the first agreement with the Raja was arrived at, his state was left under his own control and he himself was allowed magisterial powers. But constant abuses led to the whole state being finally placed under the magistrate of Ramgarh in 1816. At first the district was governed in accordance with the ordinary regulations in force in Bengal—a form of government, however, for which it was soon seen the country was not yet prepared. It was far too huge a district and too unexplored for a single magistrate to have any adequate knowledge of the vast mass of the population, which in its turn was too backward to appreciate all the regulations of a code framed for a more advanced community. Moreover, the introduction of foreigners from Behar and Bengal, not only in subordinate Government posts but as landlords, created widespread discontent, which broke out into open rebellion in 1820 and 1831.

The latter was by far the more serious outbreak, and finally drew attention to the necessity of a change. Everywhere the zemindars had been giving grants of land to the newcomers, Hindus, Sikhs, and Muhammadans, who were fast ousting the original holders of the soil. The new landlords, ignorant and unmindful of local traditions, had inflicted great oppression on the ryots. At length a particularly flagrant case occurred under the local Raja of Tamar, and the Mankis, the village headmen, sending arrows of war along all the country-side, called upon their neighbours to join the revolt. All those villages who agreed to furnish help sent back the arrows whole, while those who refused to join returned them broken. But deprived of all that they held most dear, there were few who did not welcome the chance of revenge. 'Our lives we considered of no value,' said one of the chief Mankis in giving evidence later, 'and being of one caste and brethren, it was agreed upon that we should commence to burn, plunder, murder and eat. It was with this resolution,' he pathetically adds, 'that we have been murdering and plundering those who have deprived us of both honour and homes, conceiving that committing such outrages our grievances would come to light, and that if we had any master, notice would be taken of them and justice rendered.' The Pathans and the Sikhs had dishonoured and ousted them from their homesteads, and their lives were no longer of value. There was nothing left them but to avenge their wrongs or to die.

The fighting Kols, ever ready to join in a disturbance, came up from Singbhum to their assistance, and a wild scene of disorder followed. The foreigners were everywhere attacked and in many cases killed, while their houses were burnt to the ground, the zemindars who had favoured them barely escaping with their lives. The atrocities committed were of the most savage character. 'Restless, wild, and furious,' runs the Commissioner of Circuit's report submitted a year later, 'they rushed into an insurrection scarcely paralleled for ferocity. Eager for plunder, and universally prone to inebriation and infuriated by real or imaginary wrongs, the whole population yielded to the unobstructed tide of rebellion—fire, rapine, and murder marked their paths; nor was their vindictive spirit confined to those to whom their injuries were ascribed, but madly extended to unoffending females and helpless infants, apparently with the subtle determination of extirpating a whole race.' After holding sessions at Sherghati at the conclusion of the disturbances in January 1833, Mr. Master, Officiating Commissioner of Circuit, wrote that 'the calendar presented all the possible varieties which guilt could assume,' adding that the prisoners were apparently so wholly unconscious of the fearful and revolting nature of their crimes as to excite mingled sensations of horror and pity. One form of torture they inflicted on those 'foreigners' unfortunate enough to fall into their hands was to give them seven cuts, each cut being 'named and indicating their dissatisfaction with some particular tax or duty imposed on them,' one, for instance, being for the tax that had been placed on the intoxicating liquor that every Kol loves, and another for the tax to maintain the local *dâk* (post). The Kols, in the exuberance of the first days of revolt, openly declared that all taxes were obnoxious to them, and that they were going to march to Calcutta to set up their own government and establish the one tax that they deemed sufficient—the eight anna tax on ploughs. For a time they pursued their wild career unchecked. The police force numbered only one hundred men, and they 'disappeared on the first alarm.' The Provincial Battalion consisted of no more than a hundred and fifty sepoys, and there were no other troops nearer than Benares, Dinajpore, or Barrackpore. It was thus some time before a force could be collected to cope with the outbreak, so far from the headquarters of the district and from the neighbourhood of regular troops, and it was not without opposition that order was restored. All those who had been ousted by the foreigners were to get back their land, and measures were taken to prevent a similar recurrence of the trouble.

The Kol rebellion had proved the necessity of radical changes in the administration, more particularly in subdividing the unwieldy district and supplying more officers. As a consequence, the South-west Frontier Agency, under an officer designated Agent to the Governor-General, was established in 1833 for the whole province, with headquarters at Lohardaga. With one or two small exceptions, the Agency corresponded to the present division of Chota Nagpore. At the same time, Hazaribagh, Manbhum, and a few years later Singbhum, were formed into separate districts under Assistants to the Agent, with their own local headquarters and Government officials. A series of rules for criminal justice was especially provided by the Governor-General, which continued in force until the passing of the Criminal Procedure Code in 1861. The ordinary laws for the sale of land for debt or arrears of rent had been proved to be inapplicable, and they were not again attempted to be enforced, no sale or alienation or even mortgage being permissible without the sanction of the Agent. Throughout the records of these early days of British administration there is constant evidence of the desire of those in authority to do their utmost for the welfare of all classes of the people whose fortunes had been so recently committed to their charge. Letters from headquarters at Calcutta are full of solicitude that justice should be impartially administered to rich and poor alike, and that all grievances should be carefully inquired into and if possible redressed. The letter appointing an Assistant to the Judge, Magistrate, and Collector of Ramgarh in 1826 and vesting him with special powers is only one instance among many. In it either the Magistrate or his Assistant was 'directed to make an annual tour of the district, explaining personally to the principal landholders the objects of the police arrangements proposed to be introduced, and impressing on their minds the anxious desire of Government to ameliorate their condition and that of their ryots, reporting to Government on their return from each tour on the state of the country and the condition of the people.'

Few other important changes have since taken place. In 1840 the headquarters of the Agency were transferred from Lohardaga to Kishanpur, one of the small villages of which the present station of Ranchi is made up, and which occupied the site at the northern end of the town where the gaol now stands. The name of the station, however, was very shortly afterwards changed to Ranchi, another of the small villages, which has since given its name to them all. In 1854 the designation of the province was altered from the South-west Frontier Agency to Chutia Nagpur, and the Agent to the Governor-General became the Commissioner. Since that date, Chota Nagpore, as the modern spelling gives it, has been administered as a non-regulation province under the control of the Lieutenant-Governor of Bengal

CHAPTER II

MANY RACES AND SOME QUAINT CUSTOMS

NOTHING but a special volume, devoted exclusively to the subject, could attempt to give a detailed account of all the tribes and castes that people Chota Nagpore. Their name is legion, almost justifying the Oriental imagination likening them to the 'sand on the seashore for multitude.' All the races of Northern India seem to have collected in this corner of the empire. The aboriginal tribes, with their many distinctions of custom and tradition, speaking over thirty different languages, here live side by side with a crowd of semi-Hinduised people of their own race, Hindus of every shade and caste, and a fair sprinkling of Musulmans, the conquerors of the land in the zenith of their power in days gone by. Chota Nagpore has become the common meeting-ground of them all.

The oldest and most characteristic race of the land they have made their own are the Kols. Their early doings are shrouded in mystery, and even the legends of this legend-loving people

THE SUBARNAREKHA RIVER, SINGBHUM.

throw little light on the days before they came to Chota Nagpore. Tradition ascribes to them the ruins that still remain of an earlier race in many parts of Behar, and it seems probable that they once actually inhabited that province, forming a Kol empire under the rule of the Cheros. Driven out from thence, when or how no trace remains, they gradually fell back on the plateau of Chota Nagpore. Here, admirably adapted as it was for defence, they finally made their home. The big central tableland was appropriated by the Mundas, their chief strength lying in the very heart of Chota Nagpore proper and the wilder hill tracts of the native states. The Bhumij Kols, passing on down the valley of the Subarnarekha, took up their headquarters in southern Manbhum, between the banks of the river they had followed and the Kosai. The Larka or Fighting Kols, the wildest and most exclusive of them all, went further south and, driving out the Bhuiyas, who had been before them, occupied Singbhum and entrenched themselves jealously against all outside influence in the Kolhan. Besides these three branches of the Kol family came a host of other aboriginal tribes, occupying the land from end to end,—the Oraons, like the Cheros, of Dravidian origin, settling in the north-west corner of the district, which the Mundas had passed over and left almost untouched; the Santals making their home in portions of Manbhum and Hazaribagh; the Cheros with their great traditions of an empire on the banks of the Ganges ; the Parheyas and Brijias, wild hillmen of Palamau ; the Kherrias of Ranchi and Manbhum ; the Birhors of Hazaribagh ; and a crowd of other races, each separate and distinct, speaking its own language and living its life apart.

With the exception of the Hos of Singbhum and the Santals—both of whom demand a chapter to themselves—the Mundas are physically the finest of all the aboriginal tribes. The men average something like five feet six in height, and many of them are remarkably well developed and muscular. Living the free open-air life of the fields, and with constant exercise, manual labour, and exposure to all weathers, they are always in condition, hard and sinewy and wonderfully adapted for sustaining long and continuous exertion. Their skin is of the darkest brown, almost black in many cases, and their features coarse, with broad flat noses, low foreheads, and thick lips, presenting as a rule a by no means prepossessing appearance. The women are often more pleasing, the coarseness of their features less accentuated or less noticeable on account of the extreme good nature and happy carelessness that seldom fail to mark their countenances.

Both men and women wear their hair long, tied up loosely behind or straggling over the face. The men often shave a portion of their foreheads, always, however, leaving some portion of the hair uncut. Of clothing, the tribal precept seems to be 'the less the better.' The men in the out-of-the-way villages or working in the fields are quite content with a narrow strip of cloth passed between the legs and held in place by a string round the waist. But nearer the haunts of civilisation, their one garment develops into a more ample loin-cloth, such as most of the men are wearing in the illustrations. The young of both sexes, however, in spite of the scantiness of actual clothing, are by no means above personal adornment. Round the neck are worn rows on rows of beads of all the colours of the rainbow, and more again as bracelets round the wrists and half-way up the arm. In addition to these, neck and wrist ornaments of heavy silver, bell-metal, or bone, and armlets above the elbow are considered none too many. Circles of bell-metal decorate the ankles, and these, few maidens, whatever their position in life, would be without. To get them on over the feet is a work of some difficulty. 'Il faut souffrir pour être belle,' is a saying of which the Kol maiden has bitter experience, but the delight of seeing the anklets on her feet is full compensation for the pain of getting them on there.

A group of men and girls fully decked out for a festival makes a fine show. Dancing is one of the few recreations in which Mundas and Oraons indulge, and a dance at the *akhra*—a space especially cleared and kept for the purpose in the open—is the inevitable accompaniment of every gathering. They have a great variety of dances, appropriate to special times and seasons, but one suitable to any occasion seems to be the favourite. The girls interlace their arms behind their backs, in rows of five or six abreast, and, led by the master of the ceremonies, who goes in front beating a drum, they dance to his tune, advancing or retreating as he gives the sign.

The motion of the dance is slow and graceful, a monotonous singsong being kept up all through. The steps are in perfect time and the action wonderfully even and regular. This is particularly noticeable in some of the variations of the dance, representing the different seasons and the necessary acts of cultivation that each brings with it. In one, the dancers, bending down, make a motion with their hands as if they were sowing the grain, keeping step with their feet all the time. Then come the reaping of the crop and the binding of the sheaves, all done in perfect time and rhythm, with the continuous droning of the voices, making a quaint and picturesque performance.

The costume of the girls is as fine as they can make it. The substantial part of it consists of one long piece of coarse white cloth, with a red border, which is wound round the body, reaching to the knees, the end of it caught up and thrown loosely over the left shoulder. Every ornament in the shape of bead necklace, silver collar, bracelet, armlet, and anklet would seem to have been brought out for the occasion. As for the headdress, it is the crowning-point of the turn-out. The long black hair is gathered up in a big coil, most often artifically enlarged, the whole being fastened at the right-hand side of the back of the head, just on a level with and touching the right ear. In this knot are fastened all sorts of ornaments of brass and silver, and surmounting it, stuck in every available space, are gay plumes of feathers, that nod and wave bravely with the movements of the dance. The ears are distorted, almost beyond recognition, by huge earrings that pierce the lobe and smaller ones that ornament them all round. It is nothing unusual for the dances to be kept up all night, and well into the following day, with only brief intervals for rest and refreshment.

All the aboriginal tribes alike are passionately fond of dancing. Once a year, at the time of the Jatra Festival, there is a huge gathering in Ranchi, all the dancers from the villages round meeting together in the Court compound and exhibiting their skill in friendly rivalry. It is a picturesque sight, the whole wide open *maidan* behind the Court buildings packed with a dense crowd of natives in their gay clothes of many colours, Mundas, Oraons, Kherrias, and Hindus of every caste, with a stray Musulman here and there looking on with dignified curiosity, half interest, half contempt. Scattered about among the crowd are the groups of dancers, so hemmed in by the crush that the spectators have to press back this way and that as the figures of the *nautch* evolve. The solid formation of the dance, however, takes but little room—the rows of dancers linked close together, arm in arm, and gyrating in perfect accord and unison, never breaking out of the monotonous round, but swinging first here, then there, with the regularity and evenness of a pendulum.

Only later on, when, an adjournment having been made to other parts of the town, the native liquor, freely imbibed, and the excitement of the hours of dance and song have taken effect, and the flickering fires, roughly lit here and there on the outskirts of the crowd, cast their changing lights and shadows on the ever-moving groups, does something of a wilder character, more in keeping with the appearance of the dancers, seem imparted to it. Even then the regularity is never broken. The singing is louder, hoarser, wilder, the play of limbs is less restrained and the tossing plumes wave more wildly, but the dance never degenerates into a mere *mêlée* as one would half expect. Hour after hour through the night, in unbroken monotony, it goes on. Variation is as unknown as it is undesired by these extraordinary revellers. Here and there a maiden falls out of the moving phalanx from sheer breathless exhaustion, to snatch a brief respite and a drink of toddy before joining in the dance again, refreshed and reinvigorated. Or one of the waving heads has tossed too wildly, and imminent disaster, not unknown in more civilised ball-rooms, threatens. With much laughter, and amidst the jokes of her companions, she detaches herself from the rest and, standing in full view on the outskirts of the group, performs her toilet. But the headdress is too fearfully and wonderfully constructed to be trifled with, and, no looking-glass being handy, another maiden must perforce come to the rescue and secure the thick black bundle of hair and reset the falling flowers and drooping plumes. And so, with unflagging energy, the revelry continues, till one goes away, from sheer impossibility to stand the maddening monotony longer, leaving them to dance on till the first faint light of dawn has struggled out of the east and the morning sun beats down upon them after their night of orgy.

Ignorant and superstitious, the Kols regard the sun with awe and reverence, his daily rising and setting being to them a thing of mystery. He is known among them as Sing Bonga, and stands at the head of their universe. All the other gods of their mythology are subservient to him, but they do most of the ruling of the world in his behalf. Sing Bonga is great, too great to trouble himself much with worldly matters, and the burden of affairs falls on the shoulders of his lieutenants. He is not a malignant spirit, being almost the exception in that respect among all their numerous deities. He is, in fact, of a kindly nature and well-disposed, but he either does not take the trouble or is unable to hinder the vicious intentions of his subordinates. The Kol spends his whole life in fear and dread of evil spirits. At every turn they shadow him, needing constant propitiation and demanding to be consulted on every occasion of importance. A special malignant spirit seems to watch over almost every conceivable action of any moment that he can take. At seed-time and harvest, giving in marriage and burying the dead, at the time of going on a journey or returning, and at every festival, offerings of propitiation must be made to the particular presiding deity.

Marang Buru, the Great Spirit, next to Sing Bonga, is the greatest of divinities, for in his hands lies the power of giving or withholding rain. He resides in rocks and hills, and, being a malignant spirit, requires constant attention on the part of the unfortunate cultivator. When the desired rain is long withheld, it is a sign that Marang Buru is angry, and nothing in that case will appease him but the sacrifice of the best buffalo in the village. Ikir Bonga, another divinity, requires white goats for sacrifice, otherwise he will spread disease and death through the country-side by means of the water in the tanks and wells that he presides over. Fowls and eggs are generally sufficient to propitiate the lesser deities, Garha Era, the goddess of rivers, streams, and springs, or the Naga Era, who haunt the low levels of the rice fields, but they are so numerous that the offerings form a considerable item in the annual expenditure of the unfortunate cultivator.

Every village has its own particular spirit, whose duty it is to look after the crops. He is known as Deswali, and plays a large part in nearly all the Kol festivals, most of them being connected with the cultivation of land, on which their sole means of subsistence depends. The home of this presiding deity is in the *Sarna* or Sacred Grove, a little patch of primitive jungle that, when all else was cleared for cultivation, was left as a refuge for the gods where they might dwell apart. At all seasons of the year offerings are made in the Sarna, for on the favour of Deswali depends the success or failure of their crops.

The Mundas, unlike the Oraons, have no symbols for any of their gods save Sing Bonga and Chandor, his wife. Chandor is the Moon, and the special goddess of the women. To account for her changing shape, a quaint legend has been invented. Once long ago she was faithless to her husband, the Sun, and swift was her punishment. Sing Bonga cut her in two in the heat of his anger. But Chandor was beautiful and Sing Bonga's repentance quick. So he allowed her at times to shine forth in her full beauty, though the fact that she was once cut in half could never be wholly obliterated, and is still made patent to all at stated seasons.

The Mundas relate a curious version of the Fall of the Angels and the Creation of the Minor Deities. Once upon a time, heaven was peopled by a race of divinities who were attendant on Sing Bonga. But one day they happened to come across a mirror, and, seeing their faces for the first time, found that they were made in God's image. Inflated with pride at this newly discovered knowledge, they refused further service, declaring that they were the equals of God himself. But the sin of Lucifer, Son of the Morning, as in the Biblical story, met with speedy punishment. They were promptly expelled from heaven and cast into a place known to the Mundas as *Terasi Pirhi Ekasibasi*, but popularly known in the West by a shorter and seemingly more expressive name. In these lower regions they came across large quantities of iron ore, and at once made furnaces and started work smelting it. But the fire and the smoke and the heat ascending to heaven annoyed Sing Bonga. Therefore he issued orders that they must confine themselves to work either by day or by night; he could not be worried by the continual smelting. The fallen

A GROUP OF MUNDAS.

spirits, still rebellious, refused to obey the order, and continued working night and day. Sing Bonga in anger sent two king crows and an owl to warn them, but they only flippantly waved their furnace tongs at them, trying to catch them by the tails. Then Sing Bonga sent a crow. Now the crows were formerly white, but when the unfortunate representative of the family reached the iron-workers, they caught him and smoked him black, sending him away thus disfigured to show their contempt for Sing Bonga's orders. The crows have never recovered from the indignity, and have remained black ever since.

His orders disobeyed and his messengers insulted, Sing Bonga at last determined to go himself to reduce to submission his unruly subjects. But at first he appeared incognito, waiting his time until he could take a complete revenge upon them for their insubordination. At first he lived in the house of an old couple who made charcoal, helping them in their work and amusing their children. One of the games he found them playing was a game with iron balls. He joined in with eggs, and the eggs that he threw always smashed the balls of iron. Then follows a Munda version of Alfred and the cakes. The old couple went away one day to work, leaving Sing Bonga in charge of the hut and the rice that had been laid out to dry in the sun. But Sing Bonga played with the children all the time, and the fowls came and ate up the rice. When the old people returned, they were very angry, until Sing Bonga, collecting the few grains of rice that were left, filled all the pots in the house with them. His host and hostess, however, instead of showing gratitude, at once accused him of having stolen the rice to make good the loss caused by his carelessness.

Here the story abruptly breaks off and begins again about the furnaces, which suddenly collapsed, causing ruin to the smelters. In distress they consulted the *ojha* (soothsayer), who led them to Sing Bonga. The latter, after some deliberation, said that the Supreme Being was enraged and that nothing but a human sacrifice would appease him. The smelters looked at one another in dismay, and all with one consent began to make excuse. At last Sing Bonga said that he would be the sacrifice. A new furnace was quickly made, Sing Bonga put inside, and the bellows blown. After a time they put out the fire, and, to their amazement, he stepped from the furnace uninjured, while streams of gold and silver and precious stones poured out on to the ground. All the smelters were delighted, and then Sing Bonga knew that his day of revenge had come. He tempted them and they fell. 'See what one man has done,' he said. 'If you all enter the furnace none of you will be harmed and you will have vast stores of wealth sufficient for all time.' They gladly consented to be smelted, and entering the furnaces Sing Bonga shut them in, and, with a touch of irony, ordered their wives to blow the bellows. From within were soon heard screams and cries, and the women would have stopped in alarm. But Sing Bonga urged them on, saying that they were only quarrelling over the spoil. So all the smelters were destroyed, disobedience to the Supreme Being meeting with its due punishment. Then the women turned to Sing Bonga, weeping and asking what was left in life for them now that their husbands were dead. The Supreme Being took pity on them and assigned to each of them a certain spot where they might dwell for ever, as minor deities or *bhuts* (ghosts). Some live in rocks, some in the pools and streams, and others in the hills and jungles. To the frightened Munda imagination they dwell everywhere, and, being evil-minded, need constant offerings and propitiation.

Besides the dread of these evil spirits, the Kol goes in continual fear of witchcraft and sorcery. Not content with peopling the earth with imaginary beings to thwart him at every step, he grows suspicious even of his own relatives and neighbours. If any misfortune befalls him, he attributes it at once to the anger of some unappeased spirit or to the machinations of a witch. The *ojha* or diviner alone can tell to which cause the misfortune is due, and recourse is had to him. If he decides that it is due to witchcraft or sorcery, there are several ways of discovering who has wrought the spell, though the decision in all cases practically rests with the *ojha,* giving him unlimited opportunities of gratifying any personal enmity he may entertain. One curious method, and seemingly a very unsatisfactory one, save for the *ojha* himself, is to throw a handful of pulse on to a large open dish, mentioning at the same time the name of a villager. This is repeated, with a different name each time, until the grains form a certain pattern, agreeable to the *ojha,* when the name that accompanied that throw is announced as the name of the witch. Men are frequently accused of being sorcerers; and it seems strange to find that the people suspected of the evil eye are often young or in the prime of life, bearing no resemblance whatever to the wrinkled haggard witch of Western popular imagination. In former days those denounced by the *ojha* were at once put to death, and even at the present day cases still occur where the unfortunate victim of the *ojha's* divination suffers such ill-treatment at the hands of an indignant village that death results.

The Munda and the Pahn are two important figures in every village community. The Munda is the head-man, whom the Santals know as

A GROUP OF MUNDA CHILDREN.

Manjhi and the Bhumij Kols as Sirdar. He is the great authority on all social matters, and to him the villagers go when in doubt on any point of custom or procedure. He is the repository of the Table of Consanguinity, and any question of marriage within the forbidden degrees, which are very strictly defined, is brought to him. The Pahn is a scarcely less important personage. He performs the functions of a village priest, and is always chosen from one family by the *sup* or winnowing-fan, which is used as a divining-rod and carried from house to house by the boys of the village until the choice is made. He must be the descendant of the earliest settlers, as his office has only tradition for its guidance. It is his duty to propitiate the gods and officiate as priest at the sacrifices in the Sarna. The office being practically kept in one family, he is supposed to have full knowledge of all village matters, handed down from father to son through many generations. To him the villagers bring cases of land disputes, and the party that can produce the Pahn as a witness on its side in a case before the court is confident of success. But often the word of the Pahn alone bears sufficient weight, and the villagers accept his decision unquestioningly without appeal to a higher tribunal. He makes an excellent thing out of his position as the village priest. The crops may not promise well, and the villagers in distress come to him.

The evil spirits must be at once propitiated, and there is a busy time in the Sarna. The Pahn orders one man to provide a bullock and another a goat or a fowl for sacrifice, and his word on points like these is law. Of each sacrifice he gets a share, and so fares sumptuously for many days to come. Special lands also are assigned to his office, which he gets rent-free in consideration of his priestly duties and his care of the Sarna. The Mahato, another village official, may be described as the local settlement officer, allotting the village lands, and settling and collecting the rents. Contrasting him with the Pahn, there is a local saying that whereas the Pahn 'makes the village,' the Mahato only 'manages it,' showing the immense superiority of the priest in popular estimation.

It is the Pahn who is so much to the fore in the numerous festivals that break the monotony of the dull round of daily life. Mundas and Oraons both keep the same chief festivals of the year, each with their own slight variations, and some more, some less elaborately. One of the most important of them is the Sarhul, observed with much ceremony in the months of March and April. None keep it with greater detail than the Oraons, who invest it with many quaint customs. It occurs when the sal tree is in flower, and the graceful plumelike blossoms are to deck the earth for her marriage. All the villagers assemble at the Sarna, where the Sarna Burhi, or Woman of the Grove, whom the Mundas call Deswali, resides. The festival is begun by sacrificing fowls before a small rough image of mud or stone, the Oraons differing here from the Mundas, and always requiring something material to regard as the embodiment of the spirit they worship. The sacrifice complete, the fowls are at once cooked and partaken of by all those assembled. It is the occasion of a general feast which lasts for the remainder of the day, and at night they return home laden with sal blossoms and marching to the beating of drums and the blowing of shrill-voiced horns, with much dancing by the way. So ends the first part of the festival. Next morning the maidens of the village, gaily decked with the sal blossoms, the pale cream-white flowers making the most becoming of adornments against their dusky skins and coal-black hair, start off to visit every house in the village. One carries a drum and the others baskets filled with more sal blossoms, which they place over the door of every house for luck. For this service the inmates give them rice or pice, which, when the last of the visits has been paid, they take to the Pahn. With the proceeds he purchases goats if the collection has been large, fowls if the pice are few; and again there are sacrifices at the Sarna and another feast to follow. Later on an adjournment is made to the *akhra*, and the dance is soon in full swing, to last all that night and the following day as well.

The Oraons are a singularly contented people, making the best of things, whatever comes. Many strings of beads and a brave show of ornaments, much feasting and dancing, are all they demand of life. Yet they are an industrious race, despite their love of finery, working hard and apparently enjoying it, though never bettering themselves or rising to any position of wealth or influence. Many of them have been induced to migrate to the tea gardens of Assam, where wages are higher, and they have been always welcome there as good and industrious workers. But those who have returned, with what to the villagers at home is untold wealth, have never attempted a better style of living, and most of them have soon squandered the fruits of their labour, sinking back again into their old hand-to-mouth state of existence.

Of all the other crowd of aboriginal tribes that people Chota Nagpore, making a fascinating study, with their peculiarities of language, customs, and legends, it is impossible to give more than a glimpse here. Many of them, wild races of the jungle and shunning civilisation, still live their own lives in the scattered villages of their community, knowing nothing of the outside world. The Cheros, with their great traditions of a past empire, are perhaps the most advanced where all

AN UMBRELLA CONSTRUCTED SOLELY OF LEAVES.

is backward. They affect the purity of race and the dignity of Hindus, wearing the sacred cord and looking upon themselves as Rajputs. Brahmins, with one of those distinctions so typical of the caste system, will drink water from their hands and eat any kind of food except rice which they have cooked. As a rule the Cheros are proud of their descent, scorning to labour in the fields and to carry earth upon their heads, like most of the aboriginal races among whom they live.

The Birhors, on the other hand, are at the other end of the scale, among the most backward and wild of all the tribes of Chota Nagpore. Numerically they are a small race, numbering a little over a thousand—woodmen, as their name in Mundari implies, living far away from the larger towns and villages in the deep recesses of the jungle. Their huts are of the most primitive description, made only of the branches of trees and leaves, yet so wonderfully constructed that they continue to keep out the rain on the worst of wet days. The umbrella in the illustration is a good sample of what can be done with the primitive material to hand. It is made of nothing but leaves, so carefully and closely joined together that the man beneath can keep his head and shoulders dry through the heaviest shower. It is the most primitive of umbrellas, but it serves its purpose and gives one some idea of what the first dress of all, the dress of fig leaves in the garden, most probably resembled.

Few of the Birhors have even now taken seriously to cultivation as a means of livelihood. They are quite content with what the jungle can provide, making rough rope and *banghis*—arrangements something on the principle of a milkman's yoke, consisting of a straight piece of wood placed across the shoulders, with burdens suspended by means of ropes on either side. They are essentially woodmen, for whom the jungle with its supply of fruit and game suffices. A curious tale is told of how fate allotted to them this manner of life. The ancestors of the race were three brothers who set out to make their fortunes, and settled in what is now the Hazaribagh district. Their possession of the land, however, being disputed by the chiefs of the country, they marched out to decide the question by right of battle. On the way, the headdress of one of them got entangled in a tree. Thinking it a bad omen, he returned home and busied himself in cutting wood while his brothers fought. On their return they found him thus occupied, and in derision called him a mere 'Birhor,' woodcutter, while boasting of their own deeds in battle. The result was a family quarrel, and the two brothers departed in scorn, leaving the third to his work of cutting wood in the jungle, the name 'Birhor' remaining ever since with him and his descendants.

Marriages among all the aboriginal tribes are affairs of ceremony and the occasion of great festivity. The Kherrias, a wild tribe found in the south of the Ranchi district and in Manbhum, have some especially interesting customs attached to the tying of the nuptial knot. It is the father of the family who sets out in search of a wife for his son, as soon as the latter can handle the plough and is thus considered of marriageable age. After much consultation with the father of a girl of suitable years and position—a consultation assisted by many potations of *haria* (native liquor) —the price of the bride in tale of cattle is decided upon. That is the chief preliminary, and, once fixed, the course of true love has every prospect of running smoothly.

The next step is for the bridegroom's father to bring the *lowrie* to the father of the bride. The *lowrie* is a short bamboo stick about three feet long, supposed to contain the family god. It is kept by the father of the bride for one or two days, and is then restored to the bridegroom's family as a sign that the proposed son-in-law is acceptable and that the bride's relatives are ready to proceed with the marriage. Both these visits are accompanied by great drinkings of *haria*, and the parents of the contracting parties are generally in a hopelessly maudlin state before the proceedings are over.

But, important as they are, these are only

preliminaries, and, a day being fixed for the wedding, the actual ceremony commences. Most of the duties fall upon the bridegroom's father. He has already contracted to pay so many head of cattle for the bride, and he has also to bear all the expense of the festivities accompanying the wedding. The bride and her party come to the bridegroom's house, encamping a short way off and expecting to find ample refreshments, and above all a full quantity of the best *haria* awaiting them. The night that follows is made hideous with the beating of drums and tomtoms and the blowing of horns and pipes, as a sort of preparation for the concluding ceremony that begins at dawn.

In the morning the bridegroom, seated on a stool outside his house, formally receives his bride-elect, salaaming to her as she is brought up, and seating her on his right-hand side on another stool similar to his own. Seeing them thus seated together for the first time as bride and bridegroom, the Baiga or priest attempts to look into the future and foretell their fate. Taking a small portion of the hair of each in turn, from the centre of the forehead, he draws it down on to the bridge of the nose. Then pouring oil on the top of the head, he watches it carefully as it trickles down the portion of hair. If the oil runs straight on to the tip of the nose, their future will be fortunate, but if it spreads over the forehead, or trickles off on either side of the nose, bad luck is sure to

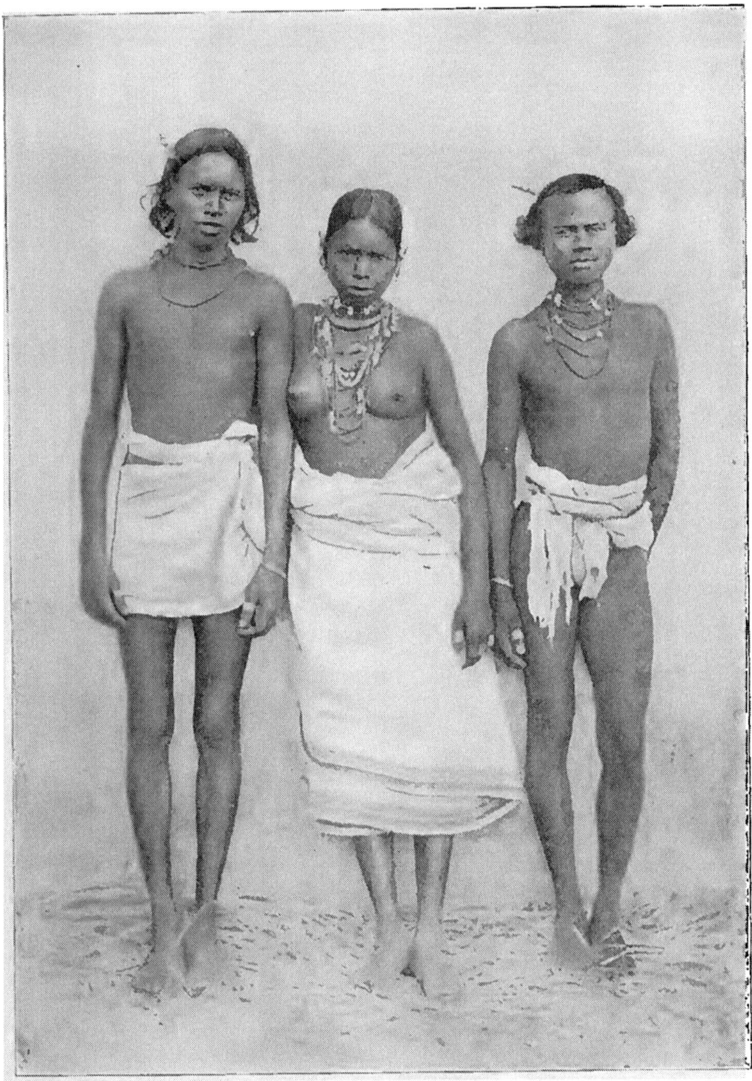

RANCHI KHERRIAS.

follow. Their fortunes told, generally to their own satisfaction, the essential and irrevocable part of the ceremony takes place. Standing up side by side but with faces carefully averted, the bride and bridegroom mark each other's foreheads with *sindur* (vermilion). Great precautions are always taken that neither shall catch a glimpse of the other during this important process, which finally makes the couple man and wife.

As soon as this is done, the beating of the inevitable drums and tomtoms begins again, and the guests dance and sing round the newly married couple. Later on an adjournment is made for refreshment, and the potations are again deep and liberal. Drinking, singing, and dancing go on till evening, when the priest, who during all this time has been doing *puja* (praying) for the newly married couple, takes them by the hand and leads them into the house, locking the door behind them. Outside, the guests collect, burning dried chillies close against the door and windows, with the object of sending the smoke through the cracks and making the unfortunate couple inside sneeze. If they should sneeze, it would be the worst of omens ; so, in order to stop the nuisance, the bridegroom, through the closed door, makes the guests an offer to desist. It is generally so many fowls or so much *haria* that they demand, and if he does not offer enough they threaten to burn more chillies, until he is forced to accede to their demands. In consideration of the fact, however, that he has just married a wife who will doubtless be a great expense to him, they refrain from asking anything exorbitant. After continuing the feasting and drinking all night, the guests depart in the morning, leaving a few pice for the bride for luck. Thus end the wedding ceremonies, and the bride's family starts for home, leaving her behind, but not forgetting to drive off the cattle that had been fixed upon as her *pan* (price). Marriage customs differ in detail among the various tribes, each having its own peculiar additions and elaborations, but with feasting, drinking, dancing, and the smearing of *sindur* as the almost invariable accompaniments of them all.

One picturesque scene in a Munda wedding ceremony is worth noticing. The bride goes to a stream or well near by with her pitcher, and, having filled it, raises it aloft on her head, steadying it with her hand. The bridegroom comes behind as she turns homewards, and, resting his hand on her shoulder, shoots an arrow along the path in front of her, through the loophole formed by her uplifted arm. The bride then walks on to where the arrow lies and picks it up with her foot, still balancing the pitcher on her head. Transferring it gracefully to her hand, she restores it to the bridegroom, thus showing that she can perform her domestic duties well, with hand and foot at his service. He, in turn, by shooting the arrow in front of her, has shown his ability to protect her and clear her path of any danger that may beset it.

The funeral ceremonies are no less elaborate, and are most punctiliously carried out by all the aboriginal tribes. The Mundas, Oraons, and Hos first burn their dead, and then bury their ashes beneath the huge natural tombstones in the grave-yards that are scattered all over Chota Nagpore, wherever these races have settled. The Santals and Kherrias, on the other hand, after burning their dead, carry the ashes whenever possible to their Sacred River, the Damuda. They all show great reverence for the departed, performing the funeral rites decorously and with an apparent sincerity of grief. When an Oraon dies, his body is borne on a *charpoy* (native bed) to the burning-place, surrounded by all the villagers, the women with their hair flying loosely and wild about their faces, and giving vent to loud cries of lamentation. Music generally accompanies the procession, the drums beating, slowly and mournfully, a weird and impressive funeral march. On arriving at the spot, the body is carefully washed and anointed, and a curious custom holds of putting rice and coins into the mouth of the deceased. If the wife or husband is present, he or she sets the funeral pyre alight. In their absence the nearest relative performs the task. The body consumed, the ashes are carefully collected and placed in an earthen pot, the coins that had been placed in the mouth of the corpse being recovered and given as their fees to the musicians! A feast is then provided by the relatives for all those who have attended the ceremony, and the vessel containing the ashes of the deceased is carefully put aside until the time comes for its final disposal.

This can only take place at one time of the year, when there is a general interment of all those who have died during the past twelve months. The day fixed for the ceremony falls in December or January, and on that date all the villagers proceed to the burying-ground, carrying the ashes of their departed relatives. The Oraons lay particular stress upon being buried in their own village, and it is incumbent on a man's relatives to carry back his ashes on the next annual day of burial, however far away from home he may have died. Huge flat blocks of stone, sometimes brought from a great distance, are placed over the remains to mark the spot, and the funeral ceremony is at last at an end and the feasting begins.

A gipsy encampment is a sight only found, as a rule, in the out-of-the-way parts of the district, or at certain seasons on the outskirts of large towns and villages. One of the largest gipsy tribes is that of the Gulgulias, a wandering race, which makes a precarious living by snaring wild animals, squirrels, and monkeys, and gleaning from the fields what is left of the crops after harvest. They generally have a collection of pariah dogs, goats, and monkeys in their camp, which they have taught various tricks for exhibition when they pay their occasional visits to the villages or to the passers-by along the roads. Squirrels seem to have a peculiar connection with the caste. One is reputed to have been their ancestor, and is thus their totem, though at the present day squirrels form their favourite food, and they have developed the greatest ingenuity in catching them. This they do with extraordinary quickness by stabbing them with a long spear, and in spite of the light agile movements of the squirrel their aim rarely fails. The legend of their ancestor is that there were seven brothers who backed themselves, one against the other, to jump off a palmyra tree. The first—the squirrel—jumped down easily and landed unhurt. But the second fell heavily and was killed on the spot. Their father, in his grief, turned his anger upon the first, whom he accused of having led the others into mischief. As a punishment he struck him with his hand, leaving the mark of his five fingers on his back, and dooming him to be always numbered among the lower animals, with only this accomplishment, that he should be able to jump more nimbly than them all. It is from this incident that the squirrel got the five marks on its back which it has ever since borne.

Full of interest, too, are many of the festivals of the Hindus and Muhammadans to be seen in Chota Nagpore. One of the most curious is the Churuk Puja, reminiscent of the old days when death, torture, and mutilation were the common accompaniment of Hindu worship. It is generally known as the Hook-swinging festival, the devotees being swung up in the air by means of hooks thrust into the flesh, and, though long since strictly prohibited by law, almost every year until recently cases of its having taken place with full rites were reported in the various districts. It is one of those ghastly exhibitions that a past race of Hindus more especially delighted in; and the devotees themselves, from all accounts, eagerly underwent the torture, probably well drugged to mitigate what would otherwise have been physical agony. Each devotee approached the priest in turn and fell full length on the ground before him, his back and shoulders bare. The priest, muttering his formula, stooped down, and, dipping his finger in a heap of ashes, made two marks on the back of the suppliant just below the shoulder-blades. His assistant, pinching up the flesh underneath these marks, thrust the two large hooks securely through. This done, the devotee rose amid the cries of admiration of the crowd, and marched off to the swinging post, swaggering

HOOK SWINGING AT THE CHURUK PUJA.

along with pride and seemingly unconscious of the wounds made by the hooks, from which blood was flowing down his back. The hooks being attached to the ropes of the swinging machine with a sudden wrench that would seem as if it must have lacerated the flesh beyond endurance, he was swung aloft, to the wild shrieks of the crowd of enthusiasts and the deafening noise of the drums. A loose band, placed round the man's chest, prevented the strain from actually causing the hooks to burst through the flesh, but so slackly tied that it mitigated little of the pain. The illustration gives an idea of the machine and the manner in which the devotee was and is still surreptitiously swung when the police are not by. Everything is complete except the hooks.

The other scene is the great Mohurrum festival held by the Muhammadans in honour of Hosain, the grandson of the Prophet, who was slain on the field of Karbola on the banks of the Euphrates. The festival lasts ten days, but the great day is the tenth, when the enthusiasm reaches its height. Vast processions carrying *tazzias* and flags and leading a gaily decorated, but riderless, horse throng the streets. The *tazzias* are wonderful temple-like structures in miniature, made of wood and covered with red and white cloth or paper, and gay with gold and silver tinsel. They are carried shoulder-high, and a crowd of them raised above a sea of heads in the dense procession makes an imposing sight. The horse—sometimes the animal itself, sometimes an effigy in wood—decked out in gorgeous saddle-cloth and trappings, represents the one that Hosain rode in his last battle, and for that reason is led riderless at the festival.

The enthusiasm gradually increases as the procession moves slowly along, the drums and tomtoms sounding their deep sonorous notes and the horns braying hideously. The noise and the heat and the dust have their effect on the dense crowd, and the babel of voices grows louder, vibrating with the rising enthusiasm. Barefooted and bareheaded, and beating their breasts, the most excited of the followers of the Prophet take up the great cry of the Mohurrum, 'Hassan, Hosain! Hassan, Hosain!' that sweeps through the multitude of the Faithful, to be taken up again and again and pass in waves of long-drawn cadences from end to end of the procession.

CHUTIA TEMPLE.

CHAPTER III

OLD CHUTIA NAGPUR

Two miles east of Ranchi lies the straggling village of Chutia. It looks a small, insignificant village, nowadays, to have given its name to the whole surrounding district. But tradition assigns it an honoured place in the annals of Chota Nagpore. It was, so the legend runs, the earliest home of the Nagbansi Rajas, the ‘ snake-crowned ’ race. But of those far-off days, time-honoured fables and legendary lore alone survive, and what part Chutia played in their history has been long since forgotten. Only the memory of a former greatness remains.

Nothing is left of Chutia save the long straggling village street with its irregular rows of tumble-down houses, and small stone shrines scattered here and there along its length. Only the ruins of the old fort-like temple at the far end of the village are left to prove its claim to antiquity and past glory. Round it on all four sides runs a massive stone wall, as if jealously guarding all that survives. Inside, in the middle of the grass-grown square, stands the temple, rising high up on a mound of earth and overlooking the walls. It is a dome-shaped building, with many flanking bastions and a well deep down beneath, approached from above by a long stone passage, gradually descending, damp and overgrown with moss and weeds to the water's edge. An old Brahmin is in charge of it, but everything is the picture of neglect, and age and exposure have long since marred the features of Ram and Sita on the rough stone images that still preside over the now deserted temple. It is hard to imagine the sleepy quiet of this out-of-the-way corner of the world once broken by the noise and stir that surround a native court.

But Chutia, long forgotten and unnoticed, suddenly woke to life again fifty years ago. The great annual fair for the whole of Chota Nagpore had hitherto been held at Silli, thirty-eight miles away on the Purulia road ; but two years before the Mutiny it was transferred to Chutia. Silli had been found to be too far removed from headquarters and to provide too little accommodation for the crowd that thronged from all directions to the fair. Chutia, on the other hand, was close to Ranchi and offered an excellent site. A grove of mango trees, covering in all something like one hundred acres, was an ideal place of shelter for the booths, and beneath their shade the bargaining, so much loved of Eastern races, could be prolonged in coolness and comfort. Near by was the flourishing Ranchi bazaar, offering abundant provisions and accommodation for the better sort who were not content to camp beneath the mango trees on the site of the fair itself. Water, too, was plentiful in the many fine tanks round Chutia, relics some of them of its past greatness: while on the other side of the village away from Ranchi runs the Subarnarekha river.

Everything was to be bought and sold at the Chutia fair. Beads 'made in Birmingham' reached the end of their journey at last, and passed, after much haggling and vociferation, into the pleased possession of some Munda maiden. Cloths of all kinds from Calcutta, shawls from Cashmir, silver work from Lucknow, and inlaid work from Jaipur made a brave show; and the local Raja from some distant corner of the district, intent on making purchases, could revel at leisure in the array of velvets and gold braid, gorgeous saddle-cloths and elephant trappings, that a Raja's heart most loves. Horses and elephants were brought from all parts of the district and beyond, finding a ready sale. Large numbers of other animals were there too, in their flocks and droves and herds—the value of them all being estimated one year at nearly ten lakhs of rupees. Other things, less expensive and of commoner use, appealed to the mass of the people. Cloths and *saris*, brass and silver necklets, and ornaments of many descriptions—in fact, everything that could ever be obtained in Chota Nagpore in those days—was to be had once a year at the Chutia fair.

It must have been a great sight, this vast assemblage, where the chiefs from the surrounding districts, each with his own following of retainers, jostled the motley crowd of merchants and money-lenders, dealers and coolies, who thronged the lines of booths under the shade of the mango trees. Every race and people of Chota Nagpore were there—the Hindu and the zemindar with his arrogant claims to Rajput blood : Muhammadans, not so numerous, but treating the rabble with all the pride of a conquering race : the dark-skinned Munda and Oraon from Chutia Nagpur : the sturdy Santal from Hazaribagh and beyond : a group here and there of unkempt Kherrias and athletic Hos from Singbhum, besides a full quota from the Native States, wild hillmen, looking suspiciously on all who were not of their race : while in and out among the throng moved the traders, of another manner of look and speech, who had brought their merchandise all the way down from the north-west to the famous Chutia fair.

Untouched by a line of rail in its earlier days, the annual fair had been started not only to develop trade and commerce in Chota Nagpore, but to bring the people of the district together and break down the isolation of the petty chiefs. It had quickly become a great success. The local potentate came to look forward to it as the one occasion in the year when he might leave home to display his pomp and state, and rival his neighbour in magnificence. Here, too, it was possible to have audience of the great Commissioner Saheb and unburden himself of a long-standing grievance, or profess his devotion to the Sirkar in the hope of blessings yet to come.

A meet was always held in the European station of Ranchi at the time of the annual fair. It was a big gathering for those days. The regiments from Hazaribagh and Chaibasa sent their contingent of visitors, which was swelled by civilians from Purulia and tea-planters from Hazaribagh and Ranchi districts. One day at Chutia was set apart for the sports of the Saheb-log. A gymkhana fifty years ago seems to have been much the same as it is to-day, though elephant, *tat* (native pony), and *bailgari* (bullock cart) races for Europeans figure more largely in the programme, and seem to have especially appealed to a past generation of Anglo-Indians.

The native sports were one of the great attractions of the fair. The Kols thoroughly entered into the spirit of such contests as sack and three-legged races, greasy-pole climbing, jumping, and running. But among all the competitors there were none to equal the Hos from Singbhum, who carried all before them. Cock-fighting has always been a favourite pastime of the Kols, and at the fair, champions from different villages, far and near, met and added to their laurels or perished in the attempt. The steel spurs, two inches long, that the Kols fix to the cock's feet are deadly weapons, and generally result in a speedy termination of the fight.

But the event that always created the greatest excitement was the ram fight. It was held in a large open space with a ring of spectators all round. Released simultaneously from opposite sides of the arena, the rams made a frantic rush for one another, meeting in the centre with a shock that often for a moment stunned them both. But a ram's strength is proverbial, and they were soon on their feet again, prepared to fight it out. As soon as one gained a distinct advantage, however, they were separated, and not much harm was allowed to be done.

But with improved means of communication and the railway at the very gates of Chota Nagpore, at Giridih and Barakar, the Chutia fair was doomed. Everything was to be obtained more easily all the year round, and there was no need to wait for the annual fair to make one's purchases. After lingering on for a time merely as a pleasure gathering, it was finally abolished altogether, and Chutia was once more left to its quiet and seclusion.

Old Chutia Nagpur is full from end to end of rough landmarks of the past. Here the Mundas have made their home, and for generations they have left signs of their presence behind them in the most permanent possible way. They built no palaces or temples to live after them, but their deaths are commemorated in rough monuments of stone that will last for ever. Scattered over the country-side in almost every village lie the Munda graveyards and memorial stones. Huge slabs of rock, unshaped as nature left them, they remain without name or inscription to keep guard over the memory of the dead. To mark the fact that the body is buried beneath, the stones lie flat, full length upon the ground. Hundreds of them are often to be seen grouped together in some sheltered spot outside the village beneath wide-spreading trees. At Chokahatu, the Place of Mourning, there are no fewer than seven thousand of them covering an area of seven acres. They form a singularly impressive natural graveyard, a place of silence eloquent with the memories of the nameless dead.

Some of the stones point north and south, others east and west; and there is a tradition among the Mundas that, placed in the former position, they indicate that the deceased died a natural death, in the latter position a violent one, caused in most cases by wild beasts or the bite of a snake. In many of the graveyards a large proportion point east and west, so that, if tradition speaks true, the number of violent deaths must have been large. Where the stones are only a memorial and the body does not lie buried beneath, they are placed perpendicularly, forming huge rough pillars, sometimes twelve or fourteen feet high—a miniature Stonehenge. It seems wonderful that the Mundas, with the primitive means at their disposal, should have been able to move and erect these huge blocks of stone, conveying them, as they must have done in many cases, great distances.

Beyond these sepulchral and monumental stones, there are few other remains of the past to be found in Chota Nagpore. Only here and there can still be seen the ruined forts and palaces that were once the houses of the Nagbansi Rajas, who seem to have changed their headquarters a remarkable number of times. They have not even kept to one particular part of the district, but have fairly dotted the land with buildings, which when finished were quickly deserted owing to some whim or superstition of the Rajas. Doisa, thirty miles south-west of Ranchi, was built by a Nagbansi Raja in 1664 A.D., as an inscription, still remaining, states. The palace was of an unusual height, being five-storied and of brick, the temples and adjacent buildings being constructed of elegantly carved granite. But it was deserted almost as soon as completed. The legend runs that the Raja, Raghunath Sahi, on the very first evening that he entered into possession, received a mysterious visit from a Brahmin, who suddenly appeared, whence no one knew. Walking straight into the palace where the Raja sat feasting, celebrating the completion of his house, the unknown visitor solemnly warned him that the house was ill-fated and that nothing but bad luck would follow him so long as he remained beneath its roof. The Raja, alarmed by the warning, spent the night in counsel with his courtiers, and the next morning sent for the Brahmin to question him further. But, to the general consternation, he was nowhere to be found, and none had seen him since he left the Raja's presence. That night there was not a living soul left in Doisa. The Raja and all his following had fled, leaving this new-built palace to crumble to decay.

Palkot was another residence of the family. The palace there was a large building but of no architectural interest, and that in its turn was evacuated for a newer residence. At Tilmi there are the remains of another fortress, once inhabited by a branch of the original Nagbansi family. It is interesting as containing one of the comparatively few inscriptions to be found in Chota

Nagpore. This one is written in Sanskrit over the top of a well within the walls of the courtyard, and states that the well was made in 1737 A.D., 'for the attainment of the four beatitudes.'

Pitoria, not far from Ranchi, is said by tradition to have been the birthplace of the first 'Snake-crowned' Raja. Here a festival known as the Ind parab is annually held in honour of the race. The important feature of it is a huge umbrella raised aloft on a long pole some forty feet high. The exciting part of the ceremony consists in hoisting it aloft, all the villagers being eager to bear a hand, and executing a kind of maypole dance round it when at last securely fixed.

There are temples everywhere in Old Chutia Nagpur. Five miles out from Ranchi is the largest and most important of them all—the temple of Jagannath. It is built on the plan of the great Jagannath temple at Puri, the most famous and sacred of Hindu shrines. Towering up on a solitary rock, that rises grim and rugged from the dead level of the plateau, it commands all the country round. It is a steep rough climb to the top over huge boulders that strew the ascent, but it is the only path up. From the other side there is no entrance, and the stout square walls rise up a solid mass of masonry as if designed to form an impregnable defence. Inside, a large courtyard leads to a smaller one

THE TEMPLE OF JAGANNATH, NEAR RANCHI.

where the gods reside, scarce visible in the 'dim religious light' of a small ill-ventilated mud-lined room.

Once a year, escorted by thousands of their worshippers, the gods emerge from their seclusion and face the light of the sun. It is a wonderful sight—the Rath-Jatra festival—in all the heat and dust of a June day. Thousands of pilgrims, attired as for a festival, crowd the steep ascent and far over the plains below. The huge car, with its cumbrous wheels that look as if nothing short of an elephant's strength could move them, is decked out in all the splendour of tinsel and the much-loved *genda* blossoms, that are never absent from a Hindu festival. Dragged as far up the steep ascent as possible by a crowd of willing hands, the gods are brought forth and seated in it ready for their journey down the slope to the smaller temple a stone's-throw from the foot.

There is something that appeals to the imagination, in spite of all the tawdriness and dirt, as the huge cumbrous chariot swings down the slope with sudden halts here and there as the unevenness of the road pulls it up suddenly or the long disused wheels give trouble and need repair. The natives, who have crowded to the front to see the car go by, press back on those behind as it lumbers down upon them, frowning and relentless as if to crush them beneath its weight, while the dense crowds behind, in their anxiety to see, surge forward, thrusting those in front almost beneath the wheels. A wave of excitement, real and intense, passes over the whole throng. Cries of encouragement to the struggling group around the car and exclamations of awe and interest, as it finally passes by, need little in imagination to swell them into the frenzy of bygone days that made the progress of the car of Jagannath a ghastly scene of sacrifice as the worshippers flung themselves beneath the wheels. But to-day the arm of the law is far-reaching, even if the fanatical desire for self-destruction still exists, and Jagannath swings on his way without a human sacrifice. For ten days he remains at the little temple down the slope, and is then drawn back to his gloomy seclusion in the fort-like temple on the rock till the Rath-Jatra comes round again.

From the top of Jagannath there is an excellent view of the heart and centre of Old Chutia Nagpur. The whole plateau lies spread out at its foot, with its forest of trees, its trimly demarcated fields and scattered *bastis*, few and far between. Ranchi, though so near at hand, is almost hidden out of sight in a wealth of foliage. There is nothing to be seen of it save the cathedral spire and the 'Pimple'—the two chief Ranchi landmarks—and bits of the military cantonment at Doranda nearer at hand. The 'Pimple,' so named from its appearance, is a steep conical

SMALL TEMPLE AT THE FOOT OF JAGANNATH.

hill surmounted by a tall temple-like structure intended for a summer-house. It is said to owe its existence to Colonel Ouseley, Agent to the Governor-General for the South-west Frontier province seventy years ago, whose name is still remembered in the district.

Ranchi itself is delightfully situated. Right in the middle of the big central plateau of Chota Nagpore, it stands over two thousand feet above sea level. It is all open country for miles around, wonderfully flat for its elevation and broken only here and there by groups of rocks and the long low Ramgarh hills to the north. The openness and the height give it an excellent climate, pleasantly cold in the winter months and escaping much of the long dry hot weather of the plains. The rains, too, quickly run off the elevated plateau, leaving none of the dampness and humidity that characterise the rainy season elsewhere, while they have the added compensation of showing Ranchi at its brightest and best, with a wealth of luxuriance springing to life under their fertilising influence. The gardens are a feature of Ranchi, and, after the rains, they are ablaze with a host of English annuals which the soil, clay mixed with gravel and sand, seems to suit to perfection.

It is a long straggling town with traces, in the scattered way the houses lie, of the cluster of separate villages that it once was. It is fully three miles from the further end of Ranchi to the military cantonment at Doranda, and the long straight road that joins them runs for part of the way right through the native quarters that lie grouped on either side. The bazaar, with its long irregular rows of rudely built shops, is undistinguished from others of its kind, save perhaps for a somewhat greater cleanliness and width of street. A typical Eastern crowd fills all the roadway, and, unaccustomed to anything more speedy than the *bailgari* and the *sagar*, only escapes from under one's horse's feet, with a start of alarm and scarce an inch to spare, at the latest possible moment. It is a busy road on bazaar days, thronged with groups from the villages round, walking mostly in single file, with their merchandise piled high in baskets on their heads.

The Katcherries, a long low block of red brick buildings with the smaller offices close beside, stand at the northern end of the town. Day after day, a noisy crowd of litigants covers the open space all round, talking of the ever-fascinating subject of pice and discussing the chances of the lawsuit that is going on inside. Here is the hard-faced petty zemindar, come himself to see that his case is not mismanaged and that his ryots escape not one jot of what is due from them: there an anxious accused, talking earnestly with his pleader and suggesting the best possible line of defence: or another accused, no less anxious but more cunning, intent on gaining over a hostile witness and cautiously offering the least possible coin in the way of a bribe: or a group of *box-walas* (pedlars) with an endless jumble of things to sell, mindful of none of these things, and come only to drive the biggest trade they can: while, piloted through the crowd by three blue-coated, red-turbaned constables, comes a wild-looking group of hand-cuffed Mundas sent up in a dacoity case from the south.

Outside the court room, spread under the trees, is a row of skins, tiger, leopard, bear, wolf, and hyæna, proudly guarded by some sportsman from a far-off corner of the district, who has just brought in his yearly bag to obtain the Government reward. He will get twenty-five rupees (1*l.* 13*s.* 4*d.*) for each tiger killed, five rupees for a leopard or a wolf, two rupees eight annas for a bear, and two rupees for a hyæna; and many a cultivator, if his aim with the bow and arrow has been straight or his snares well laid, will go home happy with his reward in much hard cash. Sometimes a larger reward still is offered—as much as two hundred rupees for a man-eating tiger—and he who bags it is a rich man and a hero among his fellows for many a day to come.

The European station seems to have followed the straggling outline of the native town, the bungalows lying in scattered groups on the outskirts of the bazaar. Many of them are charmingly placed. The Commissioner's, one of the largest, stands in a large park-like compound with the Ranchi lake close behind. This is a splendid piece of water, some fifty acres in extent, fringed by rows of trees on the further side, with two picturesque islands in the midst, and a pillared bathing ghat beyond, while, half hidden in a mass of foliage on the bank, stands a Hindu temple with Shiva's trident overhead, flashing out clear in the sunlight. The lake, like the structure that crowns the 'Pimple' behind it, owes its existence to Colonel Ouseley, during whose time, chiefly by prison labour, it was excavated.

Ranchi is full of picturesque bits, typical of Chota Nagpore scenery. The Judicial Commissioner's house, right at the northern end, looks on to a view scarcely to be surpassed for quiet charm and beauty. Away in the background, a haze of exquisite blue envelops a far-off range of hills, shading them with its loveliest tints after a storm of rain. Just below, the clearer purple hue of the nearer hills stands out distinct against them, with touches here and there of black-grey rock or patches of brighter colour lit up by the slanting rays of the sun. At their feet, a wealth of trees in every shade of changing green covers the foreground right down to the edge of the compound, with only glimpses here and there of an open space where the plough has turned up the rich brown earth. The whole picture is set off by the touch of colour afforded by the brilliant mass of annuals in the garden near at hand and framed in the graceful branches, with their delicate leaves and bright red masses of blossom, of the great gold mohur that overshadows the verandah. It is only one of the many beautiful bits to be found in Ranchi.

Doranda, the military cantonment, is three miles away, just across the Subarnarekha bridge. There have been troops of some kind here since Ranchi first became the headquarters of the South-west Frontier Agency until three years ago. For a long time it was garrisoned by the Ramgarh Light Infantry, first raised by Colonel Broughton at the end of the eighteenth century, and stationed in its earliest days at Hazaribagh. Later a wing of a native infantry regiment was always quartered here until removed under Lord Kitchener's recent reorganisation scheme. The cantonment has since been utilised as the headquarters of the Military Police of the province. It is a pleasant little station, well sheltered by a wealth of trees, that make of every road an avenue, and cover the cantonment from end to end. The lines and native quarters with the village and bazaar lie behind, with a glimpse here and there among the trees of a Hindu temple with its pinnacles and turrets, or a Muhammadan mosque with its flat dome-shaped roof. Further away, on the outskirts of Doranda, is the military cemetery, with the massive tombs that a past generation of Englishmen in India were wont to erect over their dead, towering up above its surrounding wall.

There is only one last bit of scattered Ranchi of special interest. The English, German, and Roman Catholic missions, which have worked with such wonderful success over large districts in Chota Nagpore, all have their headquarters here. Four Lutheran ministers, sent out by Pastor Gossner of Berlin in 1845, were the pioneers of missionary enterprise. Arriving in Ranchi, they started work among the Kols, labouring for five years before a single convert was made. Once begun, however, their numbers rapidly increased, until in 1869 there were about ten thousand native Christians to be found in the district. But in that year unfortunate dissensions began among the missionaries themselves. A number of younger men had arrived from home to help in carrying on the increased work of the mission, and they quickly found fault with the old order of things. They finally made various serious charges against the older missionaries, which, though proved to have been without foundation, brought matters to a crisis. The older men, outnumbered and receiving no support from home, were at last compelled to withdraw. They were shortly afterwards received into the

English Church by Bishop Milman in 1869, thus forming the beginning of the English mission in Ranchi which now numbers its converts by thousands.

The Cathedral—Chota Nagpore has had its own bishop since 1890—is a handsome building with a tall graceful spire, visible for many miles around. It is capable of seating something like twelve hundred people, and it is an impressive sight to see the long broad nave, with its two flanking aisles running its full length, absolutely bare of seats and thronged with a native congregation. There is an occasion of especial interest once a year when Europeans and natives join in a common service, partly in English and partly in Hindi. It is held on Christmas Eve, and save for the few Europeans seated at the top of the two side aisles, the church, beautifully decorated for the occasion, is filled to overflowing with a white-robed crowd of native worshippers. The absence of seats lends a singular impressiveness to the densely packed church, as the native Christians join in the service, seating or prostrating themselves on the floor of the nave. The whole congregation follows the service with remarkable attention and sings the Hindi hymns from memory to the old well-known English tunes. It is a wonderful sight with its curious mixture of Eastern and Western worship, and one not soon forgotten.

An old Moravian custom introduced by the first German missionaries is still kept up by the English Church and forms an interesting link with the past. Early before daybreak on Easter morning, the children of the mission school, with a large following of native Christians, assemble outside the Cathedral. Carrying lanterns and torches to light the way before the dawn breaks, they form into line, and, with the bishop, priests, and deacons, European and native, at their head, they pass slowly down the road leading to the Ranchi cemetery. The whole effect of the procession in the half-darkness that precedes the dawn is wonderfully picturesque. Nearly all are in white, from the bishop in his surplice at their head down to the last straggling follower, his scanty garment washed to an unwonted spotlessness for this special morning of the year. The lamps, swinging as the bearers walk, and the flickering torches throw their uncertain light over the slowly moving procession, with its banners raised aloft and swaying with the motion of the crowd. It all looks like the realisation of one's childish pictures of the East. Arrived at the cemetery, the long stream of white-robed figures lengthens out, winding its way along the paths, until, the circuit made, it moves towards the centre and pauses while the bishop gives a short address in Hindi on the Resurrection. All the native graves in the cemetery, smooth-plastered mounds of earth, uninscribed but not forgotten, have been freshly whitewashed in readiness for the day, and as they stand out dazzlingly in the early morning light they add the last touch of Oriental picturesqueness to the scene.

All three missions in Ranchi have many outposts in various parts of the district, and everywhere the number of Christians is steadily increasing. The English mission outside Ranchi is now entirely carried on by native padres, under the supervision of the English clergy at head-quarters, who visit the out-stations as often as possible. The mission rest-houses that one comes across scattered here and there about the district are of the most primitive description. In them the traveller finds no unnecessary luxury. In many of them, as in the one at Tapkara, near Bandgaon, there is only one room and nothing in it except a rough *charpoy*, and one chair sadly in need of repair.

The ground outside the same rest-house at Tapkara recalls another scene—that of a famine kitchen in full progress. It was one of many established all through the district during the last severe famine of 1897. Those admitted for relief got only one meal a day at five o'clock in the afternoon, but that one meal was substantial, and luxurious compared with their previous starvation diet which had reduced many of them to mere skeletons. One hundred recipients were provided for daily at Tapkara, and the full number never failed to put in an appearance. *Dal-bhat* (the native dish of pulse and rice) was the only course, but it was served liberally, and if they did not exactly grow fat upon it, they at least survived in comfort till the days of plenty came again.

Kunti, between Ranchi and Tapkara, where all three missions have large outposts, only within the last few years has had its own excitement. It had been long known as one of the most unruly parts of the district, and a spirit of unrest seemed to have taken possession of all the Mundas from Tamar and Kunti down to the borders of Singbhum. The leading spirit was Birsa, a young man of only some twenty-one years of age, who had been brought up in the Christian Mission School at Chaibasa. He appears to have fallen a prey to religious mania, preaching a new religion, and professing himself to be an Incarnation of the Deity. The influence he exercised over the people was extraordinary, inspiring them with a measure of his own fanaticism. His new religion, readily embraced, inculcated a belief that the days of the White Raj were over and that the time of his own kingdom had come. Birsa had been previously sentenced to two years' imprisonment, but, released before his sentence had expired, in the Diamond Jubilee year, he again began his preaching, freely advocating the use of force and arson, and the secret preparation of

SOME FOLLOWERS OF THE PROPHET BIRSA BEING ESCORTED TO JAIL BY THE POLICE.

weapons of attack. Christmas Eve was fixed upon as the time of rising, when all the officials of the White Raj and all Christian converts were to be murdered and their houses burnt.

A time was secretly appointed for the rising, and on the day fixed a Thana was attacked and a few houses destroyed, one European missionary narrowly escaping with his life. But the disturbance was quickly over and Birsa captured. It is said by those who saw him that his face bore an extraordinary resemblance to the usual portrayal of the face of Christ, a likeness which he must have seen in his early days in the Chaibasa Mission School and doubtless fostered for his own purposes. Birsa died in prison while his case was pending, and of his chief followers eighty-seven were committed to the Sessions Court, some of them being eventually imprisoned and others transported to the Andamans for life. So quickly came and went the last of the Kol risings in Chota Nagpore.

South of Kunti and close by Tapkara runs the Karo, one of the typical rivers of the district, a rushing torrent in the rains and a tiny stream in a bed of sand for the remainder of the year. Near Ramtollya is the ferry. It is a dangerous crossing when the river is in flood. There are quicksands all along its course continually shifting and making it impossible to keep a permanent ford. The only boats available are of the craziest description, and when it so happens that they are laden with a palki, the chances are considerable that they capsize. The traveller enters the boat with a rueful look at his bedding and household gods, and is not greatly encouraged by the information suddenly vouchsafed that it is necessary to land in mid-stream. Halfway the river becomes too shallow for the boat, except when the torrent is too strong to cross at all, and there is nothing for it but to get out and wade knee-deep or be carried by a couple of staggering coolies. The latter, though often the more preferable, is not exactly a pleasant method of getting ashore. One never quite loses the feeling that one may be wading oneself the next moment or, worse still, slip sprawling into the stream. The coolies cross their hands and one takes one's seat, an arm round the neck of each with an awkward clutch, as, feeling them stagger beneath one's weight, one expects momentary immersion. But those who fall by the way are few, and the coolies can be trusted to land one safely if not comfortably on the opposite bank.

There are rivers flowing in every direction like a network all over the plateau of Old Chutia Nagpur. In the rains every hill sends out its streams to work a way for themselves across the level or to join others that have already made their course. The rocky sandy beds that they hollow out are left dry for the greater part of the year, when the rushing torrent of the rains has expended itself and fallen down to the lower level of the plains. Occasionally the drop from the higher plateau is deep and sudden, and the water rushing along the upper level dashes over the fall to find its course again below. Chota Nagpore is the land of waterfalls, miniature most of them, but attaining in two places magnificent proportions. Hundru Gagh is famous as one of the sights of the province. Here, right on the edge of the Hazaribagh district, the high Ranchi plateau ends abruptly and the Subarnarekha, flowing along its level course above, comes suddenly upon a sheer drop of three hundred and twenty feet. It is a splendid fall, dashing over first in one long straight sheet of water, then breaking into a cloud of spray and leaping on from rock to rock until it reaches its new level at last in a pool of foam and pursues again the even tenor of its way across the plateau below. In the rains the fall of water is tremendous, thundering over the cliff in one broad sheet almost the entire depth, the lower falls half hidden in the spray. Clear up against the sky a forest of trees borders it on the Hazaribagh side and clothes the steep face of the cliff its full length from top to bottom, shrubs and foliage springing up between the rocks and flourishing almost in the very pathway of the waterfall.

The Dawson Falls, out beyond Palandu and

Taimara, have only a drop of one hundred and fourteen feet, but the river rushes over, a solid mass of water, falling straight down the full depth to the level below. They are broader than Hundru Gagh and the force of the water is greater, smaller falls above and below adding their quota to the deafening roar. The Dawson Falls are a perfect panorama of natural beauty, framed everywhere in a glorious luxuriance of foliage.

There is an occasional bear to be got in the jungle round the Dawson Falls, and the hills near Taimara, six miles off, offer a better chance still. Further on, along the Ranchi road, Bundu and Tamar seldom prove a blank. All the country round here is just the place for bear—range after range of undulating hills, covered with thick sal jungle. But there is singularly little else to be got. It is not so long since leopards and even tigers were to be found, but the jungles now seem to have been swept absolutely clear of life—save for the bear that a careful beat seldom fails to produce.

The shooting all over the district is nothing compared with what it once was. Only a few years ago vast tracts of jungle remained practically untouched, forming natural game preserves well stocked with tiger, leopard, panther, and bear. But Chota Nagpore is no longer an unexplored district, and there are few parts that have not been well shot over, while the rewards offered by Government have been an added inducement to the native to exercise all his skill with the bow and arrow or the European rifle, which is fast becoming an accustomed weapon in his hands. Enormous tracts of sal jungle, moreover, have been cut down in recent years, exterminating large quantities of game and driving what remains into the remoter parts of the district.

Palamau, until recently a subdivision of Ranchi but now forming a district of its own, has always been one of the best shooting-grounds in Chota Nagpore. It is a land of rivers, mountains, and jungle, and even now in many parts is absolutely undisturbed. But Daltongunj, the headquarters station on the North Koel river, is now the centre of a large coal district, and the introduction of the railway has already made great changes, threatening the peace of the jungle and foreshadowing the inevitable result of the advance of civilisation when Palamau too will cease to be a natural preserve and the haunt of big game.

CHAPTER IV

THE LAND OF THE HOS

SINGBHUM is the Land of the Hos. Centuries ago they took possession, and, clinging to it with unyielding tenacity, they have held it against all comers from that day to this. The ruling chiefs of another race, insisting on their Rajput descent and their supremacy over the Hos, claim that the country takes its name from them—Singbhum, the Land of the Singhs. It is a derivation as probable as another, and it may be that the country had acquired its name before the Hos came southwards from the uplands of Chutia Nagpur. But the Hos scornfully reject the suggestion and claim another derivation for the land they have made their own. They called it, they say, after Sing Bonga, the greatest of all their deities and the Creator of the World. Throughout Chota Nagpore, the aborigines have a fondness for naming rocks and hills after their numerous gods and goddesses, and it is not improbable that the land itself should have been given the appellation of Sing Bonga, the

A HO: FAMILY (THREE GENERATIONS).

Sun-god, who is the object of their greatest veneration.

But whatever may be the derivation of the name Singbhum, there is no doubt that from the first moment of their coming it has been the land of the Hos. The incidents of their arrival are unfortunately fragments of the vast history of Chota Nagpore long since lost in some remote period of the past and now hopeless of recovery. The Hos themselves know little of the beginnings of their race, and, a people of no great pretensions, tradition for once has not been busy on their behalf. They acknowledge their kinship with the Mundas, and that in earlier days they dwelt with them in Chutia Nagpur, whence, at some later unremembered date, they set out to make a home for themselves in Singbhum. But they deny, indignantly, and with reason, the boast of the Oraons that it was they who drove them out from their former home in Chutia Nagpur and forced them to settle elsewhere. It is a boast that a comparison between the Ho and Oraon physique, and the after history of the Hos themselves, are alone sufficient to discredit.

But why the Hos left their earlier settlement and came southwards to Singbhum is a question still unanswered. The Singhs, anxious to preserve the traditions of their own previous occupation of the country, have invented a story that the Hos first came from Nagpur in the train of the marriage procession of a bride for the Singbhum Raja. But it is nothing more than an obvious fable invented with a purpose. The Bhuiyas, with their chiefs and their claims to Rajput descent, were undoubtedly in possession of the land before the Hos appeared, and another race has left enduring monuments in stone behind it to prove how real and permanent its occupation once was. The Jains here, as in Manbhum, must have been a powerful community, and it is astonishing to find how completely they have vanished from off the whole country-side, leaving no sign whither or why they went. Only the fine stone temples they have built have lasted into another age as monuments of their piety and their one-time presence in the land.

Although so little is known of the first coming of the Hos, it is evident that they came in sufficient force and strength to take and occupy the open central plateau—the most fertile lands in all Singbhum. Here they cleared the jungle and settled down, finding it so much to their taste that they ceased their wanderings and made it their permanent home. From the first they jealously excluded all outside influence, and to this was undoubtedly due in a great measure their success. 'The Kolhan for the Hos' was their consistent policy, and they carried it out with rigid conservatism, admitting no other race within their settlements. Even pilgrims on their way to Jagannath fared badly at their hands. They were roughly turned aside and forced to make a long détour, the Kolhan becoming known far and wide as a forbidden land which no stranger might cross. It was the Tibet of Chota Nagpore.

None but a strong and warlike race could have maintained such a barrier against the outside world. Another name for the Hos is the Larka or Fighting Kols—a name they have fully justified. As far back as their annals go, they are found fighting, and always crowned with victory, driving back invaders or carrying war and devastation into the enemy's lands. They are a fine race, tall and well knit, stronger and more active than their neighbours, and with an undaunted courage and endurance found among no other race of Chota Nagpore. Living their own lives, free and unrestrained, in the jungles or on the hills of Singbhum, they developed all the best qualities of their kind, strength, courage, and endurance.

Singbhum itself seems like a land especially designed by nature for the Hos. Right away in the southernmost corner of Chota Nagpore, bordering on the Native States and the tributary Mahals of Orissa, it is a wild rugged country, walled in by range on range of hills and covered with dense patches of tree jungle. In the centre, well guarded, lies a plateau seven hundred and fifty feet above the sea. Quick to perceive its unrivalled advantages, the main body of the Hos stopped here. Once cleared of jungle, it proved to be a fertile land, well watered from the surrounding hills and yielding an ample return for their labour.

But what appealed to the Fighting Kols most of all was the natural strength of the country to hold against foes from without. It is admirably planned for defence. Shut in by a barrier of hills, massed together in a series of bold irregular peaks, the country is almost inaccessible to an invading army. On the south and west there is nothing to fear, so compact are the hills and dense the jungle. More open on the other sides it is still easy of defence at the passes through the hills by which alone entrance can be gained to the heart of the Kolhan. It was the country above all others especially suited to a jealously exclusive people like the Hos, and it enabled them to maintain their isolation long after the reserve of the other races of Chota Nagpore had been broken down.

Far away to the south, where the ranges of hills unite in the highest peaks of all, is the wildest part of the Kolhan. It is a splendid mass of rocky summits, lonely and inaccessible, the highest of all rising up three thousand five hundred feet above the sea and picturesquely named 'Saranda of the Seven Hundred Hills.' The dense jungle that covered the slopes was a safe retreat before an invading force, under cover of which they could carry out all their tactics of irregular warfare. Here lived the most uncivilised of the Hos, those who had not settled down on the plateau below but had preferred the greater freedom of the jungle and the hills. Small clearings and groups of ill-built huts mark their dwelling-places, whence they were ever ready to sally forth to the help of their kinsmen in time of need. Change has touched this part of the Kolhan not at all. To-day the Hos still lead the same simple life that their ancestors lived for generations—save only that the days of forays are over and the arm of the British law reaches even into the remotest corner of the jungle.

Nominally, in the old days, the Hos owned the supremacy of the Rajas of Singbhum. But how slight was the bond between them, all that is known of their history before and after the British occupation proves. They were ever ready to follow the local Raja when he led them out to battle, but that was probably the only allegiance they ever unquestionably gave. They were a splendid fighting race and the Rajas made full use of them, as pawns in the game, in their quarrels with each other. But often the Hos proved restive, and attempt after attempt was made to reduce them to obedience. Some time in the middle of the eighteenth century things had come to such a pass that the Raja of Singbhum called in the help of the Maharaja of Chota Nagpore. A force of twenty thousand men, headed by the Maharaja, Dripnath Sahi himself, advanced into the Kolhan, joined on the way by the levies of the local Rajas far and near. The Hos then adopted those tactics which stood them in such good stead, now and on subsequent occasions. Retreating before the invading force, they allowed it to penetrate far into their country unopposed, until, cut off from help from without, they had it at their mercy. Armed with their national weapons, bows and arrows and battle-axes, they swept down suddenly from the surrounding hills and carried all before them with their mad irregular charge. The huge unwieldy army of the invaders scattered and fled panic-stricken at the first onset, an immense number falling at the hands of the infuriated Hos. It is their first remembered battle and victory.

In 1770 came another attack from the same source. It met with a similar fate, and this time the Hos retaliated by pursuing the enemy into their own lands and laying waste the whole country-side. There was only one more unsuccessful attempt to subdue them in 1800, and then at last the turbulent Hos came face to face with the British Raj. It was forty years since the country had been made over to the Company as part of Bengal, Behar, and Orissa, but Singbhum lay on the very outskirts of this large district, and no attempt was made to deal with it till 1803. In that year, the Marquis Wellesley, then Governor-General, sent to ask the help of the Raja of Seraikela against the Mahratta chief Raghoji Bonsla. The Raja, flattered at being asked, promised his help, though he was careful to stipulate that his right to hold his land rent-free should be always respected.

For the next sixteen years there appears to have been no communication between the British Government and Singbhum. It was absolutely unexplored country, and nothing except vague rumours of their warlike deeds was known of the Hos. But in 1819, in response to an appeal for help from the local Rajas, the first British force entered the Kolhan. Under Major Roughsedge, the Political Agent, a considerable body of infantry, cavalry, and artillery advanced into the country unopposed. The Hos again adopted their old tactics. They had invariably proved successful against former invaders, and as yet they had had no experience of British troops. They made no show of resistance at the outset, but hanging cautiously on the flanks of the invading army, they allowed it to advance into the heart of their country till it reached the Roro river, not far from the present station of Chaibasa. Then, with all their old dash and courage, they began hostilities. A small party of them rashly attacked a band of camp-followers in full sight of the main force. A troop of cavalry, hastily sent out to avenge this insult, succeeded in intercepting the retreat of the Hos towards their mountain fastnesses. Finding themselves thus cut off, they turned, nothing daunted, to face the enemy. It was a hopeless attempt, the rush of ill-armed, impetuous savages against the disciplined charge of regular cavalry. As the attacking force came on, the Hos discharged their volley of arrows, but making little impression on the advancing ranks of the enemy, they threw aside their bows and rushed to meet the charge of cavalry battle-axe in hand. It was a splendid exhibition of their old fighting spirit, and nowhere in Chota Nagpore had the British troops experienced a resistance so spirited and courageous. But the Hos had met with more than their match at last, and the hitherto victorious race suffered its earliest defeat.

This encounter was only the first of many such. That they were no longer invincible was a bitter lesson for them to learn. Time after time they flung themselves with disastrous results upon the trained unyielding ranks of sepoys. They had been used to carry all before them in the first impetuous rush, and they took long to realise that the old rash onset now led them no longer to victory but to death. It was not until they had been scattered and driven back at every point that the Hos of northern Singbhum learned the lesson at last and made submission.

Their wilder kinsmen to the south, however, still remained untamed, and Major Roughsedge set out on a difficult journey through their hostile country, determined to reduce them to order. Roads there were none, only jungle-paths from village to village. Now and again the forest was so thick that it was almost impossible for one man to walk alone, and a way through had to be cut as they advanced. Range after range of hills had to be crossed where progress was slow and difficult. Always hovering round their line of advance, secure themselves in their knowledge of the locality, were the Hos ever ready to seize the moment of greatest difficulty to attack. The journey after all could result in little but to increase the respect the Hos had already acquired for the British troops, whose powers of endurance they reluctantly admitted almost rivalled their own. But they were too scattered and the country too impregnable for the invading force to make much impression, and no sooner had it left the country than the old local feuds with their Rajas again broke out.

Two years later, another force was sent down to put a stop to the constant disorder that still agitated the Kolhan. The Hos this time, in the face of British troops, readily submitted, praying only to be taken directly under Government control and not to be made subject again to the local chiefs. But, unfortunately, their petition was rejected, and they were once more ordered to pay tribute to their Rajas—eight annas for every plough. It was an impossible settlement, however, and no sooner had the troops withdrawn than anarchy once more began.

But a day of reckoning came for the Hos at last. Their depredations hitherto had been but local, and only the neighbouring potentates, unable to take care of themselves, had suffered. But the part they took in the Kol Mutiny of 1831 finally decided their fate. The news of the rising in Chutia Nagpur tempted the Fighting Hos and drew them further afield. They had none of the real grievances of their neighbours across the border, and so purely local was the disturbance that the contingent they sent to join the mutineers was the only one during the whole of the rising that was ever found far from its own home. It was simply the love of fighting for its own sake that the Hos had not been able to resist. So strong was the support they gave to the Kols of Chutia Nagpur, that Captain Wilkinson, then Agent to the Governor-General, resolved to turn his attention to the Kolhan as soon as peace was restored. It was clear that previous expeditions against them had had no permanent results and that the real trouble lay in the submission to the local Rajas, always hitherto insisted upon. Consequently it was wisely resolved to bring them directly under British rule. Two regiments of native infantry, a brigade of guns, and the Ramgarh battalion were despatched into the Kolhan—the most formidable army that the Hos had yet seen. But, undaunted by previous defeats, they prepared for a strenuous resistance, until, finally persuaded that they would no longer be required to submit to their hated Rajas, they came in voluntarily and quietly submitted to the British Government.

The new policy was at once put into force. Chaibasa became the headquarters station of the district, which was controlled by a British officer with authority over all the Kolhan, including six hundred and twenty villages, with a population estimated at the time at something like ninety thousand. The old assessment of eight annas tribute for every plough was still retained, but it was paid henceforth into the Government treasury, and no tie whatever was left to bind them to the Rajas, whose control they had so strenuously resisted. So rapidly did the condition of the people improve under these altered conditions that, less than twenty years later, the eight annas assessment was doubled without a murmur of complaint on the part of the Hos. Henceforward, with one brief interval during the Sepoy Mutiny of 1857, they have remained peaceful subjects of the British Raj.

As elsewhere in Chota Nagpore, it is only in recent years that a beginning has been made in developing the natural resources of the district. Iron ore, copper, limestone, chrome, and manganese, which have so long lain untouched, are all now being profitably exploited. The Dhalbhum iron mines are being worked by the Bengal Iron and Steel Company, the output being estimated in 1908 as 18,907 tons, with every prospect of further development. In Dhalbhum, also, Messrs. Tata, Sons & Co. have fixed upon a site for their iron and steel factory, which promises to provide not only the immediate locality but the whole of India with so important an industry. Copper and chrome ore still await further development. Difficulties of transport have not yet been entirely overcome in many instances, roads being often non-existent, and the railway so far removed as to render valuable deposits useless owing to the impossibility of placing them on the market. Two new lines, however, are already under construction that will for the first time bring hitherto inaccessible wealth within reach, one in connection with Messrs. Tata, Sons & Co.'s steel and iron works, and the other in connection with the Bengal Iron and Steel Company's iron mines in the Kolhan. A great future in this direction undoubtedly awaits Singbhum.

Chaibasa, which in 1837 became the headquarters of the new district then formed, was chosen as being the only place of any size in the whole Kolhan. Nowhere in Chota Nagpore is

THE MAIN STREET, CHAIBASA.

the population so scattered as in Singbhum. Villages, far and near, dotted over the plateau, or nestling, a mere cluster of rough-built huts at the foot of the hills, all look to Chaibasa as the centre of life. Yet even this metropolis of the Hos, with its straggling streets and wealth of trees, is of no great size. It is a picturesque little town, standing on the banks of the Roro, with a peaceful old-world air. One derivation of the name Chaibasa is the 'Dwelling-place of Rest,' and none could be more appropriate. Miles away from a railway until recent years, and even now sixteen miles from the nearest station, there is nothing progressive about Chaibasa. As it was in the beginning, so it is now, and the spirit of rest broods over it. There is another derivation of the name scarcely less appropriate—the Land of Shade. Trees flourish everywhere, bathing the sun-baked earth in grateful shadow. The long street that runs through the centre of the town is one of the most charming pictures of village life to be found in all Chota Nagpore. The shops, built irregularly on either side, with their low pillared verandahs rising scarce a man's height from the ground and filled with rice and cloth and merchandise, run the whole length of the street, while close in front of each, planted in no prim straight line but carelessly, almost as if for picturesque effect, run rows of arching *karanj* trees, their fresh green leaves casting a cool refreshing shade over road and shops and passers-by below. It is a charming glimpse of a dwelling-place of rest and shade.

There is little doing here, save the ordinary lazy round of daily Eastern life. Only for one day in the week it forms the centre of a busy scene. Every Tuesday is bazaar day, and the place is astir with the dawn. The whole country-side round Chaibasa is awake, dotted here and there with groups of Hos from every village far and near, filing in with their baskets on their heads and talking cheerfully in pleased anticipation of the day. Wending their way towards the town, they take up their places on the wide open space where the *hât* (market) is held. Here may be seen a little company just arrived from the same village ten miles away and busy setting out their wares for sale. Close by stands a group of Ho women, with their free, independent carriage, a striking contrast to their shrinking Hindu sisters in the foreground, who instinctively crouch back and cover their faces as one approaches, with an irresistible impulse bred of long centuries of seclusion. But as far as the Hos are concerned, and they are in the majority, it is a light-hearted, good-tempered crowd, eager to buy or sell and to strike a bargain, but with none of that loud-voiced wrangling and vituperation so typical of an Eastern bazaar.

Once a year Chaibasa is the scene of a greater

A SNAKE-CHARMER AT THE 'MELA.'

gathering still. Then not only Hos from the villages round, but men from distant Dhalbhum and Seraikela, from Porohat and far-off 'Saranda of the Seven Hundred Hills,' crowd in and set the little town astir with life. It is the time of the great annual fair held on the closing days of the year in the middle of the Indian winter. Here, as at every native *mela*, pleasure and business are combined, and, the bargaining and selling done, the night is given up to dancing and festivity. The last day of the fair is reserved for races and athletic sports. Active and energetic, the Hos delight in these feats of strength and skill. Their ingenuity offers some novel devices for the obstacle and the more familiar wheelbarrow race, which boys and spectators always thoroughly enjoy. Many of the men who take part in the contests are of splendid physique, and, accustomed to an out-of-door life, are capable of a tremendous amount of bodily exertion. They seem at times absolutely tireless and able to do with a minimum of sleep. None but a race living, as the Hos have done for generations, the free open-air life of the hills and jungles, could pursue the chase on foot all day and dance all night in the way they do.

But, fine race as the Ho men are, they have to give way on many points to their women-folk in stature and development. There is no mistaking the Ho women. None of their sex elsewhere in Chota Nagpore can compare with them. Generously built, tall, overtopping the men, and perfectly formed, with a free graceful carriage, they are a splendid race. As they walk, stepping out with an unrestrained independent air, swinging their arms and holding head and shoulders erect, they present a charming picture of unstudied grace of motion. They wear but one garment of long coarse cloth, white with a red border, draped round the waist, and then caught up and thrown carelessly over the shoulder. It is a wonderfully becoming dress, showing off the figure to perfection and leaving all the limbs free, the long strip that hangs over the shoulder adding its touch of grace to all their movements. As a rule, they wear few ornaments, save a string of coral round their necks, and the brass or silver bracelets and anklets that the native woman of the East is rarely found without. They have little love for the gaudy strings of beads so dear to the hearts of the Mundas and Oraons, and their ears and noses they are happily content to leave unadorned.

All their art of decoration the Ho women reserve for their hair. Flowers only are used, and none that are bright and gay come amiss in the arrangement of the headdress. The hair is gathered up in a knot behind, which the Ho maiden does not scorn to enlarge artificially if Nature has not been sufficiently generous. The knot is worn on the right-hand side of the back of the head and gives free scope for decoration. It is the most important part of their toilet, and they take elaborate pains to make it a success, revelling in the effects of the bright red of the *palas* and the cotton, or the pale yellow of the sal against the jet-black background of the hair. Thus simply and tastefully attired, they attend the dance, to meet with the admiration they deserve.

Yet, charming and handsome as the Ho ladies are, it is proverbial that to find an old maid one must go to the Kolhan. Old maids are so rare a commodity in India that it seems strange at first sight to find them here, where the women are so fine a race. But it is not that they fail to receive their due meed of admiration from the men. Of that they get their full share; but what is the use of admiration, as they themselves say, if it does not lead to a proposal? The great drawback from the man's point of view is that the price of a wife in the Kolhan is extraordinarily high. Fathers, insisting on the dignity of their families, demand a large *pan*—the price due from the bridegroom to the father of the bride. It is usually payable in cattle, and the intending bridegroom must be a rich man who can pay the *pan* demanded for ladies of the best families. There is no such thing as child marriage among the Hos, and a girl must wait until she is chosen by a man who can afford sufficient head of cattle to satisfy her father's dignity. It is hard luck on the ladies, as the men hang back afraid of the price, and they realise themselves that they must be doubly attractive to tempt the hesitating swain. Once when a snapshot was being taken of a group of these ladies, who, in spite of their attractiveness, were still unwed, it was suggested to them, just as the photograph was going to be taken, that one of them should marry a day labourer. As the price of each of them was about thirty head of cattle, the ladies, immensely taken with the joke, smiled broadly, to the ruin of the photograph.

It is at the village dances that most of the courting takes place. But even though the momentous question of the *pan* has been settled, many things may occur to prevent the course of true love running smoothly. The Hos, like the Mundas, are a prey to superstitious fears, and the bride and bridegroom spend an anxious time before the wedding-day arrives, lest bad omens should appear to cause the ceremony to be postponed or perchance abandoned altogether. But, all dangers successfully avoided, on the fateful day the bride is escorted to the bridegroom's village by all her young female friends, with much singing and dancing by the way. The bridegroom, with all his relatives, comes out to meet the bride's procession, and together they return to the village to feast and drink the inevitable rice beer. There is no proper marriage ceremony. The bridegroom pledges the bride, pouring some of the liquid from his cup into hers, and she returns the compliment. Henceforward they are man and wife, and it can almost invariably be said that they live happily ever afterwards. Their domestic relations are singularly fortunate. The wife is the companion of her husband, a careful housekeeper and absolutely contented with her lot, while she receives every mark of respect and affection from her spouse. In fact, so happy is the lot of the wife that it has been whispered that henpecked husbands are not unknown in the Kolhan.

The funeral ceremonies of the Hos are interesting for one especially curious custom that prevails. After the body has been cremated, the ashes are placed in an earthen vessel until the arrangements for interment have been completed. Then the chief mourner, carrying the vessel with the remains of the deceased on her head, leads the funeral procession to every house in the village, the inhabitants of which come out and pay their last tribute of respect to the dead. The deep solemn notes of the drums and the low-voiced grief of the women form a weird funeral march as the procession winds from house to house, returning at last to the grave prepared close to the house of the deceased. Rice and other food is first thrown in, and then the vessel containing the remains is lowered into the hole and covered over with earth. A huge uncut slab of stone is placed over the spot to mark the grave and guard it against desecration. Outside the village, the Hos, like the Mundas, put up another monument to the deceased's memory in the form of a huge pillar of rock varying in height from four to twelve or fourteen feet.

Quiet and well-mannered as the Hos are at all other times, there is one season of the year when they throw off all restraint, giving their primitive instincts full play. It is at the end of harvest, during the Magh festival, when the work of the fields is done and the people are free to cease toil and celebrate the gathering-in of their crops. Then, after the long spell of labour in the fields, they are ready to plunge into a whirl of pleasure, feeling, in their own words, 'full of devilry.' Intoxicated with excitement, they abandon themselves to a period of perfect riot and debauch. Men and women, old and young, alike let themselves go in pure reckless enjoyment of the moment, obeying the first impulse that comes uppermost in their minds without restraint. The result is a scene of wild orgy. Not content, too, with their own local celebration of the festival, they arrange that it shall be held in different villages at different times, so that, passing from one village to another, all may take part in a

HO MEMORIAL STONES.

long succession of celebrations until even the energetic Ho has had his fill. Dancing, the invariable accompaniment of every festival, plays a large part here. But the slow stately measure of the ordinary dances is flung aside and the steps grow lively and spirited, until, the excitement increasing with the frantic beating of the drums and the imbibing of much liquor, the whole ends in a wild mêlée and pandemonium of sound.

Except for this annual outbreak, the Hos are a remarkably steady, self-respecting people. An excessive fondness for rice beer is a weakness of theirs as of all the Kols, and the liquor shop in the village is the most popular of resorts. But their potations seem to have little after-effect upon them, always in condition as they are from constant exercise. Crime is rare among them, and, although one derivation of the word Chaibasa is the 'Home of Thieves,' it is a tradition now, whatever their reputation may have been in the past, that the 'Hos don't thieve.' They have a contempt for the concealment that is the necessary accompaniment of theft, and it is a noticeable trait that when they do commit a crime they are at no pains to conceal it. They have been known in several cases to give themselves up voluntarily after the commission of an offence and ask that punishment might be meted out to them. For the same reason, they are as a rule a truthful race, scorning a lie as exhibiting a want of courage, a charge that, as they themselves proudly boast, has never been made against a Ho.

Another trait, peculiarly characteristic of the race, is their extreme sensitiveness. So remarkably developed is it that it has become proverbial with all who know them. A harsh word or a public slight wounds their feelings to an extraordinary degree. The women are particularly sensitive. A sharp rebuke evokes no reply, but it weighs upon the mind of the recipient, who broods over it in silence, becoming for a time depressed and inconsolable. In that condition it is unsafe for her to be left alone, or suicide may be the result. There is a saying among them that for the woman reproved by her husband 'nothing remains but the water at the bottom of the well.' Suicides in the Kolhan have been of common occurrence, and instances have been reported where Ho women have drowned themselves, heartbroken and despairing, because of some harsh word from their husbands given in a moment of anger, or some slight put upon them by another. It is owing doubtless to this common sensitiveness that the Hos live peaceably and amicably among themselves. Quarrelling is the exception, even among the women, and to hear their voices raised in anger is a rare event indeed—a pleasing contrast to the often shrill-voiced, volubly abusive woman of the East.

With this gentle kindly nature one would have imagined that they furnished hopeful ground for the Christian Missions that are established in the district. But here again the barrier of rigid exclusiveness they have always maintained comes into play. Though without the caste prejudices of the Hindus, they have no mercy on anyone who disobeys the traditions of their race. No Ho would take water or food from one of another race, and as such any one of their number who embraces Christianity is considered, being outside the pale of the Ho community and not participating in the rites and festivals of his family. Converts thus fare badly among the Hos, and few adults have broken through the rigid customs of a lifetime and adopted the Christian faith. It is to the children that the missionaries chiefly turn their attention, and, as in Ranchi, the Anglicans, Roman Catholics, and Germans all have stations here with their churches, schools, and native padres and outposts in the villages round. Not least important is the English church in Chaibasa. In the English mission schools the boys and girls number something like five hundred, and there they may be seen at various kinds of manual labour, learning useful lessons that will enable them to earn their living later on. The English church lies at the far end of Chaibasa, in Nimdhi, the city of nim trees, a long, low building with its picturesque bell-tower strangely reminiscent of a rustic church in some far-off English village.

In the illustration some of the boys of the mission school are showing how the Ho shikari lays his snares for the tiger that has carried off his cattle and terrified the village. A bow is fixed flat on the ground, fully drawn, with the arrow in position. A string carefully fastened so as to release the arrow at a touch is attached to it and fastened, a foot above the ground, to pegs on either side of the path which the tiger is known to frequent. If he takes that path again, his fate is sealed. By knocking against the string he releases the arrow, which, if carefully fixed, cannot fail to hit him. To avoid the serious danger that such a contrivance might be to anyone passing along that way, another string is fastened across the path a few yards on either side, three or four feet high. A man coming down the path must brush against the string, which is so contrived as to release the arrow, thus discharging it well in advance of the passer-by, and avoiding all chance of mishap. It is an ingenious method of dealing with a wily foe not always to be otherwise caught.

But the Hos, though they know well how to set a snare, are noted shikaris on more legitimate lines. They are keen sportsmen and straight shots who have made good use of their national weapon—the bow and arrow—from their earliest

THE HO METHOD OF SNARING A TIGER.

years. There is no finer hunting-ground in Chota Nagpore than their country, which affords a wonderful variety of game, big and small. Away to the south, the jungle lies undisturbed, a glimpse of what the whole district once was in the days before even the earliest of settlers had made it their home. Only recently a single day's beat in the thick tree-jungle brought out no less than six tigers, a fair record for even the best shooting-grounds in India. Here too in the deepest recesses of the forest is the haunt of the bison and the wild buffalo. It is a long tramp after them, far from any camping-ground, and there is no way but on foot. Yet a spice of danger lends excitement to the chase, and a fine pair of horns more than repays the day's exertion. Right away in Dhalbhum, small herds of elephants sometimes find their way up from Morbhanj, but they are rare visitors, and prefer the still greater seclusion of their home in the Meghasanni hills across the border in Orissa.

The Hos, in common with most of the aboriginal tribes of the district, keep up the great national hunts in the month of May. Each jungle has its own local beat, but it is no uncommon thing for the Hos to travel far afield and swell the ranks of a bigger hunt than their own small jungle can provide. Then parties of Mundas cross the borders from Tamar, and Hos collect from every quarter, from the far west of Anandpur and Saranda of the Seven Hundred Hills and the far-off eastern limits of Dhalbhum to the nearer tracts of Porohat and Seraikela, a crowd of mixed races from all quarters hunting in one vast assemblage. They form a striking array of huntsmen as they stand at ease waiting for the hunt to begin. Prominent among them all are the Hos, keen sportsmen, unpretentious in dress and appearance, yet ever first in the chase: the Munda and Oraon, gorgeous in ornaments of bead and brass and silver, armed with *baluas* (axes) of many shapes: the Santal, tall and strong, with well-knit frame adapted for the chase, armed with his deadly bow and arrows: the Kherrias, sturdy hillmen from Manbhum and a crowd of followers besides, breaking the perpetual silence of the jungle with far-sounding drums and deep-voiced horns. Here and there one prouder than the rest is armed with a matchlock of wondrous make and size, a weapon that looks more dangerous to its owner than to his intended prey. Last of all, if he grace the proceedings with his presence, comes the local Raja or zemindar to take his seat on the *machan*, towards which it is the object of the beaters to drive the game.

But the beat is far too huge and half organised for things to turn out exactly as they should. The usual ending is for groups of scattered beaters to straggle out in front of the *machan* instead of formed in one long wide-spread line. The whole beat is not without its distinct element of danger to man as well as beast. The excitement is intense as the drums beat and the horns are sounded and the wild cries of the men pass along the line. No sooner does an animal emerge from the undergrowth than a dozen arrows are let fly, some of which go wide of the mark and fall perilously near the straggling line of beaters. Even the *machan* of the Raja is not exactly a haven of safety. The wave of excitement reaches its height as the beat nears its end, and the arrows fly more wildly as the animals make their last dash for freedom across the open space around the *machan.* It requires some nerve on the part of the occupant to maintain his position when an arrow whizzes past his head and sticks in the tree behind. A straight eye and a steady aim, too, from the *machan* itself are needed to bring down the frightened quarry as it dashes from cover with a crowd of shrieking, gesticulating natives closing in on all sides.

It is a wonderful collection of game laid out in the open when the drive is done. Only occasionally is there a tiger, leopard, or panther to grace the spoil, or a wild buffalo or bison for a highly prized trophy. But bears seldom fail to swell the bag, and sambhur, cheetal, and barking deer are also there, unless the drive has been particularly unsuccessful. The pigs have fallen an easy prey to the arrows of the beaters and have rarely reached the *machan* to run the gauntlet of the superior weapons of the Raja's party. Hares, peacocks, jungle-fowls, partridges, doves, and even squirrels complete the bag, a sufficiently varied one for a single beat.

CHAPTER V

LIFE IN A SANTAL VILLAGE

No Saheb, so the villagers say, has ever been this way before. It is nothing but a ragged collection of huts, this smallest of Santal villages, buried far away in the deep recesses of the Tundi jungle. Riding along the rough *sagar* track that winds for miles through the forest, one comes upon it suddenly, half hidden among the trees. It stands in the middle of an open space, cleared of the jungle, with tiny patches of garden and cultivation beyond and the forest of trees closing it in again on the further side.

There are not more than a dozen habitations all told, clustering together as if for company in the midst of the surrounding loneliness, and so closely and irregularly built that one can scarce tell where the one begins and the other ends. They are the most lightly constructed of buildings possible, nothing but wattle and earth, sal stakes planted firmly in the ground, interlaced with light bamboos and covered liberally with mud. Generally the roof is of thatch, but sometimes tiled with the *kapra* (native tiles), of which the potter, busy at his wheel, seems to be always making ready an inexhaustible supply. All the houses are small, the largest of them not more than fourteen feet square by eight feet high, and windows there are none, only an open verandah on one side, giving access to the rooms within.

Outside is a tiny courtyard, fenced in all round with rough wooden stakes and with, perhaps, a crazy shanty in the corner to serve as shelter for the goats and fowls. Over the fencing, and often higher up on a trellis-work of longer sticks, grows the bean creeper, a thick mass of green with white and purple flowers that affords some measure of shade and privacy to the courtyard and the house. Here and there about the village a tumble-down shed, built like the houses, affords a doubtful shelter for the cattle.

The sun has scarcely risen yet, and that glorious breath of fresh cool air that comes but once in the twenty-four hours now that the hot weather has begun is passing with its life-giving touch of exhilaration over the land. But, early as it is, the whole village is astir. A herd of cattle is moving slowly down the one narrow road between the houses, the buffaloes in front, with their long foolish heads stuck forward, sniffing the air with satisfaction. They look indescribably vacant and stupid, these heavy slow-footed creatures with their lazy, swaying gait ; and one can appreciate, as one looks at them, the story the native tells at their expense. When the first created man saw the animals that God had made, it is said that he presumptuously, over-rating his powers, asked that he too might be given the creative power to fashion others like them. God granted his request and man tried his prentice hand. But the result was the buffalo, and man seeing that it was not good, asked in disgust that the creative power might be taken back again from him for ever. The buffalo, however, remained as the only living handiwork of man.

From one of the ramshackle sheds at the further end of the village, a pair of bullocks, with their placid, mildly expostulating eyes, are being driven out to begin the day's work in the fields. With the most primitive of ploughs, slung across his shoulders, the cultivator follows, while his son, a strip of a lad of ten or twelve, marches proudly along beside him, carrying the yoke that the oxen might well have borne, but which, with youthful desire to play his part by his father's side, he insists on bearing himself, shoulder high. The promiscuous crowd of goats that no village was ever without has already begun to browse on the dried-up patches of grass that border the road, wandering daily further afield in a vain search for something fresh and green, on the parched and dried-up earth.

Inside the courtyard, the women are busy

sweeping with their short handleless brooms of twigs, to sweep with which would break the back of any but an Eastern housewife. Everything is wonderfully neat and trim within. The hard sun-baked floor seems never to have been swept enough, and one female member of the house is always busy with the broom. The outside walls and the verandah are often whitewashed, adding their look of cleanliness to the whole. There is not much else to be kept clean in the Santal's house. A single *charpoy*, a network of coarse string on a rough framework of wood supported by four legs, and a few brass pots, standing up against the wall, to keep which spick and span is the housewife's pride, are all that the average Santal possesses in the way of furniture. A drum, however, and occasionally a flute or horn, placed carefully in a corner of the verandah or hung from a rafter in the roof, are prized possessions that make their owner an honoured guest at marriages and festive gatherings. A row of earthen *gharras*, those vessels of many uses, stand in a line against the wall close beside the most primitive of fireplaces that occupies the centre of the floor. This is nothing more than a hole dug in the ground, the earth piled up around it as a stand to hold the cooking pots and pans. Chimney there is none, and the smoke, rising up at times in clouds, fills the whole verandah and darkens the walls inside to a uniform tint of black. The Santal makes his plates and drinking-cups of leaves gathered fresh daily and used but for one meal. Fitted ingeniously into one another, leaves make excellent plates for holding *dal-bhat*: while one large sal leaf, twisted round to form a hollow, holds *haria* quite satisfactorily for the short time necessary for its passage from the pot to the bibulous Santal's lips.

As one rides up, the whole village stops its work for a moment and comes out to look. The womenfolk, broom in hand, appear at their doors with frank pleasing curiosity, and none of that shrinking from public gaze that to Hindu women has become second nature. The Santal women never cover their faces, and their bearing has an independence and freedom from self-consciousness unusual in their sex among Eastern races, and only to be equalled among the Hos. Their features are pleasant rather than actually good-looking, beaming over with good nature and good spirits. Laughing and talking gaily to one another, they snatch the smallest of the children from the middle of the roadway where they have strayed, almost beneath one's horse's feet. The men of the village have gone to cut wood in the jungles or take their cattle to the grazing ground, or, if there has been a shower of rain, to work in the patches of cultivation that lie behind the village. Only a few of the oldest remain gossiping with their neighbours and discussing the prospects of the crops, the next marriage ceremony, or some approaching festival.

The oldest of them all is the *manjhi*. He is the head-man and a great personage in all village affairs. Outside his house is the *manjhi than*, where the spirits of his ancestors reside and where all the important meetings of the village are held. It consists of a raised mound of earth and mud, about two feet high and eight feet square, covered by a ragged thatched roof on wooden pillars. The floor is kept carefully swept, like all the courtyards in the village, and in the centre stands a small block of wood daubed with red. Attached to the central pillar is an earthen vessel containing water for the spirits to drink. In winter, it is left unfilled: the spirits need no water then. But in the long hot weather it is always carefully kept full to the brim: the spirit is sure to be thirsty in the heat of the day. When asked why he only provides water for the ghosts of men who probably in life much preferred rice beer, the Santal shakes his head knowingly and says that a continual supply of *haria* in the *manjhi than* would cause it to be too much frequented by the spirits, a consummation evidently not altogether desirable.

Yet it is in the midst of the presiding company of the spirits at the *manjhi than* that the most solemn conclaves of the village meet. Has anyone been accused of witchcraft, or a mysterious disease,

THE MANJHI THAN.

attributed to the evil eye, spread among cattle or villagers, the old men gather here to judge and pass their sentence that carries the weight of law with every member of the small community. The *manjhi than* is the judgment hall, and many an unfortunate victim of their superstitious fear of witchcraft has received her sentence from the wise men of the village there assembled. But on other points a rough justice is administered without fear or favour, and many a knotty point of Santal custom has been wisely settled at the *manjhi than*.

The *manjhi* himself is quite willing to talk, and after a while, when his confidence has been gained, to tell what he knows of the manners and customs of his race. For everything that cannot be explained by his limited intelligence the Santal has woven a legend, and there is none more interesting than the one invented to account for the beginning of all things, the creation of the world and the creation of man, which the *manjhi* relates in his own vague rambling way.

In the beginning, so runs the quaintly contrived fable, a waste of waters covered the earth and there was no land. Only Thakur, the Supreme Being, and Marang Buru, the Great Spirit, brooded over the face of the waters, surrounded by a multitude of lesser and attendant divinities. At last it occurred to some of these latter that human beings should be created, and they approached Thakur to ask his sanction. The Supreme Being gave the undertaking his approval and appointed a female spirit, Malin Budhi, to prepare the outward forms that the human beings, when created, might inhabit. Malin Budhi, obeying the command, made two human forms and laid them out in the sun to dry. But before the sun had fully done its work and while they were still moist, Sing Sadom—the Day-horse—came down that way to the water to drink and trampled them under foot. Malin Budhi, in distress, carried her complaint to the Supreme Being, who commanded her to make them over again, at the same time directing Sing Sadom to take more care not to destroy her handiwork.

So once more Malin Budhi made two human forms, and this time they dried fully in the sun without any mishap. There remained nothing but that the Supreme Being should come and give them life. Thukur, accordingly, came to see Malin Budhi's handiwork and found that it was good. Thereupon, he ordered her to return to his house and bring 'the gift of life.' His instructions to her were explicit. In his house, he said, there were two kinds of spirits—the bird spirit, that stood above the door frame, and the human spirit higher up on the rafters. The first she was not to touch, but to reach for the higher one and bring that with her. But Malin Budhi was short and the human spirit out of reach, so, contrary to her instructions, she took the one that stood above the door frame and brought it to the Supreme Being. He imparted it to the bodies she had made, not knowing the mistake, and they at once became birds and flew away over the waters.

For twelve months, or it may have been twelve years, the Santal adds with a careless wave of the hand—time is of no account in Santal-land—the birds flew round and round, finding no resting-place anywhere on the vast expanse of water. But at last they greatly desired a home and came with their request to the Supreme Being. 'You have made us beings,' they said: 'be pleased now to give us a place in which to rear our young.'

This was a difficulty that had not presented itself before, and all the ingenuity of the spirits was required in order to meet it. The Supreme Being summoned his council. After much deliberation Sole Hako—a fish—offered to raise the earth above the face of the waters, and Thakur deputed him to undertake the task. But after many fruitless efforts, Sole Hako had to acknowledge that it was beyond his power. Then the Crab tried and failed, and the Earthworm took up the task. He placed himself with his head resting on the land at the bottom of the water, so that the earth which he ate might pass through him and fall on the surface, thus forming dry land. But as fast as he raised up the earth, it sank back again into the water, and the Earthworm, too, had to acknowledge that he had failed in his task.

Then the Centipede came forward with a proposal. The Tortoise, he said, lived in the water and his back was broad and high. On him it might be possible to pile up the earth so as to make it rise above the face of the waters. So they chained the Tortoise to a certain spot with four iron chains, and the Earthworm raised the earth on his back until an island appeared and dry land was at last obtained. On this island, gradually increasing in size, the Supreme Being caused a tree to grow and planted grass beneath its shade.

Here the birds found a home and the female laid two eggs. From these eggs sprang the first human beings—a boy and a girl—the progenitors of the human race. The Supreme Being made Marang Buru their guardian, and he taught them how to cultivate and initiated them into the mysteries connected with the manufacture of rice beer. The Santal to-day still points to this fable to excuse his excessive fondness for the liquor, referring to it as a 'gift God-given.'

These two first human beings were known as Pilchu Haram and Pilchu Budhi. From them sprang a family of seven sons and seven daughters, whose descendants the Santals are. But after their children had grown up, Pilchu Haram and Pilchu Budhi, who should by that time have known better, fell out and quarrelled, as husband and wife sometimes will. Pilchu Haram in anger took his seven sons and went off into the jungle, while Pilchu Budhi, not to be outdone in the expression of her wrath, took a diametrically opposite direction with her daughters, and it was many years before any of them met again.

The reunion took place in this way long afterwards. The sons of Pilchu Haram grew to man's estate and became mighty hunters, penetrating far into the jungle in search of game. One day, their steps were arrested by the unusual sound of low sweet-voiced singing, and peering through the trees they saw seven charming maidens swinging on the branches of a wide-spreading banyan tree and disporting themselves gaily in the shade. These were their own sisters, but so long had they been separated that each failed to rocognise the other. The young men quickly introduced themselves and they soon paired off, spending the rest of the day dancing and making love. Proposals were quickly made and accepted, and the seven newly married couples made a clearing in the jungle on the spot, leaving their parents, who knew nothing of their doings, to take care of themselves.

As his sons did not return, Pilchu Haram at length set out in search of them. During his wanderings he came upon a clearing in the jungle, and, seeing a house with an old woman standing at the door, he went up to ask fire of her to cook his food. They got into conversation, and, quickly discovering their relationship, made up their quarrel and settled down together again.

There is another version, however, of the reconciliation, in which Marang Buru, the guardian of the first couple, plays a beneficent part. Pilchu Budhi, so this version runs, was in tears at the disappearance of her daughters whom she had failed to find, when Marang Buru came across her and inquired the reason of her grief. He assured her that her children were safe and happy, adding, 'You have been too long at variance with your husband: come, I will lead you to him and you shall make up your quarrel.' After this had been done, Marang Buru told them what had happened to their sons and daughters. Later on, the whole family was reunited, but when the sons learned that they had married their sisters they were very angry with their parents for not having warned them, and they would have killed them had not their guardian spirit Marang Buru once more come to their help and hidden them in a cave. That is the end of the story of the first two human beings, for from that cave they were never known to emerge.

As the descendants of Pilchu Haram and

Pilchu Budhi increased, they became divided into groups or tribes named after the seven sons of the old couple, five other groups being added later. One of the sub-tribes is named Chilbindhu, the Vulture-slayer, and a curious legend survives in connection with it. The Santal mother always lays her infants in the sun in order that their skin may develop a healthy colour. But long ago the land was infested by two huge vultures, who found these babes to be exceedingly tasty morsels, and consequently brought grief and consternation to many a Santal home by promptly carrying off the hope of the house. So serious did their depredations become that the very existence of the race was threatened, and strong measures were resolved upon. All the men turned out and followed the vultures, tracking them until at last they came upon them in their nest in a *sohoda* tree. The female was sitting on the nest, which was so carefully constructed, mostly of agricultural implements, that it seemed impossible to shoot her. However, a hole was at last discovered in an *argom* or clod-crusher, and two brothers, Kara and Guja, the most skilful bowmen of the tribe, were chosen to shoot her through this opening. Kara, the elder brother, took first shot, steadying himself with his foot on an ant-hill, and so true was his aim that his arrow pierced the breast of the vulture. The bird flew out of the nest, but being mortally wounded fell to the ground. So huge was she that the force of her fall made an impression in the ground which has since become a lake.

After destroying the vulture, the Santals started home again ready with their bows and arrows for any game they might come across. The only thing, however, that they saw was a nilgai, and this they easily managed to kill, carrying it home in triumph. Great preparations were at once made for a feast, the necessary duties entailed being distributed among them all. To one was given the task of wrapping the flesh in leaves before cooking it. This he performed, but, as a storm of rain suddenly came on, he also disposed of his only garment in the same way, it being the custom among the Santals to divest themselves of their clothes and bury them among the fallen leaves, when caught in a storm, to keep them dry. Unfortunately, however, the owner in this case got the parcels mixed and consigned the one containing his wearing apparel to the fire instead of the joint of meat. Consequently, when the guests had prepared their plates of leaves and the packet was hauled out of the fire, the mistake was discovered, and instead of finding the flesh ready cooked they found nothing but the charred remains of the man's clothing. The others, extremely disappointed and annoyed, abused him, saying, 'We desired you to roast meat, and you have given us your *bhagwa* (garment).' And ever afterwards, the fable ends, he was looked upon as a great fool.

These are only a few of the vast store of legends told in Santal-land. The old *manjhi* in the village is a veritable treasure-house of folk-lore and quaint information, but he has turned now, with keen anticipation, to the still more pleasing subject of a marriage with all its attendant festivities that is to take place on the morrow. The village is not always the quiet scene depicted, A wedding ceremony transforms it with its feasting and dancing and crowd of guests from the villages far and near. The hot weather, when there is little doing in the fields, is the favourite time of the year for marrying and giving in marriage, and the villagers celebrate each event with unwearying zeal and enjoyment. The parents of the parties have previously held long consultations and settled the price to be paid for the maiden, often with the help of the wise men assembled in conclave at the *manjhi than*. All arrangements made to their mutual satisfaction, the happy day is fixed. Failing a calendar to mark the time, they tie a number of knots on a piece of string corresponding to the number of days that must elapse before the day fixed arrives. Each morning one of the knots is untied, until the last is reached, when the parties know that the wedding day has come. Invitations to the villagers, surely the most primitive ever issued, consist of a similar string of knots, so that they too, by striking off one each day, can arrive at the date fixed.

When the last knot has been untied the bridegroom and his friends set out for the bride's house, thus reversing the practice in custom among the Hos. All the villagers come out to meet the bridal party, washing their feet and escorting them to the bride's house with the noise of drum and flute and with much dancing and singing by the way. The bride is then brought out, carried in a basket by her brother or other near relative, the bridegroom being at the same time hoisted on the shoulders of one of his friends. In this exalted position the marking with *sindur* or vermilion takes place, the bridegroom daubing it on the bride's forehead in five long horizontal streaks. This is the most essential part of the ceremony, constituting the couple man and wife.

Then follows a feast at which the newly-married couple sit and eat together for the first time. During the whole ceremony the beating of drums and a monotonous singsong has been going on without a pause in the open space just outside the *mandhwa*, where the final ceremony has taken place. It is a weird picturesque sight. Darkness has fallen by the time the feast begins, and torches have been lit and disposed here and there among the crowd, casting their flickering lights and shadows on the ever-moving figures in the dance that never ceases. All the village is assembled. The quiet rustic street with its row of straggling houses, as seen in the early morning, is transformed now with the stir and noise of revelry. The pick of the Santal youth for miles around are dancing the *Pak Don,* the sword and shield dance, the uncertain light intensifying the wild effect of their rapid movements and gyrations. Wearing no clothes but a loin-cloth and rows of jingling bells as anklets, their limbs have full play, showing off their athletic curves and outlines as they flourish aloft their clubs and shields or spring into the air, whirling round at the same time with a savage and unearthly yell. Only the very flower ot the Santal youth are chosen to dance the *Pak Don,* and in the old days it was danced with wild excitement on the eve of battle or with yells of triumph after victory. But it is too energetic a dance to be kept up without constant potations of *haria,* and each of the performers falls out from time to time to take a drink, the dance keeping on all through with tireless energy. The *haria,* however, frequently imbibed, tells at last, and the sword and shield dance perforce gives way to the quieter performance of the girls—quieter, however, only as regards the steps, the beating of the tomtoms and the shrill notes of the horns and flutes going on unceasingly.

The girls have many dances, appropriate to the different seasons, and all are wonderfully effective. In one, a solid phalanx of dancers, joined hand in hand, moves slowly round in a circle, in perfect time, the drummers and musicians directing the dance from the centre of the ring. In the illustration, the group of Santal maidens and musicians was taken just before the dance began, as it was found impossible to get a clear photograph after the rapid movements had once commenced.

The girls are gaily dressed for the dance, with their rows of beads, bracelets, and anklets of bell-metal, and flowers in their hair. The weight of ornaments some of them are carrying is surprising. Their bracelets often weigh from two to four pounds each, and anklets, necklets, and bracelets together sometimes weigh as much as thirty pounds—no light burden to sustain hour after hour through the unvarying movements of the dance. All night the carousal goes on. The old men, their dancing days over, are quite content to sit idly by and watch the younger generation, imbibing always long draughts of the much-loved *haria*. It is a scene of drunkenness and debauch, kept up with unflagging zeal until the dawn disperses them to their various duties, which they take up with no interval for sleep and perform as casually as if they had not spent a night of orgy.

GIRLS AND MUSICIANS AT A SANTAL DANCE.

But the scene at a wedding ceremony is only a small reproduction of what takes place at the greatest of all their festivals. The Sohrae is a time of still more unbridled license. As it draws near the old men of the village assemble to arrange, according to immemorial custom, for the fitting performance of the festival. One of their formulas, repeated regularly on this occasion, is quaint and characteristic : 'Now at this time one must close one's ears with cotton-wool, so that one may not hear, and put clay upon one's eyes so that one may not see, what one's neighbour says or does.' It is only another way of saying that during the Sohrae whatever moral code the Santals possess is in abeyance and each man does as he pleases. Then, when the festival is over, the old men meet again and make offerings to atone for the flagrant misconduct that has accompanied it.

Among many other curious customs is the 'trial of luck' during the Sohrae festival. A space is cleared at the end of the village street and a thin layer of rice is spread in a circle over the ground, with an egg placed carefully in the centre. Then down the street, from the other end, are driven all the cattle of the villagers, their owners keeping a careful watch to see which animal breaks the egg, each one hoping that it may be his own. It is strange to see how the cattle avoid the circle of rice, swerving off it one after the other and passing it by untouched. But at last a cow or buffalo, or perhaps a goat, comes heedlessly on and smashes the egg beneath its feet. It is the luckiest possible of omens, and the owner of the animal is sure of good fortune for the year to come until the trial is made again.

There is an *ojha*—that important factor in Santal life—living in the village, and he strolls up as one finishes one's talk with the *manjhi*, who has proved more than usually garrulous and communicative. The *ojha* has grown fat and looks as if his trade had prospered. Not every village possesses an *ojha*, and neighbours from miles around come to consult this important personage with the occult powers. In his hands lies the ordeal. If any one's crops or cattle or relatives are bewitched, the *ojha* can detect the whereabouts of the evil spirit. He may resort to the ordeal of planting grains of damp rice for each of the villagers, and he or she whose grain is found to have sprouted during the night is the guilty sorcerer or witch. Or he may plant branches of trees on the edge of a tank, and the one whose branch fades first is guilty of the sin of witchcraft. Or if he wishes to keep the decision more in his own hands, he can pour oil over a quantity of sal leaves and rub them in his hands, reading at last in their distorted shapes, in language unknown to any but himself, the name of him with whom lies the power of the evil eye. The *ojha* too, with his divining rod, can discover the hiding-places of thieves and stolen property. So it stands to reason that the *ojha* is a man of great influence and much respected in the village.

There are a multitude of other interesting customs and festivals that make up a Santal's life—the arrow-shooting competition in the *Sarhul*: the *Jom Sim*, a great festival held in honour of the Sun, when sacrifices are made with mysterious rites in the depths of the forest: and that most extraordinary of family festivals whose origin it is impossible to guess. Each family shuts itself within its own doors, every member stuffing his or her ears with cotton-wool so that no sound shall penetrate. Then sitting round on the floor, father and mother, sons and daughters, they all at a given signal start shrieking the most obscene things their fertile imagination can conceive. No one, of course, can hear what another says, yet until obliged to stop from sheer exhaustion they shout abuse at each other at the tops of their voices. The Santals themselves, when questioned, can give no idea as to the meaning of the observance: it is an immemorial custom, and as such they religiously keep it. To the mere onlooker, however, it appears a festival of much subtle humour, and one that might meet with due appreciation in far more civilised circles than those of Santal-land. To be able once a year to unloose the vials of one's wrath and tell other people to their faces, even though they could not hear, exactly what one thought of them, would surely give one's pent-up feelings much relief.

If it happens to be the month of April, the village may present yet another scene. The great national hunt formerly took place in May, but for several years in succession violent thunder-storms broke up the meet, several of the beaters being killed by lightning. The Santals, superstitious in the extreme, looked upon this as the worst of omens, and permanently changed the date of the meet. All the men within a certain radius, from the youngest of untried youths to the venerable master of the hunt himself, meet at an appointed place, fully equipped for the chase. The hunt is begun with much ceremony. Before leaving home, the master of the hunt has performed an act prescribed by tradition from time immemorial. He has laid his wife, bound hand and foot, on her bed, placing beside her a bowl of water. She must lie there without moving, looking always into the bowl until she sees the water turn to blood. Then she will know that the chase has begun, and she may rise and go about her household duties. The master of the hunt himself is bound, with his back against a sal tree, while he performs the sacrifice that has to be made at the rendezvous before setting out for the chase.

At last, however, the sacrifice is completed,

and the hour of noon arrived, the huge company of beaters moves off in line in a pre-arranged direction, to meet again at sunset in another part of the jungle, where water is to be had and where arrangements have been already made for spending the night. Big game is avoided in these national hunts of the Santals, but nothing in the way of smaller game comes amiss to their unerring aim.

Until evening the beat goes on. Then, when all have met again and refreshed themselves with food and drink after the exertions of the chase, a solemn conclave of the whole assemblage takes place. It is the Santal High Court of Justice, and here all appeals are heard from decisions of the local *manjhis* and village wise men, and any important questions that are agitating the clan receive consideration. The Dihri or Master of the Hunt, who is an authority on all points of Santal law and custom, presides, and every adult member of the clan has a voice in its proceedings. Social questions are discussed, and those who have broken the strict rules of the Santal Table of Consanguinity are severely dealt with. Only in this great meeting of the nation, and after careful decision of his case, does any man receive the full penalty of the law and become an outcast from the tribe.

When the solemn conclave is at an end, the usual feasting and dancing begin. In spite of the long and tiring tramp through the jungle during the day, there is no thought of rest, and the wild measures of the dance are kept up with unflagging zeal till daylight comes and the chase is once more resumed. At noon, just twenty-four hours after it commenced, the great shikar festival comes to an end, and the huntsmen, carrying their trophies, make their way home again, to tell the women and children, who have remained behind, the story of the chase.

It is a far cry back to the village whence one set out in the morning, hours ago. It is neither Sohrae nor Sarhul, hunting nor marriage festival, there to-day. Often as they come, breaking the monotony of its life, the natural aspect of the village is one of absolute repose and seclusion. It is towards sunset now, and the short Indian twilight, the 'hour of union' as the Santal picturesquely calls it, quickly merging into night, seems to intensify the sense of rest and peace, folding all things in its softer light after the fiery heat of the day. The deep musical sound of the wooden cow-bells, as the cattle slowly wend their way towards the village, comes through the jungle near at hand, and fainter still from away on the upland slopes. Unled they come, passing slowly down the village street and making straight each for his own home, knowing it with unerring instinct and intelligence. Only a pair of buffaloes seems to have needed guidance, and their owner follows close behind, urging their slow pace, and

SANTAL WOMEN CARRYING PITCHERS FROM THE WELL.

bearing raised aloft on his shoulders a huge broken branch that he has taken from the jungle to serve as firewood to cook his evening meal. A line of women, carrying water from the stream beyond the village, come with their graceful even tread, balancing their *gharras* on their heads. The whirr of the potter's wheel, in the tiny courtyard at the end of the street, ceases suddenly, making the silence felt and seeming to break the last link with the departing day. The cry of the jackal, beginning, as the native says, at the foot of the Himalayas and passing on from village to village to the furthest limits of the south, already in the distance breaks the stillness, to be taken up close by and answered back again and yet again, until the last cry dies out of range and all is still. So the 'hour of union' passes, and the Santal village, leading the life of nature, is quickly wrapped in sleep.

CHAPTER VI

THE SACRED HILL OF PARASNATH

RIGHT on the very edge of the Hazaribagh district, the Sacred Hill of Parasnath stands like a sentinel, dominating the land on every side. Hazaribagh and Giridih lie at its feet—a wide expanse of plain, backed to the west and south by a range of hills. The Grand Trunk Road, one long fine line of white, runs, as if fascinated, straight beneath its shadow. Far away into Manbhum, the western sun frames its distant peaks in a halo of light, while even in far-off Ranchi the eye of faith can trace its faintest outline against the rain-cleared sky.

Its name of the Sacred Hill is well deserved. Nowhere could a more fitting home for the gods be found. So must have thought the countless multitudes of pilgrims who have trodden the well-worn road to Parasnath from the utmost limits of India. Thirteen hundred miles from Bombay, a month's journey on foot from Murshedabad, three days by train from Guzerat, from every part of distant India where the Jains have made their home, the long continuous stream of pilgrims wends its way towards the Sacred Hill.

Parasnath cannot fail to be impressive, from whichever side it is approached. To-day by far the greatest number of pilgrims is to be seen along the Giridih road, the railway bringing them to within sixteen miles of the foot of the hill. It is a modern way of pilgrimage, in all the comfort or discomfort of a third-class native railway carriage, but the line stops short at Giridih as if arrested in its course by the frowning mass of Parasnath with its surrounding crescent of attendant heights, that spread out their arms east and west as if to bar the way. But once the railway is left behind, the pilgrimage takes up again all its old-world conditions. To most it means a dusty tramp on foot, to a few only the luxury of a *palki* or the still more primitive *dooli*. The latter is the most lightly constructed of conveyances, and from its appearance promises little in the way of comfort. It consists only of a long pole, carried on the shoulders of coolies, from which, suspended by ropes at either end, is a flat oblong seat, made roughly of pieces of bamboo or wood nailed crossways. There is necessarily little room for the occupant, who must perforce sit in an Eastern attitude with crossed legs, tailor fashion. Six miles of this, most of it at an angle, sometimes acute, as the road ascends, would appeal to none but the native born, on whom the cramped position and the jogtrot of the coolies makes no impression.

It is a silent journey for the most part along the sixteen miles of road to the foot of Parasnath. Contemplation is a part of the Jain religion, and, the noise and bustle of the long railway journey left behind at Giridih, a sense of peacefulness and content falls on the wayfarer along the quiet country road that ever points the way to the foot of the Sacred Hill. The end and object of the pilgrimage are in sight, and, vague and imaginary as it has always been to them before, it at last assumes all the proportions of reality. Now, as these people of the plains lift up their eyes towards the hill which their religion has pictured for them from their earliest days, they acknowledge with a sigh of wonder and content that it far exceeds in beauty all that they had imagined. They are a people of strong imagination, and the great silence and grandeur of the towering throne of their deities cannot fail to impress them after the noise of the crowded bazaars and the busy cities whence they come. It is to them an experience unique and never to be forgotten, perhaps the only glimpse of the great outside world that they are ever destined to see. For this they have saved and hoarded and haggled in the dust and heat of some far-off city of the plains, that they might once visit the Sacred Hill before they pass into the great

A DOOLI.

unknown. Above all, the maimed, the diseased, and the blind have kept the thought of it ever in their minds as the only hope that life held, and faith has never wavered though others have returned with no outward signs of the beneficence of the gods.

Nothing is more striking than the numbers of old men and women that throng the road to Parasnath. Haggard and wrinkled women, huddled up in their *doolies* with their chins resting on their knees, haggard and wrinkled as they only can be in the East, have come but just in time to propitiate the gods before death calls them. Occasionally such a one passes up, all alone, save for the bearers who carry the *dooli*, and as one looks into the deep-lined anxious face one cannot but marvel at the strength of a sentiment that has conquered the ingrained superstition and timidity of a lifetime, and brought her through the unknown perils of the way to the far-distant home of the gods. The road is strewn with the graves of those who have succumbed before they reached their journey's end. Starting in old age or sickness, all too late, they have died from sheer exhaustion by the way, often at the very foot of the Sacred Hill, with their eyes fixed on the temple of Parasnath, that they might never reach, soaring high above them.

But most often the pilgrims come in groups, friends and relations taking the road together for mutual company and safety. Here may be seen a band of Jains from Bombay, busy clerks and merchants, snatching a well-earned rest from temporal things to make their offerings to the gods thirteen hundred miles away. Or there again a family of four generations plods slowly up on foot, only the frail old man, with a child in his arms, in a *dooli*, the latter making its pilgrimage early in life and thereby gaining grace. A group further on is too pitiful to linger by—maimed and stricken with disease, the ascent for them must be one long agony, and the descent into the world again uncleansed more painful still.

But, for all, there is rest from the toil of the road at Madhuban, nestling with its multitude of glittering domes and pinnacles, right at the foot of Parasnath. Immediately behind it the ascent begins, and Madhuban itself is sacred ground. To one coming suddenly upon the temples from a bend in the road they present a wonderfully striking appearance. The bell-shaped domes, dazzling in their whiteness, tower up against the background of the hill, and the countless pinnacles tipped with gold peep out here and there among the trees, giving to the whole a sense of size and grandeur. Flags of red and yellow surmount the turrets and float gaily in the breeze, while spotless coats of whitewash give the temples a look of cleanliness and care, so strangely foreign to most religious buildings in the East.

There are three separate temples at Madhuban, and the pilgrim makes his way to the one of his choice. The first, lowest of all and furthest from the ascent, is the Nichli Mandir, belonging to the Digambaras. The Jains are divided into two sects, the Digambaras or sky-clad and the Svetambaras or white-robed. The differences between them to the uninitiated seem small, but the distinction is great nevertheless. The Digambaras, whose name would imply that they wore no garments at all, probably did at one time discard all clothing. But at the present day the only survival of this rigorous practice exists among the Munis or ascetics, who have renounced all things of the world external. The other followers of the sect content themselves with laying aside the headdress and the garments of the upper part of the body only before sitting down to eat, and leaving the images of their gods unadorned. The Svetambaras, on the other hand, clothe their images, covering them with the jewels that the pilgrims offer at their shrines. The ascetics of this branch of the Jains also observe the most rigorous customs, using a face-cloth to keep defilement from the lips and a brush to sweep away insects when they take their food. But they always observe the most scrupulous care to kill none of these insects, for 'no killing,' even of the smallest life, is the motto of the Jain religion. Even the plucking of a flower and the trampling of a blade of grass is against their tenets, and though in the world these things must be, no true Jain would knowingly injure any living thing.

The Nichli temple is a handsome building. It is of comparatively recent date, having been built by a Calcutta merchant just over a hundred years ago, but there is nothing obtrusively modern about it. Covered up in its freshly applied coat of whitewash, with a quaint gilded figure of the Tirthankaras, the deified saints, seen far off across the paved courtyard with its cloister-like seclusion and arched doorways, the temple has rather the appearance of age. Only across the first courtyard can the booted foot of the stranger go. Nothing more than a glimpse of the Holy of Holies can be seen from the court of the Gentiles. One feels a strange desire to enter, but it is a curiosity born only of the prohibition, for one knows that, having seen the outside of most Indian temples, one has exhausted all that there is worth seeing. Inside, there is nothing but the bare floor, well swept and garnished, and the painted figures of the gods that fail to appeal to Western imagination, in a row against the wall, decked with blossoms of red and yellow.

So, with a look from the archway, through which one may not pass, across the forbidden courtyard where the curtain swings in the breeze before the shrine, disclosing here and there a flash of a golden god or the prostrate figure of a worshipper, one passes out through the gateway and on to the second of the Madhuban temples.

The Murshedabad or Majhli Mandir, as it is generally called from its central position, stands slightly higher up the slope of the hill. This is the temple of the Svetambaras, who claim sole rights over all Parasnath and the custody of the temples on its summits. They are a wealthy sect, and presents of gold and silver ornaments, earrings, bracelets, and necklaces, the gifts of devotees, adorn the figures of their gods. But outwardly this temple much resembles the first. Here again there is an outside courtyard with a high wall running all round it, and a raised verandah and lodgings for the pilgrims along one side. At midday the court is thronged by a crowd of mendicants, waiting for the distribution of the daily dole of rice. Being the richest of the three temples, the crowd here is the largest and most varied. It is a motley gathering, mostly women and children, drawn from the very poorest of the pilgrims, and many hangers-on who once were pilgrims but have found this a comfortable halting-place where food is to be had for the asking and no labour is required. Here, too, congregate pitiable specimens of humanity, the leper and the diseased, knowing that if ever the hand of charity will be open, it will be here on the threshold of the gods.

The last temple, covering with its building and gardens the largest area of ground, is the one right at the foot of the ascent. It is the Gwalior Mandir, belonging like the first to the Digambaras. The oldest of the three, it has two large courtyards with galleries all round, built as lodgings for the pilgrims, and during all the winter months these never want for occupants. Over the gateway leading to the inner court is a musicians' gallery, faced with wooden carvings, where flutes and drums mark the passing of the hours with their weird monotonous music. Just now it is tenantless, save for the flight of pigeons that circle round and make of it a moment's resting-place. The drums have ceased, and only the soft motion and flutter of wings break the stillness. The silent-footed figures, moving to and fro across the paved court, pass by without a sound, and the wonderful sense of rest and peace that has fascinated the myriads of Jain pilgrims, as they lingered at the foot of the hill, seems to have settled over the glittering domes and pinnacles. Only occasionally, from the roof of the pilgrims' lodges, comes the sound of voices, where the women, their washing done and the bright-coloured garments laid out in the sun to dry, are arranging their hair, finishing their toilet in full public view with typical Eastern unconcern. Even these cease at last, and the chattering groups of bright-green red-beaked parrots, that had settled in the pepul tree in the far corner of the garden, have flown away with a parting screech, as if they feared longer to break the all-pervading silence. The spirit of contemplation broods over courtyard and temple, and the weary pilgrims, resting on the house-top or in the galleries, sink imperceptibly from day-dreams of the greatness of the gods into the unconscious slumber of oblivion.

It is hard to tear oneself away from the Gwalior temple with its fascinating air of absolute repose. But it is the last of the three temples, and the road to Parasnath runs, in its first gentle rise, beneath the wall, overhung by the venerable trees of the Gwalior garden. Groups of gaily-dressed pilgrims, mostly women from the Bombay side, having made their offerings at the shrines, are just starting on their journey upwards. All go barefoot, some scattering further offerings by the way, for every stone is sacred and every inch of ground a shrine on this most holy hill. A tiny child of four or five, in all the bravery of necklet, bracelet, anklet, and silver charm, steps out half staggering beneath the weight of another little bit of humanity, that as yet scarce counts its age in months, devoid of all clothing save a row of coloured beads, and seated contentedly astride across her hip. It is an everyday sight along the way, but the road up Parasnath is long and steep, and one wonders how that small couple will ever gain the top. But there are many pauses along the ascent, and for the pilgrims it is holiday time and they have less cause for haste even than usual. There is a small shrine just where the first straight bit of road ends and the zigzag path begins. They can stop there awhile and make an offering, and further on, halfway up the hill, there is a rest-house where they can break the journey and enjoy a longer rest.

The first two miles of the road offer every inducement that they can to linger. To say that it is the most charming bit of Parasnath would only be to contradict oneself later on, but Chota Nagpore can offer few such exquisite pictures as this. The path, ever upward in its course, runs through a perfect forest of trees, bordering it above and below. Here and there, through the branches, where the phalanx thins for a moment, one catches a glimpse of a view of surpassing beauty. Down below, at one's feet, lie the plains, stretching away as far as the eye can reach, with their wealth of foliage and plots of cultivation here and there, the Giridih road a tiny line of white, appearing for a moment, then lost again beneath the trees. It is a wonderful panorama, smiling and peaceful, with scarce a sign of the habitation of man, the villages nestling so close amongst the foliage that they are almost lost to view. Right at the foot, in the shelter of the ascent, lie the domes and pinnacles of the

Madhuban temples, flashing white and gold in the sunlight and clothed in a garment of green. There are trees everywhere, with their delicate shades of yellow, emerald, and brown, hiding all the temples below, save the cupolas and turrets that soar above them or peep out here and there in their dazzling brilliance. It is a charming scene and one that changes with every step, each turn of the zigzag road disclosing some fresh row of glittering pinnacles and hiding others out of sight.

After the first two miles the trees grow thick and there is less to be seen, but every now and then comes a glimpse of the plains, though the temples of Madhuban have long since disappeared below. Halfway up, where the ascent is less steep, the road passes through a tea garden, closed in on every side by thick tree-jungle, and as we pause for the midway halt, it recalls to mind, what we would fain forget, the strife and controversy that have so long invaded the peaceful precincts even of the Sacred Hill. It is an old story now, and the dispute, complicated from time to time by outside interference, seems as far from settlement as ever. From the earliest time the Svetambaras claimed sole rights over the Sacred Hill, pointing to Sanads granted by the Emperor Akbar in 1593 and by the Emperor Ahmed Shah in 1760 confirming them in possession. But although Parasnath is their Sacred

Hill, few Jains even in those days lived in its immediate vicinity. The times were troublous and the hill all but inaccessible in the midst of an unknown country, and the pilgrims gladly welcomed the protection of a neighbouring zemindar who then professed their own religion. Gradually it came to be recognised that the Raja of Palgunj had the right to keep watch and ward over the temples on the hill, and this eventually developed into a claim on his part of proprietary right over the hill itself. Disputes grew constant between the Rajas and the Svetambara Jains with regard to the offerings at the shrines, and many of them found their way into the civil and criminal courts about the year 1866. To bring these unseemly disputes to an end, a compromise was attempted and agreements were entered into between the Raja of Palgunj and the representatives of the Svetambara Jains in 1872 and again in 1878. In these agreements the possession of the hills by the Svetambara community was acknowledged by the Raja, as well as its right to any site on the hill itself or in Madhuban for building temples or *dharmsalas*. The Raja bound himself not to interfere with the Svetambaras in the performance of their religious observances, and in return they undertook to pay him an annual sum of R.1500 in lieu of all his claims to offerings at the shrines.

Subsequently to these two agreements occurred

what is undoubtedly the most astonishing event that has ever happened in connection with the Sacred Hill. The Raja of Palgunj in 1876 leased out two thousand acres on it to an Englishman, a Mr. Boddam, who began by cultivating tea, coffee and cardamoms. Finding, however, after eleven years' work upon it, that the garden was not paying, he suddenly resolved to set up a piggery there. To the Jains, to whom all killing is an abomination, such a proceeding was a desecration too horrible to contemplate. That pigs should be kept and slaughtered in large numbers on their Sacred Hill, of which every foot of ground was holy, outraged their deepest feelings as nothing else could well have done. It is said that the piggery was only started in the ingenious hope that the Jains would bribe its proprietor heavily to close it. On the other hand, Mr. Boddam's partner is stated to have said that they expected to make R.80,000 a year from the business, which was begun in March 1888. The Jains immediately protested, and failing to get satisfaction from the proprietor, appealed to the courts for an injunction to prevent the further desecration of their Sacred Hill. More than one hundred pigs, however, had been slaughtered by the month of May when, by what the Jains must have regarded as a timely interposition of Providence, the business was brought to a sudden conclusion by a fire which destroyed all the buildings of the factory as well as the pigs themselves. Immediately afterwards came an order of Government temporarily forbidding the carrying on of the business until the matter in dispute had been referred to the courts. The case that was subsequently tried before the High Court, Raj Budri Das Bahadur and others on behalf of the Svetambara Jain community against the Raja of Palgunj and Mr. Boddam, was a famous one of its day and a final decision was not arrived at until June 25, 1892. In the end, while the suit against the Raja who had granted the lease failed, a perpetual injunction was issued against Mr. Boddam restraining him from slaughtering pigs and carrying on the manufacture of lard on the Sacred Hill.

The troubles of the Svetambara Jains, however, are not yet at an end. Beyond their still unsettled dispute with the Raja of Palgunj, there was for long another danger that threatened them. Parasnath is the only hill that tops four thousand feet in Bengal south of the Himalayas, and as such it has always offered tempting ground for the establishment of a small hill station. Though not sufficiently high for an ideal summer resort, four thousand feet make a very appreciable difference in temperature from the intense heat of the plains below, and there is no doubt that but for the religious difficulty it would have been exploited long since. The establishment of a sanitarium for British troops in the middle of last century met with strong opposition as violating the sacred character of the hill, and chiefly on account of its unsuitability for the purpose the scheme, after a brief trial, was abandoned. Recently, however, the estate of the Palgunj Raja came under the management of Government under the Encumbered Estates Act, and the question of utilising the hill for residential purposes was revived. In this connection both the Svetambara and Digambara Jains were consulted, which the former consider improper, since they maintain that they alone have rights over the Sacred Hill and that the Digambaras have never been associated with them in their efforts to protect it from desecration and encroachment. The final decision of Government on the whole question is still awaited.

Continuing the upward way the road grows steeper again, on past the native rest-house and the rustic bridge beneath which the stream is never altogether dry, and past the ruined grass-grown barracks, long since deserted, until at last the European bungalow is in sight right overhead, and the last few zigzag windings bring one to its level.

The bungalow was once a part of the barracks built here more than forty years ago when Parasnath was made a sanitarium for the troops in Bengal. But it was only used for four years, as it was soon found that the site had disadvantages for such a purpose. There was absolutely nothing in the way of amusement for the men and not much space for exercise, and the sanitarium, in spite of its proved healthiness, was given up in 1868. The principal building is now the European rest-house. It stands right on the edge of a spur, below the summit, commanding magnificent views of the plains that lie in one long vista to the north and west below.

But the stream of pilgrims passes on, for the summit is yet to be attained. It is not far off now, and the winding path brings one at last to the topmost ridge over four thousand feet above the sea. It is a splendid elevation. The drop is steeper on the southern side and the towering cliffs fall in rough irregular escarpments, almost sheer down the full depth to the plains below. Away to the east the ridge runs on in graceful curves and scattered peaks, dropping at last to the long low range of hills that stretch away through the Tundi jungle to the banks of the Barakar. Beneath, at its feet, lie the groups of hills about Topechanchi, a mass of thick tree-jungle, that look little more than mounds and hillocks from the exalted heights of Parasnath.

There is but one more ascent and the journey's end is reached. Towering up against the western sky is the temple of Parasnath itself, perched on the highest peak of all. Only one path leads up to it: on every other side it looks straight down the face of the rock to the precipice below. It almost makes one giddy to gaze up at its dazzling wall of white, straight in line with the rock on which it stands, without an inch of space to spare. The western sun is catching it now and bathing it in a flood of light, the cupola, brilliant white and gold, standing out like a watch-tower against the sky. Pilgrims, like moving specks, are passing up and down the broad white steps of the approach, that seem, so high they mount, to stretch from earth to heaven.

To one standing at the foot of them they are curiously impressive. Straight up they go, seventy-nine deep wide steps of dazzling whiteness, and above them towers the temple of Parasnath, the end of all things. The religion that made this its holiest place and the home of its gods knew well how to appeal to the imagination of its followers. As the pilgrim from the plains mounts the long flight of steps his mind cannot fail to be impressed by a sense of detachment from earth and earthly things. If there is any place in the world set apart for contemplation and inspiration, it is here on the topmost step of the temple of Parasnath, with the world a distant vision far below.

The sun has set at last over the Ramgarh

hills, and the temple stands out white and deserted in the moonlight. The pilgrims have gone down the hill again, for no Jain may eat or drink or spend the night upon the Sacred Hill. Only those of other religions, whom mere curiosity has drawn to the summit, remain in the bungalow and rest-houses. Tigers are not unknown on Parasnath, and those who pass the night upon it huddle together, behind closed doors, before darkness has fallen, or sit close round a crackling fire of twigs.

There is much to be done in the morning before the pilgrimage on Parasnath is over, and with the dawn the stream of worshippers once more begins the ascent. They have made their offerings in the greatest temple of all, but there are other shrines that demand their devotions, and not one must be omitted. This is written on the top of Parasnath in the bitter cold of a January morning, as the sun rises over the last peak of the ridge, clothing it in a haze of golden splendour. Far away across the plains, the horizon is tinged with an exquisite pink, merging into the gold that is lost again in the perfect blue of the gradually lightening sky. The hills below, scarce visible at first, emerge from a mist of pink and grey, slowly casting off the shadows and appearing in their own unequalled beauty of exquisite green. The numerous shrines, flashing white and gold, dotted here and there along the ridge, catch the earliest rays of the coming sun and glitter against the darker background of the hill—all save the farthest away, that soars up clear against the sky to be lost in the glory of the golden haze, as it adds its own sparkling brilliance to the sunlight full behind it. If the setting sun brings peace and contemplation, the rising sun over Parasnath is itself a hymn of praise.

There are twenty-five shrines in all, quaint dome-shaped structures three or four feet high, raised on flat round masses of masonry, and each approached by two or three broad steps. They contain nothing but the models of the soles of the feet in black marble of the twenty-four Thirthankaras, the deified saints of the Jains, no less than twenty of whom, so tradition states, attained Nirvana on the Sacred Hill. The shrines are erected over the places where their feet are supposed to have last touched the earth, and one stone is carefully preserved bearing the mark of the foot of the great Parasnath himself.

The remains of votive offerings, rice and flowers, strew the floor of the shrines, and the saffron marks show up in bright round spots on the black marble feet. It is a long round to visit them all, entailing a tramp of several miles, but at last the pilgrimage is done, and, with one more look along the ridge towards the Sacred

Temple that few of them will ever see again, the stream of pilgrims begins the downward path. The never-to-be-forgotten visit to the home of the gods is over, and the worshippers merge again in the common daily round of life below.

CHAPTER VII

THE GATEWAY OF CHOTA NAGPORE

MANBHUM is the land of the cultivator, the coolie, and the Bhumij Kol—the cultivator pursuing the dull round of daily life and fighting with each recurring season the battle of existence; the coolie hurrying or hurried on through the Gateway of Chota Nagpore, to dreams of exile or the reality of better wages beyond, whichever his mind may choose to dwell upon; the Bhumij Kol, half aboriginal, half Hindu, sometimes the coolie, sometimes the cultivator, but always restive and uncertain, as wild and unkempt as the jungles he has made his home.

It is a land of contrasts. The north, with its long monotonous stretch of paddy fields as far as the eye can reach, is almost Bengal; the south, hilly, jungle-clad, precipitous, is unmistakably Chota Nagpore. On the one hand perhaps the most Hinduised of any of the five districts of the province, on the other it is the home of some of the wildest and most backward of all the aboriginal tribes.

Just south of the Damuda lies a long flat stretch of country. Only, here and there, a solitary hill, rising abruptly out of the plains, breaks the level. All else for miles and miles is one broad expanse of paddy fields, where, the jungle long since cleared, the busy cultivator has ploughed and sown and reaped for generations. The slight undulations that mark all the face of the country alone distinguish it from the monotonous dead level of the rice plains of Bengal. Here the paddy fields lie in ridges, terrace on terrace, each with its own banks and dams, so arranged as to retain the last drop of moisture long after the rains have ceased.

The fields are almost deserted in the hot months of the year when the ground is hard and dry, but it is a busy scene when the ploughing season begins with the first fall of rain in June. Then every cultivator is astir in his own plot, guiding the oxen or buffaloes that draw his primitive wooden plough up and down and across its full length, widening with every turn the patch of rich brown earth that contrasts strikingly with the hard dull colour of the portion still untouched. It depends upon the nature of the soil and the variety of the crop how often it is necessary to go over it with the plough. If it is *gora* (upland) paddy that is to be sown, the

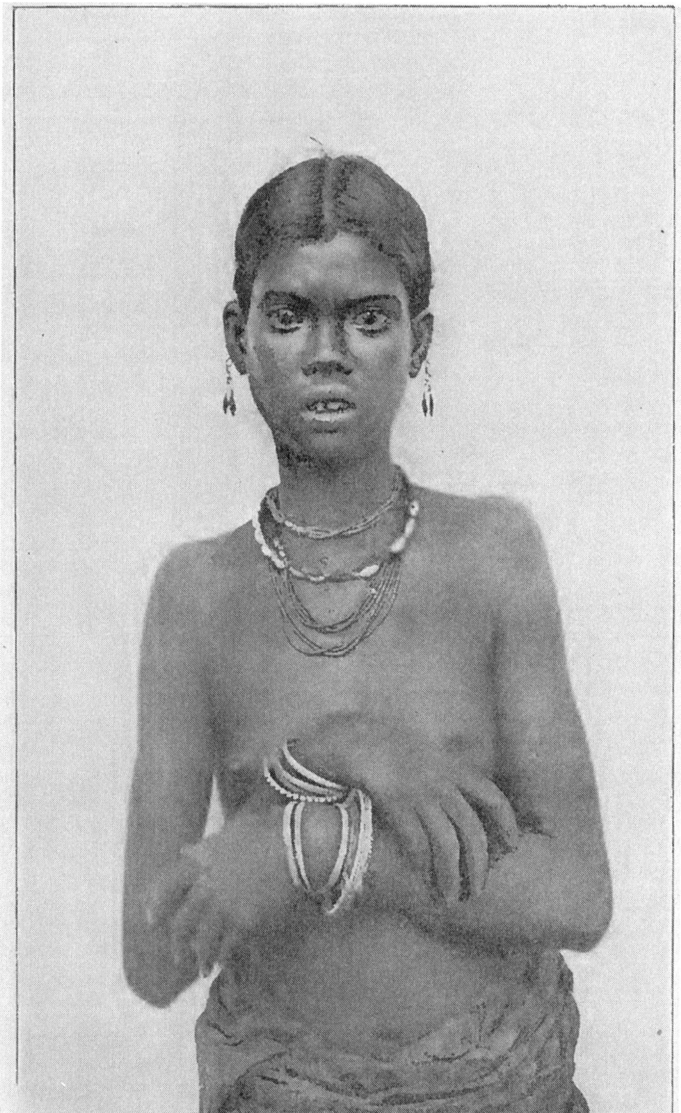

A MANBHUM KHERRIA GIRL,

soil must be ploughed many times, for, as the cultivator puts it—

> 'Baro mash, tero chas:
> Tabe karo, gora ash'—

'Plough thirteen times in twelve months and then hope for *gora* paddy.'

It is probable that the low embankments that separate the fields may want repairing or strengthening against heavy rains, and the ryot is busy with his *kodali* (hoe) making all secure. Or, where the rush of water has become too great, a group of cultivators may be seen busily engaged in baling it out, to prevent their fields becoming too sodden or their earthworks being swept away. It is an ingenious if primitive contrivance they have invented for the purpose. A long shovel-shaped basket, roughly made of straw or bamboo plaiting, is suspended by strings from the four corners. Swung by two men rapidly backwards and forwards with clockwork regularity, it scoops up the water on the downward swing and empties it on to the other side of the dam. It is a slow process, but the Manbhum cultivator has not yet devised a more convenient plan.

When the paddy is ripe for transplantation, the fields are filled with a crowd of workers. Standing often knee-deep in the water and mud, they uproot the young shoots, laying them aside in bundles conveniently for carrying away to be planted again elsewhere. Twelve women are calculated to uproot seedlings enough in one day to cover an acre field, but it takes twice as many hands to plant them out again in the new ground. Each woman takes a bundle and simply makes a hole with her thumb and finger in the mud into which she thrusts a few shoots. Transplanting, well on in the rainy season, certainly takes place under the greatest discomfort. But moving long hours in the sodden mud of the fields, with the rain descending overhead, has little effect upon the cultivator, who rejoices in the abundance of moisture that alone will ensure a good crop, and who cares nothing for physical discomfort so long as there is the promise of a good harvest to come.

Until the young plants have taken root, great care has to be exercised by the ryot that the terrace is not overflooded with water. If there is a danger of that happening, an opening is made in the earthworks and the excess of water drained off. But towards the end of the rainy season the reverse is to be feared, and it generally becomes necessary to make all secure so as to retain the last drop of moisture as long as possible into the dry season of the year.

The crop is often gathered in, later on, under much the same conditions as accompanied the transplantation. The rain still lies heavy on the land, and the reapers with their short sickles have to wade knee-deep again to cut the crop. But if the harvest is sufficient to assure them of immunity from famine for another year, it is all they ask or expect. On these three critical months of the rainy season the whole prosperity of the coming year depends, and the poor cultivator, realising their tremendous importance, expresses his dependence upon them in the well-known Indian proverb, 'If out of twelve months three are gone, what remains? Nothing.'

But while the rains have been quickly bringing the crops to maturity, the ryot has not been idle. Their safety still depends to a large extent upon his exertions. In many parts of the district he has had to build himself a *machan* or rough straw hut where he can watch over his fields, protecting them from being trampled upon and destroyed by denizens of the jungle or stolen by dishonest neighbours or wandering tribes of thieves. At transplanting time and harvest he has to be particularly wide-awake. Then the paddy, bound up in small bundles, may be easily carried off, and, unless the cultivator has caught the thief red-handed, it will be almost impossible to identify it later on.

Besides watching his crop, the ryot has had to prepare his *khanyan* (threshing-floor) in readiness for the coming harvest. It is a simple affair, merely an open space of ground, well cleaned and swept and made even with a careful plastering of mud. But the ryot spends much time and infinite pains on making it as hard and level as he can. If his fields are close by, he places the *khanyan* just outside his house: if they are far off, on some adjoining level space where he can build a temporary hut to guard the grain, over the growth of which he has so long kept watch.

The Chota Nagpore ryot knows none but the most primitive form of threshing. A thick layer of rice stalks is spread out in a circle over the floor, and a row of bullocks, tied in a line, are driven round and round, until the grains are well trodden out. As the bullocks pass, the straw is sifted with a pitchfork so that the grains fall underneath and suffer no injury from the animals' hoofs. When one layer has been well trodden out another is placed over it, and so on until the straw becomes too deep for the bullocks to make their way through it. Then at last the monotonous sound ceases, and the straw is carefully removed so that the rice and the chaff remain on the threshing-floor. Placed in a *sup* or winnowing basket, which the ryot holds on his head, this uncleaned paddy is then shaken to and fro, in order to separate the grain from the chaff. The former, being heavy, falls straight to the ground, while the lighter chaff and dust are blown away by the breeze and the shaking of the *sup*.

With the paddy threshed and cleaned the

ryot's work is nearly done. But, unfortunately for him, there are many claims to be satisfied before he can proceed to store it for future use. After the harvest is the time for paying off his debts. First of all there is the grain to be restored with interest to the *mahajan* from whom the ryot was forced to borrow in order to sow his fields. Then there are the labourers' wages to be paid, if outside help has been necessary, so much paddy for each day's work and a further amount for the hire of the bullocks at ploughing and threshing time. The *lohar* (blacksmith) and other village functionaries also claim some small share of the harvest for services rendered without payment all through the past year. Consequently, the amount of his crop that must last all through the hard times of the year to come is considerably reduced, and it is essential that he should guard carefully what remains against the many pests that threaten it. The safest plan and the one usually adopted by the ryot is to store it away in *moras*. A *mora* is made of straw, and looks something like an enormous beehive. The paddy is first placed in a layer of straw, which is then bound tightly round and round with plaited straw ropes. The whole thing must be made as tight and compact as possible and the rope wound close, coil by coil, so as to preserve securely the grain within from any possible harm.

The highest of the solitary hills rising abruptly

out of the wide stretch of paddy fields just south of the Damuda is Pachete. It is only some twelve hundred feet high, but, standing up boldly out of the surrounding level, it forms a conspicuous landmark for many miles around. At its foot lies a mass of ruined masonry, the home, in days gone by, of the once powerful Rajas of Pachete. It is more than a hundred and fifty years now since the place was deserted, and the jungle, grown dense in every direction, has clothed its decay in rampant luxuriance. Ruined tanks, gateways, towers, and massive stone walls cover the ground, giving some idea of the extensive building it must once have been, with its innumerable rooms and winding corridors, and verandahs everywhere in all the promiscuous profusion of an Eastern palace. Placed like watch-towers three hundred feet up the side of the hill are two temples, crowning the fortress below and still attracting, by their reputation for holiness, a crowd of worshippers from the district round.

Further away to the south is a scattered group of rocky hills of bold irregular formation with great masses of grey-black boulder jutting out above the close shrub jungle. One more precipitous than the rest, with a clear drop of thirteen hundred feet from an immense boulder at the top, is still known as Execution Hill. In the old days it was a name that struck terror into all the countryside. Taken to the topmost rock, approached by a more gradual ascent on the further side, the unfortunate victim of the Raja's justice or revenge was thrown straight over the face of the cliff, to be dashed to pieces on the rough stones at its foot. It was a summary form of punishment long since disused, but the native who lives beneath its shadow still looks up with a shudder to the giddy height of Execution Hill. Going home at nightfall he avoids it carefully as haunted ground where the spirits of the dead return to visit the scene of their violent departure from the earth.

To the south the scenery of Manbhum is much more typical of Chota Nagpore. The long range of the Bhagmundi hills runs crescent-shaped towards the Ranchi border, rocky and tree-clad, with their curiously shaped and jagged summits clearly outlined against the sky. Further away still to the south, running almost east and west along the banks of the Subarnarekha, where it forms for a time the Manbhum border, are the Dalma hills, more undulating and less bold in outline but with their crowning peak rising to the imposing height of three thousand four hundred feet. Cutting a channel through the range, the Subarnarekha pursues its tortuous course southwards, winding in and out among the hills, with its rocky bed laid dry and bare for the greater part of the year.

Manbhum is a land well provided with riverbeds, but rivers there are none till the rains bring them sweeping down from their rocky sources on the higher plateau or among the hills near at hand. Then for a time, without bridges or boats, the country is wellnigh impassable, and the native stays at home, crouching in his mud-built straw-thatched hut, busy keeping out the rain or diligently looking after his crops, a duty from which the worst weather never deters him. The roads are deserted save for those whom necessity takes abroad or a group of villagers waiting patiently on the bank for some rushing torrent to subside and leave the way clear for them to hasten on for their lawsuit in Purulia. They know from old experience that the waiting will not be long. The river will soon subside with almost startling rapidity as soon as the rain has ceased. 'Wash your hands while the river runs' is a proverb born of climatic conditions, the vagaries of which in another form and another country have given rise to the corresponding saying, 'Make hay while the sun shines.'

The rains are a busy time in the Katcherries. Although the worst season of the year to set out upon a journey, yet, if his neighbour cut or steal his paddy, the outraged cultivator has no choice but a tramp to Purulia to vindicate his rights. There is no time like the cultivating season in the rains for disputes. Then comes the opportunity to seize forcibly some one else's land and hastily plant a crop there, to give a semblance of possession, or better still, wait till harvest, and then coolly claim the paddy that some one else has sown and guarded to maturity. It is extraordinary how many claims to land, that have lain dormant all the year, crop up again as the cultivating season approaches, and many an unfortunate ryot has to resort to litigation to enable him peaceably to secure the fruits of his toil.

The cultivator of Manbhum, like his class all over Chota Nagpore, knows little of manufactures or any form of industry. His fields are to him the beginning and end of life, and on them, from season to season, he depends for a precarious existence. The manufacture of *tussor* cloth at Raghunathpur is one of the few recognised industries of Chota Nagpore. It is made by a class of Hindus known as Tantis. All the processes are performed here except the rearing of the silkworms, which is left to other parts of the district. Cocoons are obtained from Singbhum, several thousand rupees' worth being imported every year. The working of the looms is a slow process, one loom being calculated to turn out no more than thirty yards of cloth a month. But the actual working of the machine only requires one man and the return for his labour more than covers his simple wants, while often in the cultivating season the weaver deserts his loom to reap his harvest in the fields besides. Lac is produced in larger quantities in Manbhum than in any other part of Chota Nagpore. It is a resinous substance secreted by an insect round the branches of the *palas*, *pepul*, and other trees. Gathered twice a year, it forms a profitable employment and an extra addition to the cultivator's income. There are altogether 102 factories at work in Manbhum employing as many as 4,871 workmen. Coal, however, is by far the most important industry in the district, the coal mines being situated for the most part in the Dhanbaid Sub-division of Manbhum, which will claim attention later on.

Purulia, well in the centre of the district, is the headquarters station of Manbhum. The passer-by catches charming glimpses of the town with its avenues of fine old trees running through the bazaar, their huge branches meeting overhead and sheltering long stretches of the road beneath. One of the finest leads down to the lake, known as the Saheb Bandh, and runs along the water's edge. The lake is a splendid piece of water, covering over fifty acres, with a picturesque tree-clad island in the centre, and stone-pillared bathing *ghats* standing out among the trees on the bank. The story goes that the Deputy Commissioner, in the days when the lake was in course of excavation, devised a somewhat novel plan to secure an abundant supply of labour. No one was allowed to present a petition or

THE SAHEB BANDH, PURULIA.

complaint until he had done a full day's work on the Saheb Bandh. So the excavation proceeded rapidly, and, complaints being numerous, the lake is large.

Some way off, and nearer the native portion of the town, is one of the handsomest mosques in the district. Standing on the side of a small tank, with the water in the rains washing its steps and flanked by an array of trees on the further side, its multitude of domes and minarets, decorated walls, and cornices, show off their full effect. Close by in the centre of the bazaar is the *golghar* or municipal toll-house, around which, flanked by its rows of shops, the daily market is held. Further away, at the end of another avenue of trees on the outskirts of the town, lies the Jail.

It is not often that the quiet daily round of life in Purulia is broken. Yet a few memories recall it vividly to mind under unusual aspects. First there passes into view the gaily decorated main street, awaiting the arrival of the Lieutenant-Governor on his annual visit to the town. The Indian is an adept in the art of street decoration, producing the gayest possible effect with the scantiest materials. A striking contrast to this festive scene, there comes to mind the picture of a famine hotel, opened during a time of great distress in 1897. The children, seated in rows, are about to enjoy their daily meal of *dal-bhat*, which has just been served out to them. A third scene that recalls itself is on the banks of the Saheb Bandh, where a huge crowd of the poorest classes in Purulia were collected together and fed on the day of Queen Victoria's funeral. It was a striking gathering, and one remarkable feature of it was the presence of a large number of native gentlemen of the highest caste superintending the work of charity, barefooted and bareheaded, as a token of their grief.

But Purulia is best known as the gateway of Chota Nagpore—for the traveller, the push-push and the coolie. It is only within the last seventeen years that the railway has come as far as this, and until four years ago Ranchi still lay seventy-five miles away from this, the nearest line of rail. Purulia, the nearest station, is a well-remembered halting place to those who have passed this way to Ranchi, with its line of push-pushes waiting outside. They come as rather a shock when one sees them for the first time, unless one has been prepared for them in detail. Already tired out by a long railway journey, one pauses appalled at the thought of seventy-five miles by road in one of those lumbering vehicles drawn by six undersized coolies. They are like nothing so much as a bathing-machine on two wheels, only not half so high or roomy. They are only about four feet high inside, and one can just sit up straight, or rather half lie or sit tailor-fashion. It is impossible even to lie full length comfortably if one is anything beyond the average height, as one's feet in that case hang helplessly out of the door. Stretched over the top is a semicircular roof of matting, and beneath this go one's baggage and servants, and other impedimenta, stowed away with amazing Oriental compactness.

Six panting coolies struggle with the push-push, toiling up the slopes with much grunting and groaning or running along the level or down the inclines with a rousing cry. Each team of coolies runs a *dâk* of eight miles, showing sudden energy as with a pleased shout they approach their journey's end, where the fresh relay of runners waits.

It is an uphill journey by road from Purulia, and rarely at the best of times takes less than twenty hours. That is short compared with what it may take one in the rains. Then the going is heavy and the discomforts of the road increased tenfold. A sharp downpour, beating in at the windows, drenching the almost naked coolies from head to foot, and running off their dark shiny bodies in streams, does not add to the cheerfulness of things. Later on, the rain begins to trickle down through the cracks in the roof, and one knows that one's baggage above is well soaked, while there is a very probable chance of a similar fate overtaking oneself inside. With the windows tightly shut to keep out the rain, the atmosphere is close beyond description in the push-push, and there seems little else possible in the way of discomfort. But the worst is still to come. When the end of the *dâk* is reached at last, the runners rush for the shelter afforded by the crazy verandah of the coolie hut, leaving the push-push balanced at an awkward angle with the handle-bar resting on the ground. The new coolies, dry and comfortable under cover, cower still further back in the verandah and absolutely refuse to come out, while the rain continues to beat down on the push-push and the unfortunate occupant inside. With the water trickling through in tiny streams, and the maddening sense of being altogether helpless, one anathematises push-pushes in general and one's own in particular. It is impossible to get out in the pouring rain, and expostulating in one's best vernacular with a crouching mass of unresponsive coolies, through a slit of the window cautiously opened to avoid letting in the rain, would be comic if it were not happening to oneself. It is a situation not conducive to the preservation of an equable temper, and men have been known to sally forth from the standing push-push and attempt to supplement expostulation by a show of force. But such a proceeding has also been known to have had disastrous results in a rapid flight of coolies, leaving the unfortunate passenger stranded on the road for hours to come.

The only redeeming feature of the journey is

WOMEN ON THEIR WAY TO ASSAM TEA GARDENS.

the scenery by the way, and that gets more charming and picturesque as one leaves the plains behind and begins the ascent to the higher plateau of Central Chota Nagpore. At Tulin is the half-way rest-house between Ranchi and Purulia, where, a few miles further on, the road leaves Manbhum and enters the Ranchi district. But few will choose to travel by push-push now that the railway has been opened and the journey can be accomplished in comparative speed and comfort in under four and a half hours.

It is down this road that many of the coolies came in the old days on their way to the tea gardens of Assam and Bengal, induced to emigrate by the hope of better wages, or by difficulties or scarcity at home, or perhaps the victims of the threats, promises, or persuasions of a recruiter who was not to be denied. Chota Nagpore is one of the great recruiting-grounds for the labour districts, and emigration has been active ever since the first occupation by the British and the increased knowledge among the coolies of the world beyond. So long ago as 1827, the magistrate of Ramgarh speaks in one of his reports of a large number of Kols annually leaving the district to work on the indigo plantations of Behar and Bengal. Ever since then a steady stream of emigrants has been flowing out of the district, mostly to the tea gardens of Sylhet, Cachar, and Assam on the one side, and Darjeeling and the

Duars on the other. Those who go to the former bind themselves to work for a term of years, and when that is over they have the option of renewing the contract for a further period or of returning to their own homes. But those who go to Darjeeling and the Duars are all free labourers. They enter into no contract, and come and go as they please. Large gangs of them are to be seen leaving their homes in December after the harvest has been gathered in. Marching up to the tea districts on foot, they often work there for the best part of a year, returning home again at the close of the tea season in October and November. Having earned high wages, they can bring home a good round sum as savings, while their own plots of land have not suffered by lying fallow for a year, and their mud-built straw-thatched huts are easy to repair. A large number of Kols and Oraons are also found working nearer at home, in Calcutta and the Sunderbans, where many have settled down more permanently with their own houses, cultivation, herds of cattle, and all the accessories of village life.

The most recent Act relating to emigration to the labour districts of Assam (Act VI. of 1901) was passed to check the abuses that had grown up round the recruiting system. In their anxiety to get coolies, many of the recruiters and their agents all over the district did not scruple to use force and fraud, and many an unfortunate labourer has been taken off to Assam against his will. Various circumstances cause the supply of coolies to fluctuate, and all the energy of the recruiter is often needed to induce the unwilling to emigrate. If the paddy season has been bad, there is no difficulty. Then, the fear of scarcity at home being one of the most powerful inducements to seek well-paid labour elsewhere, the number of emigrants after the December harvest is enormously increased. In a year of plenty, however, the people are much more reluctant to leave their homes. In 1900, a year of scarcity, the emigrants numbered no less than 65,190, while in 1901 the total only reached 30,777. The number has still further decreased in recent years, until in 1909 the total was only 15,492. There are other reasons contributing to this enormous decrease, which if it continues will become a serious matter for the Assam gardens. The coal-fields that have been opened out close at hand in Gobindpur and Giridih offer every inducement of high wages and proximity, unfettered by any form of contract. At the time of the passing of the recent Act, too, wild stories were circulated of the restrictions about to be imposed, and this doubtless helped to account for the decrease in emigration.

The Bhumij Kols, the characteristic race of Manbhum, have furnished a large quota to the total number of coolies that annually emigrate from the district. They are settled in the centre and south near the rivers Subarnarekha and Kosai, and the range of hills that cuts down through their country has been productive of an extraordinary cleavage among them—a striking instance of the influence of geographical conditions. They are undoubtedly all of the same race and closely allied to the Mundas of Chota Nagpore proper. Those to the west of the range of hills who still live side by side with their kinsmen of the higher plateau admit their relationship, call themselves Mundas, or Muras as they use the word, and speak the Mundari language. Like the Mundas they build no temples, but worship in the Sarna, observing the Sarhul festival at the same time and in the same way, marrying and giving in marriage like them, and committing their dead to the earth beneath the protection of similar rough-hewn tombstones.

But on the east of the range which has formed a complete barrier to ordinary communication, time has worked a great change. Shut off from their kinsmen, they have been thrown into close contact with Hindus from Bengal. The Mundari language has been forgotten, and the people, disowning all connection with their original stock, call themselves Bhumij Kols and speak Bengali. They have adopted Hindu manners and customs, retaining many of their own side by side with the new, but dropping all those that clashed with

A REPRESENTATION OF VISVA KARMA, THE HINDU VULCAN.

the gradually increasing influence of their neighbours. They present an interesting study of a race whose entire code of life is still under process of a great change. To-day they stand halfway between Mundas and Hindus. Only one of the typical instances of this compromise between the old and the new is that they still retain fowls as an article of diet, while they have given up eating cow's flesh in deference to Hindu prejudices. Most of the Hindu festivals they have readily adopted, retaining side by side with them their old tribal meetings for dance and song, for which they have lost little of the original passion of the Kol.

They have always been a turbulent race, ever ready in the past to join in any attempt that meant plunder, arson, or murder, and to-day they form the most refractory class in the Manbhum district. In appearance, they bear a striking resemblance to the Mundas, short and strongly built, with coarse features varying in colour from dark chocolate to light brown—a resemblance that at once sets at rest any doubt as to their origin.

Side by side with their strange worship of invisible gods in the sacred grove, the Bhumij Kols have acquired a special reverence for Visva Karma, the Hindu Vulcan, and for the goddess Kali. The story goes that the latter was forced to flee from a demon in Pachete and took refuge with a washerman. In gratitude for the shelter she had received, she gave her protector a young Brahmin girl, a ward of her own, to wife, and from this couple descended the Rajas of Dhalbhum. In honour of the goddess Kali, a festival called the Bindparab was held annually in past times. Two buffaloes were driven into a small space enclosed all round by a raised platform, from which the Raja and his attendants shot arrow after arrow into the unfortunate beasts. Goaded at last to madness, they fell upon and gored one another, arrows still being discharged to keep them up to the necessary pitch of fury. When at last their strength was spent and they fell exhausted, the people rushed in with battle-axes and literally hacked them to pieces. Only a few of the oldest men can now remember having seen this brutal spectacle, but from all descriptions it appears to have been a singularly cruel performance, entirely foreign to the Kols' ritual and owing its origin among them solely to Hindu influence.

Some of the most interesting remains yet brought to light in Chota Nagpore have been found in Manbhum, on the land that the Bhuiyas and Kols have long since made their own. Scattered over the country, at Palma and Boram on the Kosai, and at Chhara and Pakhira, are the ruins of what must once have been magnificent temples. They are evidently the work of a people far more advanced than the present possessors of the land, but of whom every other trace has disappeared. Here stone figures are still to be found scattered about the ruins of the temples they once adorned. The sculptures, consisting of perfectly nude male figures, are extraordinarily well preserved, with every detail of their magnificent Egyptian head-dresses still clear and distinct. Some of the figures are crouched in a sitting posture, others standing stiffly with feet together and arms hanging straight down against the body, the hands curved inwards and touching the thighs. All round the figures are elaborate carvings on which time and exposure to all the elements have had little effect. Many of them are almost as perfect now as when they left the hands of the workmen centuries ago. There can be little doubt that the sculptures are representations of the Tirthankaras, the deified saints of the Jains, whose sky-clad figures are familiar to the visitor to Parasnath.

The Damuda and Barakar valleys, from the number of ruins that still remain, seem to have been the favourite haunts of the Jains. At Telkupi, on the south bank of the Damuda, there is a remarkably fine collection of temples, some falling or already fallen into decay, others still used by worshippers and decorated with the inevitable strings of leaves and *genda* blossoms. These temples have long since been appropriated by the Hindus, who, however, can give no account of their builders, and in one temple at least worship unquestioningly an image that evidently represents one of the Jain saints. When they were deserted, or why the general exodus of their builders took place, nothing is left to show. Only the ruins remain as memorials of their skill and the firm and long-enduring hold they must once have had over the land.

To the north, across the Damuda lies the Dhanbaid Sub-division of Manbhum. Until recently its headquarters were at Gobindpur, which gave its name to the Sub-division, and in the passing of the one headquarters station and in the rise of the other is to be read the history of the change that has so rapidly and completely changed the face of the whole countryside. The Grand Trunk Road was the making of Gobindpur. The decay of the one depriving the other of whatever importance it once possessed, now threatens its very existence. Robbery, dacoity, and murder, which the courts were placed at Gobindpur to control, have long since ceased to threaten the traveller along the Grand Trunk Road. Traffic has deserted its former highway, and the whole interest of the Sub-division centres in the coal lands to the south. The days of Gobindpur have been already numbered, and with the removal of the sub-divisional headquarters to Dhanbaid two years ago, it has fallen again to its first insignificance as but one of the many small villages that cluster on the Grand Trunk Road.

It was inevitable that Dhanbaid, an important station of the New Grand Chord Line and the centre of a big industry should supersede Gobindpur, which the line of modern advance has passed by. The railway that has sprung into existence with the new industry here passes far away from the Grand Trunk, and seven miles of dusty road, not always in the best of condition, separate Gobindpur from Dhanbaid station. Jherria itself, the heart and centre of the coal-fields, lies four miles further off still, on the other side of the line. The coal lands for the most part stop short south of the railway, and, while one part of the Sub-division has undergone extraordinary development, Gobindpur has been left isolated, as primitive and untouched as fifty years ago, and miles away from the centre of industry that recently looked to it as its administrative headquarters.

In every way the change from Gobindpur to Dhanbaid has been a great one—a passing from the old to the new in every sense of the word. Gobindpur, in spite of the busy scene of activity so close at hand, has preserved all its old-world seclusion. Nothing more than a cluster of houses on the Grand Trunk Road, the noise and life, that are the making of Dhanbaid, have passed it by. It is a perfect 'Sleepy Hollow,' undisturbed by the advance of time. Seen from any one of the group of rocks, black and grass-grown, that lie scattered here and there behind the village, it is a landscape of absolute rest and content. Below lie the buildings that were formerly the Sub-divisional Magistrate's house and the Katcherries, almost hidden out of sight in a mass of foliage, one huge cotton tree, a mass of bright red blossom without a single leaf of green as the cold weather ends, forming a flaming landmark of red against the brilliant blue of the sky for miles around. Further on, the lake, with its island, like a speck of green on the glistening face of the water, stands out clear in the sunlight, with the Bandh running straight as a die beside it up to the tiny village that clusters, in patches of red roof and white stone, among the trees. Away beyond lies the mass of the Tundi hills, framing the picture in a perfect setting of delicate blue-grey haze. Away to the right, the land is more cultivated, only a hill occasionally arising abruptly out of the level like the great round-shaped mass of Girua, covered from foot to summit with its thick shrub jungle.

The hills round Gobindpur form a wonderful line of light by night during the hot weather. The natives kindle jungle fires all along the slopes as soon as the undergrowth has fully dried, in order to make way for the fresh young grass that will spring up with the first breaking of the rains and provide welcome fodder for the half-starved cattle, which have fared badly on the parched-up land during the long hot weather. Smouldering for days, the fires creep on in zigzag lines from end to end of the hills, invisible by day, but standing out clear and distinct, a brilliant line of light, by night.

A solid range of hills just behind Gobindpur hides all the view to the south, forming, as it were, a barrier between the old and the new. To the north lies Tundi. It is the only one of the five big zemindaries of the district that has not been benefited by a discovery of coal, and the Raja of Tundi looks with envy on his neighbours' lands across the Grand Trunk Road. Not a trace of coal has been found here, and the great rush of capital and labour that has come to the Sub-division has left his estate untouched. The seams of coal nowhere, except at Pandra and Nirsha, extend north of Gobindpur, and the noise of pick and steam has never as yet invaded the seclusion of the Tundi forests.

There could be no part more out of the world than this. Thick tree jungle stretches for miles along the slopes of the hills, that run right round from the Barakar, like a semicircular array of giants, to the Sacred Hill of Parasnath, towering above them as if presiding at their conclave. It is a perfect scene of quiet charm. No one ever goes to Tundi save the magistrate or policeman on tour or a stray shikari attracted by the hope of bear or the rumour of a leopard on the banks of the Barakar. Ten or twenty years ago it was a splendid place for bear, but many have been accounted for since then, and an epidemic of ruinous timber-cutting has disturbed the jungle and sent them further afield for shelter. They are still to be got, however, and no place is more likely than Jhitpur, right in the very heart of the jungle, where there is no *basti* for miles, save a rude collection of huts here and there whose population scarce numbers a score all told. It is all undulating country, covered with the inevitable sal and palas and clumps of delicate willowy bamboo. Nearer Tundi, on more open ground, a stretch of paddy fields provides an excellent snipe ground, where the birds lie thick in December and January, and a good morning's bag there will compensate somewhat if the tramp after bigger game later on in the day proves a blank.

On the edge of the Tundi jungle, near the banks of the Barakar, lies Pokhuria. It is a name that has become a household word among the Santals all along the north of the district, and it owes its existence to one man. Thirty years ago the village was deserted. Convinced by an unfavourable omen that the place was haunted, the inhabitants had fled with all their belongings to find a home elsewhere. It offered an excellent site to a member of the Free Church Mission who had just arrived in the district. Settling down there, he began his work. As time went on and the superstitious Santals saw that no harm came to him in the village they had deserted, they gradually returned, filled with respect for the man who had defeated the designs of the malignant spirit. Starting with the smallest of beginnings and coming alone with no advance guard in the shape of converts or mission buildings, he set himself to live the life of the people, by so doing, if possible, to gain their confidence. A mud hut in the village and a daily fare of *dal-bhat*, *chapatis* (the native substitute for bread), brinjals, and, when these grew scarce, of mahua, were only small incidents to the man who had come determined to make his way. The result after thirty years' work is a marvellous success, and it is hard to realise now that it has been throughout but the work of one man. His own house, a long low bungalow with a deep verandah, and the numerous buildings round, the schools and children's and teachers' quarters, were all built under his own direction and design, the bricks made locally and the timber cut from the jungle near. Most of his work has lain amongst the Santals, and living amongst them for thirty years there are few things about that most interesting of races that he does not know. He is an honorary magistrate of the Sub-division, and the Santals, realising his interest in and knowledge of their affairs, take their cases to him or appeal to him to arbitrate in true patriarchal style.

The cultivation of *tussor* silk cocoons, carried on all over the Tundi estate, employs many hands at Pokhuria. The silkworm is reared from eggs hatched artificially. As soon as they are laid, they are smeared with ashes and turmeric and placed on trays of leaves to hatch in sheds, especially provided for the purpose. When hatched, the worms are put out on the *asan* tree to feed upon the leaves and eventually form cocoons. It is during this stage that the untiring vigilance of the native cultivator is necessary to keep off the crowd of enemies, such as birds and bats, that threaten the existence of the worm before it has formed its cocoon. The rearing of the silkworm is almost the only occupation besides the ordinary round of cultivation that the people in this part of the district engage in, but it keeps them busy for several months in the rains before the cocoons are ready for sale in September. They have never attempted yet to manufacture the silk themselves, though this is largely done at Raghunathpur in Manbhum.

Far away to the south-east corner of the district, on the banks of the Damuda, the land is almost as undisturbed as in the north. Five miles below the Grand Trunk Road, the Khudiya joins the Barakar river, and a mile further on, almost at right angles, the Barakar and Damuda meet, forming the eastern and southern boundary of the Sub-division. Close by the Grand Trunk

Road and the Barakar bridge, the land is black with coal; but further south, where the three rivers meet, the paddy fields remain unbroken, and the daily round of life goes on undisturbed in all its primitive simplicity. Only at night the furnaces of Kumardubi and Laikdih light up the face of the country with a ring of glowing fires.

The Damuda and Barakar are splendid rivers after heavy rain further up among the hills. Then the wide expanses of sand, showing bare and dry for most part of the year, are covered by a rush of swiftly flowing waters, bearing on to swell the larger and more stable rivers of Bengal. Strong, impetuous, foaming in their haste, they carry all before them, and there is no safe crossing until their force is spent. Even when their first flood has subsided, quicksands make the fording dangerous, and boats are few. Yet to get to Purulia from Gobindpur by road the Damuda must be crossed. The Bengal-Nagpur line from Ardra to Katras, recently constructed, includes a bridge twelve hundred feet long over the river at Boojoodih, but the traveller on foot will still have to make his way across as best he can and pray that his journey be not in the rains.

Dhanbaid and the Jherria coal-field that lies beyond it present an entirely different scene. Dhanbaid, with its one long street of native bazaars and blocks of railway quarters on either side of the station, is astir night and day with its endless succession of passing trains, while away to the south of the line, the sky is black with smoke from the hundred chimneys of the Jherria coal-field. Less than twenty years ago all this country was as primitive and untouched as the most out-of-the-way part of the province. To-day it is a centre of life and activity, with one of the largest local European populations in Bengal outside Calcutta. Nowhere can India furnish a more striking example of rapid change, or one so unexpected and complete. The opening out of the coal-field has altered the whole face of the land as if by magic. The jungle has disappeared, leaving only occasional patches here and there, and the land for miles is black with chimneys vomiting their clouds of smoke, while heaps of coal and dust lie everywhere in disregarded confusion. Huge boilers and furnaces glowing with light and heat, engines pumping water continuously on to the land, and shafts at work landing the tubs of coal above the surface, meet the eye everywhere. Sidings creep like network over the country, and an endless succession of tubs laden with coal or returning empty to the pit pass up and down continually. The throbbing of machinery, the monotonous sound of the pumps at work, and the noise of the trains moving in endless succession, or shunting with a rattle and clatter of tubs, seem never to cease

GROUP OF COOLIES' CHILDREN.

GLIMPSE OF THE JHERRIA COAL-FIELDS.

night or day. Only on Sundays there is relaxation. It is pay-day and the general time of reckoning, and the workings in the mine are stopped, save for the pumping of the water from the pits that goes on all through the week without a break, never daring to pause for a moment while the mine is worked.

Throughout the huge group of collieries, which numbered two hundred and seventy-three, and turned out over seven million tons in 1908, it is the same scene of constant activity. The coolies, grimed from head to foot with black dust, work as many of them have never worked before. Haste is foreign to a native's composition—'no one runs unless he has a daughter to dispose of,' says the Eastern proverb—but here there is continual movement everywhere, and relays of coolies carry on the work without a pause, urged to the utmost by the knowledge that their pay depends upon results. One after another, gangs of perspiring coolies emerge in straggling groups up the inclines, balancing the coal in baskets on their heads. Outside they pile it on the ground in neat stacks, one foot high, to be measured later when the day's work is done. The coolies get about one rupee for every hundred cubic feet thus stacked. A good worker will make his ten annas a day, and that with no more than six hours' labour. The coolies always work in gangs, often the whole family, men, women, and children, combining to divide the labour. Their task is quickly done thus, and the hundred cubic feet soon stacked, the men cutting the coal below, and the women and children carrying it away up the incline and putting it in place above.

Further on, where another seam is worked by means of a shaft, coolies receive the tubs as they come up in the cage, and, emptying them, send them down again to be refilled. At Sijua, one of the largest collieries in the district, the shaft is one hundred and sixty feet deep. The descent is worth making, showing one the striking difference between an English and an Indian coal-mine. The cage drops the distance to the bottom of the shaft in six seconds, and coolies, bearing flaming torches that cast a weird flickering light on the moist shining surface of the coal all round, show the way. It is an extraordinary sight, after the carefully protected lights in an English mine, to see the torches carried thus, unguarded: but there is no gas in an Indian mine, none of the pits here descending to any great depth.

From the foot of the shaft, a main level, ten feet wide and one thousand one hundred feet long, runs the full length of the seam. Along it, occupying nearly all its width, runs the tram line that carries the coal in tubs to the foot of the shaft. Each tub is run straight on to the cage and so raised aloft with the greatest possible facility. The floor of the gallery is on a slight slope, and the tubs once started run down of themselves to the entrance to the cage, coolies steadying them here and there along the line. There are outlets every twenty-five feet along the main gallery, and the noise of the picks of the miners at work sounds dead through the huge thicknesses of coal, until one comes suddenly upon them working out another gallery at right angles to the main level. To the left run the inclines that give access to the miners.

The whole coal-field provides work for over seventy-two thousand coolies every day, and to swell this number many have come from distant parts of Bengal and the north-west, attracted by the wages that to them mean wealth. Some work only for a time, going back home to enjoy what they have saved and returning again when it is spent. The labourer who lives close by scores most of all. Plots of cultivation flourish right in the busiest centres of the collieries. Patches, here and there, close by the pumping shafts, owe everything to the opening out of the coal-field. They have gained a regular supply of water that never fails—that greatest of all needs of an Indian cultivator—and while the land around grows baked and hard under the scorching sun, they are fertilised and always moist. It looks almost incongruous to see the bright green patches of paddy right under the smoking chimneys at the very mouth of the inclines and cut across by trolly lines, bearing their heavily-laden tubs of coal. The lucky ryot cultivates his well-watered fields and earns besides a good day's wage in the colliery close at hand.

Less than twenty years ago all this country was unmarked outwardly by any sign of the coal that lay beneath. It was not till 1893 that the first workings were begun. Ranigunj and Giridih, neighbouring coal-fields, had been started long before, and though the Geological Survey of 1866 had proved the existence of coal, no serious attempt to work it was made for more than twenty years afterwards. Jherria laboured under great disadvantages in those days. The railway ended just across the Barakar river that separates Chota Nagpore from Burdwan. Jherria lay twenty miles away from the terminus ; and the Gobindpur Sub-division, backward then in every way, was almost entirely lacking in roads. Beyond the Grand Trunk Road, there was scarcely another worthy of the name, and this was of little use to the Jherria coal-field, as the nearest seam began miles away to the south, over practically impassable country. Some doubt, too, seems to have been thrown on the quality of the coal even after the enormous extent of the field had been discovered, and this again delayed its opening. It is said that the Raja of Jherria of that day offered to a Calcutta firm his entire interest in coal for fifty thousand rupees. And, more astounding still in the light of the present day, the offer was refused.

But with the survey of the land made by the East India Railway Company in 1890 and the beginning of the Jherria extension line from Barakar, the possibilities of the coal-field suddenly opened out. It was a tremendous windfall for the local zemindars. Bare patches of land that had lain untouched for generations, too poor even for the meanest of ryots to find worth cultivating, suddenly revealed apparently inexhaustible wealth, and the paddy fields that had been held by ryots at merely nominal rents, and often at no actual rent at all, became all at once of interest to the outside world and the object of a rush of companies and individuals to which India can furnish few parallels. For the first time in their history, the modern force of competition entered in and endowed them with a value beyond all comparison with that which they had possessed under the old feudal conditions. From a poor local zemindar, in an out-of-the-way district, the local Raja of Jherria, on whose estate the chief seams lay, became at one step a man of wealth and influence, courted by individuals and companies alike in their race for lands. Had the Raja at the time of the first opening of the coal-field possessed any idea of business or careful management, the Jherria estate to-day might have

O 2

been immensely wealthy. But the intrigue and peculation and flattery that surround a small native potentate were redoubled when the prize grew so much more worth having. The Raja, without any capacity for controlling these new forces, was fleeced right and left. Even as it is, the royalties on the Jherria coal lands amount to something like five lacs of rupees, but, with a capable manager at the head of his affairs when the first rush began, the Raja's income might have more than quadrupled that amount.

Many stories are told of the way in which coal lands were acquired from the local zemindars, some true, some doubtless enlivened with a touch of Oriental exaggeration. One, however, is sufficient to show what happened, and, incredible as it may seem, its truth can be vouched for. A certain Raja, a tottering imbecile though in the matter of years he had not yet reached the prime of life, was fleeced beyond all the others. Entirely in the hands of one of his satellites, he was soon reduced to bankruptcy, though originally the owner of a splendid coal-bearing estate. One particularly ingenious method of securing grants of land for anyone who paid him a sufficient consideration was resorted to by the chief favourite. A deed of gift was written out beforehand, with only a space left blank at the bottom for the Raja's signature, and carefully turned back so as to show none of the writing above. With this concealed about them the applicant and the favourite appeared before the Raja, and, without a word as to the real object of their visit, began a long course of flattery, in which, for high-flown imagination and floweriness of speech, no one can beat an Oriental, and by which, strangely enough, no one but an Oriental would be deceived. 'But have you ever been blessed with a sight of the Raja's handwriting?' the favourite would say at last to his confederate, after having exhausted his rhetoric on every other possible attribute of his master; 'the writing of the Raja far excels in beauty any other writing in the world—his hand has the cunning of the engraver for roundness of outline and the skill of the artist for perfection of form.' 'Alas, that I have never been blessed with a sight of it!' the other would reply, and so, coaxed beyond credibility with impossible flattery, the imbecile Raja, pleased and gratified, would smilingly scrawl his illegible signature on the blank space at the foot of the deed that granted away his choicest lands. It is small wonder that his estate was soon bankrupt, and that his unfortunate successor lives on the pittance left from what might have been a magnificent inheritance.

But wiser counsels prevail now, and the days when such lavish gifts were thrown away indiscriminately are past for ever. Most of the coal lands have been already taken up, though disputes as to possession are still rife. There are few plots that at one time or another have not been the subject of disputed ownership, and when these coal-bearing tracts suddenly became of immense value, the old questions of possession between local zemindars, tenure-holders, and ryots were renewed with tenfold intensity. Claimants, often without the shadow of a claim, appeared to contest the ownership of land, making buying and selling precarious. There was too great a rush at the outset to decide definitely who was and who was not the legal owner. Possession was the first thing needful. The seller was often only too glad to get rid of his doubtful claim to a purchaser for whatever it would fetch, while the latter in many cases welcomed immediate possession, however shadowy the right of ownership might be. But it was a dangerous game, as many found when things quieted down and appeals were made to the courts, with the result that those who had sold lands were often found to have been without the slightest claim to it whatever.

Right away on the west as far as the Jumoonia, the Jherria coal-field extends, including the lands of the local zemindars of Nowagarh and Katras. The railway which only a few years since ran no further than Katrasgarh has since become the Grand Chord Line, while the Bengal-Nagpur Company has also linked the southern portion of the coal-field with their main line on the south of the Damuda. Dhanbaid is the great centre towards which all the coal traffic converges. Here all the trucks of coal must be weighed before they can pass on down the line on their way to their destination. Long trains bearing as many as forty-five trucks, each with from twelve to thirty-five tons of coal, pass continually in, first over the weigh-bridge, then shunted on to a siding to be sorted and await their final transport to Calcutta. The output of the Jherria coal-field, which was estimated at 2,143,814 tons during 1901, valued at approximately four million rupees, had risen to 7,062,036 in 1908. Formerly Dhanbaid was the only exit by rail, and though the extension of the Bengal-Nagpur line to the south has provided another route to Calcutta, by far the larger portion still passes through Dhanbaid, keeping the station officials busy night and day.

The lack of good roads was at first a great drawback to the coal district. Beyond the one from Gobindpur to Jherria, itself not always of the best, there was none that could properly be called a road. The European population of the coal-field, numbering something like two hundred, is extremely scattered, each manager living on his own colliery, and in some cases almost entirely cut off from his neighbours, with no driving road anywhere near. But much has been already done. Government some years since granted half a lac of rupees for the construction of twenty-five miles of road which now thoroughly intersect the coal-field and supply a long-felt want.

Seven years ago the question was seriously discussed of transferring the whole of this Sub-division from its old allegiance to the neighbouring Commissionership of Burdwan. It would have been a greater and more radical change than most transfers would entail, owing to the fact that the Sub-division is now part of a non-regulation province, while Burdwan is administered in accordance with the ordinary regulations in force in Bengal. Between the two there is a great distinction. Chota Nagpore, with its many aboriginal races far behind the rest of Bengal, was made a non-regulation province with special laws adapted to its own particular needs fifty years ago. These needs, scarcely less great, still exist to-day. To take only one case, which has exercised great influence on zemindars and ryots alike, the Encumbered Estates Act is a special law passed to grapple with the special conditions of Chota Nagpore. When the British first entered the district, it was evident that the local zemindars, half Bhuiyas, half Rajputs, were far inferior to their neighbours outside the province in general intelligence and business capacity, and that if some measures were not taken to protect them, they would quickly fall a prey to their own incompetence and the rapacity of up-country mahajans or astute Bengalis, who quickly spread over the land under the peaceful sway of the British Raj. It was not long, in fact, before the majority of the local zemindars or self-styled rajas were in a critical position. The hold that they had maintained over the land for centuries was fast slipping from their grasp, lost in overwhelming burdens of debt, and the intimate relations that had existed between them and their ryots were on the verge of being broken in favour of new landlords—'foreigners,' as the ryots termed them—without knowledge of or sympathy with their new tenants. It was clearly a case for Government interference. The zemindars themselves may have had little claim to demand protection from the results of their own incompetence, but at least they were better from every point of view than the men who were ousting them. The mahajans and land-seekers from outside could have none of the patriarchal and sentimental interest in the land that the existing race of zemindars had. Their object was simply to draw from it every pice they could: custom and tradition counted with them not at all.

The unfortunate ryots were far from being in a position of defence. They were a poor, ignorant, backward people, depending for assistance to a large extent on local customs that had governed their relations with their landlords from time immemorial. In some parts—to take but one of many instances—the ryots were entitled by long unquestioned usage to the produce of all the mahua trees on their holdings without extra rent. Here and there one of the new class of zemindars forced his way in, and, intent only on profits, ruthlessly disregarded the custom that had long come to be looked upon as a right. The demand for rent for the mahua trees fell hardly upon the ryots. It appears a small thing, but the crop is one that they had hitherto largely depended upon as a necessity. It ripens during the hot weather, the season of greatest scarcity for the ryot, and it has regularly tided an improvident people over the critical time of the year. Now they not unnaturally indignantly refuse to pay rent where they have always held rent-free. It is the land of *dustur* (custom), and change in any form is unwelcome to the native, more especially when it means a serious pecuniary loss. Moreover, such a hand-to-mouth existence is that of many of the cultivators of the soil that in many cases it is not a question of being willing but of being able to pay this extra rent. The new landlord, finding he can get no rent for the trees, has in some cases begun to cut them down, partly out of spite, partly for what the timber will fetch. Should this become general the ryot, deprived of the usual mahua crop, will experience a want that he will find it hard to fill.

A GROUP OF LOCAL RAJAS IN THE GOBINDPUR SUB-DIVISION.

The Dhanbaid Sub-division furnishes an excellent example of the utility of the Encumbered Estates Act if the old zemindars are to be retained at all. Three out of the five big estates are now being managed under its provisions by the Deputy Commissioner, and the other two are probably only saved from a like fate by the vast increase of wealth the discovery of coal on their lands has brought them. Under the Act, Government takes over the management of an estate when it becomes involved and on the verge of bankruptcy, delivering it back again to the Raja when it has been placed in order and its solvency well established. It was obvious that this part at least of Chota Nagpore was not yet ready to become an integral part of a regulation province, and that for the present its special laws and regulations needed to be retained.

The transfer, however, was suggested chiefly in the interests of the coal industry. Each of the three coal-bearing areas, Ranigunj, Giridih, and Dhanbaid, though adjoining, forms a subdivision of a different district, and the collieries are thus subject to the decisions of magistrates at three different headquarters, separated by great distances. Until the extension of the Bengal-Nagpur line a weary journey by rail lay between Purulia and Dhanbaid. Though the distance is only forty miles by road, a long detour by rail *via* Asansol was necessary in the old days, while Ranchi, where appeals lay, was still a seventy-five miles push-push journey even beyond Purulia. The recent rapid extension of the railway, however, has brought this corner of Chota Nagpore into much closer touch not only with its own headquarters but with the rest of the Province. Thus one of the chief arguments in favour of the transfer of the Sub-division to another Commissionership has lost its significance, and this weighed largely in the decision against the transfer which was finally arrived at. The Dhanbaid Sub-division, with its varied interests and sharp contrasts of the old and the new, is still to remain a part of Chota Nagpore.

CHAPTER VIII

PALAMAU

WHERE all is vague and legendary, Palamau can boast a history, imperfect and incomplete as it is, yet fuller and more authentic than that of any other part of Chota Nagpore. Situated in the north-west corner of the Province, it lay right in the path of the great trek that took place when the world was young. This way from the far north-west beyond came the long procession of many tribes and many races in search of the fertile uplands that seemed designed by nature to await their coming. Almost every one of the numerous aboriginal tribes of Chota Nagpore has passed this way, carrying with it into other lands the legends of its passing. Being nearer the earlier centres of civilisation, moreover, it was not the absolute *terra incognita* that further Chota Nagpore so long remained, and its early annals consequently figure more largely in the first pages of recorded history. It was for centuries the battleground of many races—Cheros,

Oraons, and Kharwars each claim in their heyday to have been the ruling race, while in later days the Muhammadans and the British made here their first entry into the Province. If Manbhum can claim to be the modern, Palamau may justly be called the ancient, Gateway of Chota Nagpore.

Whence Palamau derived its name is as uncertain as most things connected with the early days of Chota Nagpore. Of the three derivations generally given only one seems probable. It is suggested that the word comes from *palānā*, meaning a place of flight. Truly in its early days no place could have better deserved the name. As tribe after tribe came down from the great north-west, each one urged onwards by the hurrying footsteps of the tribe behind it, they formed one long continuous flight. It was a time of trouble and unrest, of movement and uncertainty, each race fleeing from the one that followed after or putting to flight the one that lay in its path ahead. It may well have been that they gave this land of unrest the name of 'The place from which men fled.' Another derivation given is from the Dravidian *pall-amm-u*, literally the Fortress of the Teeth, from the fact that where the chief fort of the Cheros was placed on the Awanga, the river is studded with rocks which, rising out of the water, have all the appearance of gigantic teeth. Yet another derivation suggested is from *pala,* the frost, and *mu,* dead, the land killed by the frost, from the fact that the higher portions of the district are liable to frosts of a severity unknown elsewhere in this part of Bengal.

It is a wild hill country with few level stretches of any considerable size. Some 1200 feet above sea level for the most part, its highest peaks in the south, where it borders on Sirguja rise almost to 4000 feet. It is the terrace leading from the flat alluvial plains of Behar, that stretch away interminably to the north, and the gentle rolling uplands of further Chota Nagpore to the south and east. A network of spurs and rocky heights covered with thick jungle, the landscape presents an infinite variety of ever-changing scenes. For miles, as far as the eye can reach, stretches the long succession of range on range of rocky tree-clad hills in every conceivable formation, bold, imposing, or fantastic. Far down below some tiny stream winds its way like a line of silver along its broad and stony bed, waiting for the rains to sweep down from the heights beyond to wake it into an impetuous torrent. Every exquisite shade of green and brown seems to combine, and once a year, as the hot weather draws near, the whole forest clothes itself in the gorgeous garment of the brilliant scarlet *palas* blooms. For sport, the jungles vie with the best in all the Province. These rocky tree-clad slopes, untrodden for the most part by the foot of man, abound with tiger, leopard, bear, bison, and deer of many kinds, to whom the thick tree jungle affords a safe retreat.

All three aboriginal races who played so large a part in the early and long since forgotten history of Palamau claim to have once held sway in the great fortress of Rohtasgarh, which, lying outside the present district, commands all the plains to the north. The Kharwars point to the days of Pratapadhavala, one of a long line of chiefs who ruled there in the twelfth century, as the time of their greatest prosperity. The Oraons, tracing their wanderings from the far-off Carnatic, the birth-place of their race, claim that they likewise came eventually to Rohtasgarh and built a fort there. Of their final loss of it they tell a dramatic story. It was the occasion of one of their chief festivals, wherein many potations of the much loved rice beer had played so prominent a part that all the men of the tribe lay senseless from intoxication as night fell. Only the women remained sober, and they were powerless to guard the fort. It was the opportunity for which the enemy had long been waiting, and unopposed the Muhammadan army took possession of the fort which all their strategy had failed to wrest from its defenders. Almost the whole tribe, taken unawares, was annihilated. A few, however, sobered by the sudden alarm, escaped, and dividing into two companies, one made its way to the Rajmahal hills, the other to Palamau. The descendants of the former are the Mal Palarias, while from the latter come the Oraons of Chota Nagpore. Another legend still current gives a different ending, doubtless designed to strengthen the claims of the Oraons to alliance with the Brahmin caste. This tradition says that only one man among the Oraons escaped from the wholesale slaughter at Rohtasgarh. Even he only escaped with great difficulty, and being hotly pursued he took refuge with some Mundas, whom he found eating a cow. Seeing his pursuers rapidly advancing he hastily divested himself of the sacred thread, and throwing aside caste prejudices sat down among them and began to eat, as his only chance of escaping discovery. When the Muhammadans came up and asked if they had seen the fugitive, the Mundas, since he had become one of them by joining in their feast, denied all knowledge of him, adding that he was certainly not among them, as they were all eating beef and none was wearing the sacred thread. An Oraon would never, they said, have been seen doing the one or without the other.

The traditions of the Cheros are far more pretentious. They claim to have reigned not only in Rohtasgarh but over all the surrounding country, finally extending their conquests even over the Rajput rulers of Palamau. A wild, lawless border tribe on the confines of the Muhammadan Empire, their bold raids and depredations made them feared far and near. So turbulent did they become under their chief Maharto Chero in the early part of the sixteenth century, that they held possession of the main road to Lower Bengal and practically blocked communications. In 1538 the great Sher Shah sent one of his generals to subdue them, and the re-opening of the road, which he rendered safe again for all travellers, was always counted by the men of his day as one of the three chief benefits that his rule conferred upon the province.

When the Cheros invaded Palamau is uncertain, but all accounts agree that it was a Rajput Raja of the Raksel family whom they conquered. As to whether they came in company with the Kharwars or found them already there on their arrival, traditions differ. According to one account they came as allies, eighteen thousand Kharwars and twelve thousand Cheros, and to this day they speak of themselves as belonging to the *Athara-hazar* or the *Barahazar*, the eighteen thousand or the twelve thousand. According to another story, the Kharwars were among the conquered people, but being so numerous the Cheros are said to have conciliated them and allowed them to remain in a position of practical independence in the southern portion of the district. Vague as these early annals are, here and there a great name or famous deed stands out clear and instinct with life. There is the story of Sahabal Rai, the fifth Chero ruler, who after many victories over the Muhammadans was finally taken prisoner by them and carried captive to Delhi, where, on account of the fame of his great physical strength, he was set to fight a tiger single-handed for the Emperor's amusement. It was his son Bhagwat Rai who is said to have conquered Palamau, setting up a dynasty there which lasted for two hundred years. Medni Rai, surnamed the Just, is another of the earlier rulers whose memory has survived, more for his justice even than his conquests. He is said to have subdued all the surrounding country, penetrating far into Chota Nagpore, vanquishing the Maharaja and destroying his capital of Doisa. With the spoil he built one of the forts at Palamau, which played so important a part in the subsequent history of the district. His son Pratap Rai began the building of the other fort there, but in his day came the beginning of the great Muhammadan invasion which, long resisted, was destined finally to break the power of Chero rule.

The famous Shaista Khan was Governor of Behar, and he was not the man to submit to the peace of his borders being disturbed by men whom he considered 'robber chiefs and heathenish zemindars.' He applied at once to the Emperor Shahjahan for permission to proceed against them, and the order promptly came in the forcible words of the Padishahnamah, 'to clear the country of the filth of their unprofitable existence.' In October 1641 he invaded Palamau and called upon the Cheros to submit and pay tribute. Trusting in their impenetrable jungles and rocky fastnesses to protect them, and ignorant of the nature of the new forces with which they had to contend, they disdainfully refused and sent back an insulting message of defiance. But Pratap Rai, that 'vain and misguided ruler,' as the Muhammadan chronicles style him, was soon to discover that an army of five thousand horse and fifteen thousand foot was not to be lightly defied. Slowly and with infinite precaution Shaista Khan advanced. 'Wherever he pitched his camp he had trenches dug, the earth of which was formed into a wall surrounding the whole of the encampment, and matchlock men were placed as guards in the trenches to frustrate night attacks. A large party was employed to cut down the jungle and make a road wide enough for the army to advance. All settlements on both sides of the road were plundered and destroyed. The wretched enemies withdrew on every occasion to the jungles and hills and trembled like victims in the hands of the butcher. The swords of the soldiers delivered many unto "the fire of hell"; others escaped half dead with fright. Of our troops also some were wounded and a few fell martyrs in this holy war.' Fort Palamau was soon taken, and Pratap, convinced at last that resistance was useless, submitted, agreeing to pay an annual subsidy of eighty thousand rupees, whereupon Shaista Khan and his army evacuated Palamau.

The misfortunes of Pratap Rai, however, were not yet at an end. His ill-success against the invaders had weakened his hold over his courtiers and dependents, giving his uncles Durga Rai and Tej Rai the opportunity they had been awaiting of ousting him and taking his place as chief of the Cheros. Treacherously making terms with the Muhammadan authorities at Patna, they seized the unfortunate Pratap and imprisoned him, Tej Rai being made Raja in his place. Thereafter occurred one palace revolution after another with true Eastern unexpectedness and rapidity. The authorities at Patna demanded that Pratap should be given up to them, but this Tej Rai refused, being already occupied with his own domestic troubles. His brother, Durga Rai, dissatisfied with his share of the spoil, was already intriguing against him. Turning again to Patna for support, he promised that in return he would hand over Fort Deogon to the Muhammadans as the price of their assistance. The Governor of Behar, annoyed at Tej Rai's refusal to give up Pratap, sent Zabardast Khan to help Durga Rai, who in accordance with his promise duly handed over the fort in October 1643. Making this his base of operations, Zabardast Khan fortified it and prepared to set out against Tej Rai at Palamau. But things had already gone ill with Tej Rai in his own home. 'By the help of the good luck which so signally furthers the policy of the Imperial Government,' says the Padishahnamah, 'it happened that on the 3rd Ramayan Tej Rai left Fort Palamau with a hunting party.' During his absence his courtiers suddenly declared for Pratap, who was still in prison, and releasing him, they placed him in command of the expedition designed to check the Muhammadan advance. But when in November Zabardast Khan drew near, Pratap was forced to recognise, as he had done once before, that an effective resistance was impossible. Determined to make the best of an unfortunate position, he wrote to Zabardast Khan saying that he 'looked upon the arrival of the Imperialists as a deliverance sent him by God.' The Muhammadan leader, suspicious of so unexpected a welcome, replied that if his submission was sincere he must prove it by coming with him to Patna, there to do homage to the Governor of Behar. At this Pratap procrastinated until Zabardast Khan, losing patience, sent him an ultimatum that 'he would either have to go to Patna or perish.' Pratap, choosing the lesser evil, agreed to go with Zabardast Khan on receiving a letter of safety, and accordingly on

November 19, 1643, they set out from Palamau on the eighty miles journey northward to Patna. The Governor of Behar, pleased at Pratap's submission, which promised a cessation of troubles on the southern boundary of the province, wrote so favourably of him to Delhi that the Emperor appointed him a commander of 1000 horse and restored Palamau to him in return for a yearly payment of two and a half lacs of rupees.

So for a time there was peace in Palamau. Of how temporary a nature it was, however, the third Muhammadan invasion eighteen years later shows. This was the most determined attempt of the three and the one that has survived most vividly in the memory of the Cheros. It was led by the Governor of Behar himself, the famous Daud Khan, who brought in his train not only the largest Imperial army that Palamau had yet seen, but a number of chiefs and zemindars with their retinues whom he had already subdued. On his arrival he found three forts guarding the northern frontier of the Cheros—Kothi, Kundu, and Deogon. The first was abandoned on his approach, but so dense was the jungle that separated it from Kundu, only fourteen miles away, that he took a month in reaching it, so careful was he to secure a safe line of communication with headquarters as he advanced. On finally reaching Kundu on June 3, he found it also abandoned. During the rains no advance was possible, and with true Oriental patience he encamped his army to await their passing. It was not until October 25 that the army was again in motion, and although the jungle was here less dense it took nine days to cover twenty miles. With its near approach the Chero Raja deemed it time to begin negotiations, but the demand of Daud Khan that he should tender his full submission, embrace Muhammadanism, and hold his state as a tributary chief were terms which the proud Cheros found it difficult to accept, and on December 3, the negotiations having fallen through, Daud Khan arrived within two miles of the Palamau forts. Then began the famous battle of Palamau, in which the Cheros proved themselves no unworthy antagonists to their Imperial foes. For many days the struggle lasted. On the first day, runs the graphic account in the Padishah-namah, Daud Khan advanced 'within reach of the enemies' bullets, threw up earthworks, and commenced a bombardment which was continued till sunset. The fighting on both sides was obstinate. Tahawar Khan, who was nearest to the enemy, had sixteen men killed and fifty men and many horses wounded, and retreated towards evening at Daud Khan's orders upon the centre. During the night the enemy brought two large guns from the fort, placed them on the earthworks and managed to kill several of our men and horses.

The Raja also sent a message to Daud to say that he refused his Majesty's conditions. The fire of the enemy did in the meantime much damage, directed as it was from an eminence on Daud's trenches, which were much lower. He therefore occupied the hills which command the fort, threw up other earthworks, placed upon them several guns and commenced a well-directed cannonade.'

'On the third day the enemy could no longer hold the trenches, retired nearer to the fort on the banks of the river, and threw up new earthworks. The space between their position and the Imperial camp being overgrown with jungle, Daud for two or three days cut down the trees, and having cleared a road, advanced against the enemies. The attack was simultaneously commenced on three sides and the ground was warmly contested till the second watch. The enemy was repulsed on all points; many were shot and cut down and others escaped. It had been Daud's original plan to occupy the trenches dug by the enemy and commence a siege, but the soldiers could not check their fury, and rushing to the river they crossed it and attacked the fortifications which surround the town at the foot of the fort. The enemy got bewildered and withdrew to the higher fort. The Raja now sent his whole family and valuables to the jungles and continued the defence. The Imperialists in the meantime had taken the lower fortifications and stood before the gate of the upper fort, where the fight raged till the first watch of the evening. Half a watch later the Raja fled to the jungles, when the whole fort was occupied by the victorious army.'

'The town was cleared of the filth of the existence of the infidels,' ends the triumphant chronicle, 'their idol temples were destroyed and Islamitic prayer filled the place.'

For a time Daud Khan remained, making his conquest good. Then, his forts built and garrisoned and his arrangements made for the administration of the country, he returned to Patna. Palamau was at first left under the control of Mankli Khan, who was appointed Faujdar, but a few years later, in 1666, it was brought under the direct surveillance of the Governor of Behar.

For nearly a century little of importance happened in Palamau. During all that period it remained under Muhammadan supremacy, though beyond exacting tribute and garrisoning its fortresses, the Muhammadans appear to have interfered but little in internal affairs. In the north a few nobles were granted lands by Imperial order ousting the original holders, but in the south the petty Chero chiefs maintained a show of independence undisturbed. The most famous name in the annals of the time is that of Nawab Hedayat Ali Khan, at one time Deputy Governor of Behar. In the earlier part of the eighteenth century the

Emperor Muhammad Shah granted him the two perganas of Japla and Belaunge which had been formerly in the possession of the Raja of Sonapura. The latter did not give them up to the newcomer without a struggle, and it was only after much fighting that the Nawab succeeded in getting possession of a portion of them. He afterwards founded the town of Husainabad, and there spent the last years of his life. The Nawab's chief claim to fame, however, rests largely on the fact that he was the father of the still more famous Ghulan Husain Khan, the author of that amazing history of the Muhammadan Court, the 'Sair-ul-Mutakharin,' the 'view of modern times.' The latter, when, in his grandiloquent words, his father 'was pleased to depart to the merciful mansion of the Omnipotent King and was intombed in the town which he had founded,' succeeded to his inheritance, immediately setting out for Murshedabad and getting his succession confirmed in 1765, the famous year in which the domains of Bengal, Behar and Orissa were ceded by the Nawab to the British.

It was only seven years later that the first British force entered Palamau. Once again there was a dispute as to the succession among the Cheros, and the British in their new position of authority were forced to interfere. Jai Kishan Rai, the head of the younger branch of the Chero royal family, had murdered the ruling chief Ranjit Rai and usurped the *gadi*. He in turn was shot a few years later in a skirmish with some of Ranjit Rai's friends, and one Chitrajit Rai became Raja. Gopal Rai, the grandson of Jai Kishan Rai, however, escaped to Patna and was taken before Captain Camac, then the Company's agent there, with a request for help to restore him to the *gadi* as the rightful heir. It was some time before Captain Camac could be induced to interfere in these tangled bypaths of political intrigue, but the fact that Chitrajit Rai had openly repudiated British authority finally induced him to espouse the cause of Gopal Rai. At the head of a small force he entered Palamau and reached the Palamau forts unopposed. Here he met with an unexpected and obstinate resistance. Even the British artillery could make no impression upon the solid stone walls of the fort in which the enemy had entrenched themselves. There is a story, however, that though outwardly uniform, there was one spot in the walls which was composed only of mud, having been especially so designed by Medni Rai, the builder of the fort, to make certain of recapturing it should it ever be taken by the enemy. The secret was known only to a few, but one of these, named Udwant Rai, who had accompanied Gopal Rai on his escape to Patna, was in the British camp, and he disclosed the weak spot in the walls to his allies. In consequence a break was quickly effected and the fort captured.

Chitrajit Rai fled to the neighbouring province of Sirguja and Palamau was formally taken possession of by the British, Gopal Rai being installed as feudatory chief.

The man, however, for whom so much had been done, soon proved himself utterly unworthy of trust. Jealous of Udwant Rai, to whom he owed his life and position, he finally had him treacherously murdered at Shahpur, on the banks of the Koel river, and once more the tide of revolt and intrigue was let loose. Udwant Rai's relatives appealed to a small detachment of troops which Captain Camac had left behind at Lesliegunj, and with their help Gopal Rai was surrounded and taken prisoner. Taken to Chatra for trial, he was sentenced to imprisonment at Patna, where he ended his short and stormy career in 1784. His successor, Basant Rai, died the same year, and his brother, Churaman Rai, a minor, succeeded. He soon showed signs of hopeless incompetence, and in 1800 a general insurrection of the Cheros broke out which needed a force under Colonel Jones to subdue it. Once more the insurgents fled to Sirguja, which proved so safe and convenient a refuge whence they could harry and ravage Palamau.

In 1814 the Government revenue was so far in arrears that the estate was put up to auction and purchased by Government. So wild was the nature of the country and so lawless the inhabitants, that it was said that 'the realisation of the revenue partook more of the nature of voluntary contribution than of that active and punctual enforcement of the rights of government which was practised in all the other districts, from which the landholders of Palamau had no special claims to exemption.' It was thus essential that the local chief responsible to Government should be a man of strong character and worthy of trust. Churaman Rai, 'nearly an idiot in understanding, dissolute, extravagant, and thoughtless,' was utterly incapable of administering so turbulent a charge, and he was finally set aside, the last Chero Raja of Palamau.

On the recommendation of Major Roughsedge, then commanding the Ramgarh battalion, the rights that Government had acquired were conferred on Raja Ghansham Singh of Deo in the Gaya district, who had proved himself eminently worthy of confidence. But so little success did he have in controlling the unruly Cheros that they again broke out into open rebellion in 1817, and in the following year Government revoked the grant, taking the entire estate under its own control, and including it within the district of Ramgarh.

In the great Kol rebellion of 1831–2, which was directed against the Hindu and Muhammadan oppressors, the Cheros played their part, but they indulged in none of the excesses which characterised the rising in other parts of Chota

Nagpore, and the disturbances here were soon quelled. Two years later, on the redistribution of the province, Palamau was transferred to the Lohardaga district. Nineteen years later, in 1857, it was made a sub-division of the same district with headquarters at Korda on the Jamira Pat plateau in Sirguja, though Lesliegunj remained the headquarters for the troops and for the collection of the revenue.

Four years later came the last stirring event in the history of Palamau. The mutiny of the native troops in Ranchi and Hazaribagh was an opportunity not to be lost by the turbulent tribesmen of Palamau. The Cheros, deprived of their ancient line of chiefs, were no longer the prime movers. The leading spirits were the Kharwars, and more especially a section of them known as the Bogtas. They were a class of lawless raiders inhabiting the high plateau that lies on the borders of Sirguja. Cut off from the lowlands of Palamau by a range of hills of which they held the passes, they occupied an almost unassailable position. Just before the outbreak of the mutiny their chief had died an outlaw, but the British Government, ever anxious to conciliate, recognised his two sons Nilambar and Pitambar Sahi as his heirs. Pitambar, the younger of the two brothers, was in Ranchi, chafing under even the slight restraint put upon him, when the sepoys mutinied at Doranda and all the officials withdrew from the station. Thinking, like many others, that this must assuredly be the end of British rule, and that a time of anarchy and licence had arrived, he hurried off to join his brother. Together they raised the standard of revolt, throwing off their allegiance and declaring themselves independent chieftains.

But for two neighbouring loyal chiefs, Raghubar Dayal Singh and Kishun Dayal Singh, who held the fort of Chainpur, the Bogtas would have swept the whole countryside unchecked. These two loyal zemindars deserve that the memory of their loyalty should survive, for without them the whole of Palamau would doubtless for the moment have been lost and the small detachment of Company's troops cut to pieces. There was apparently only one English official in the whole of Palamau at the time of the outbreak. Lieutenant Graham was acting as Assistant Commissioner, but he had no more than fifty men with him. With these, however, he pluckily advanced against the rebels on hearing that they had attacked Lesliegunj, burning and destroying all within their path. Reaching Chainpur he joined the loyal Raghubar Dayal. Further advance, however, was impossible, and unable to withdraw, he hastily fortified the zemindar's house and prepared to stand a siege. For months he was shut up, unable to escape from a position of great danger, owing to the overwhelming number of the rebels. All the surrounding district was up in arms, and he himself was the only Englishman to inspire the little company of loyal troops with confidence and courage to continue what at one time appeared an almost hopeless resistance.

The troops that eventually came to his relief were two companies of H.M.'s 13th L.I. from Sasseram under Major Cotter, the Deo Raja adding a contingent of his own followers. Fortunately it was winter and marching was less difficult. On the 8th of December he succeeded in joining forces with Lieutenant Graham, and after one or two small encounters the insurgents rapidly dispersed in face of the larger number of organised troops opposed to them. Fort Palamau, however, still held out, and in January Captain Dalton, the Agent to the Governor-General, with 140 men of the Madras Native Infantry under Major Macdonell, a small company of Ramgarh cavalry, and a party of matchlock men under the loyal Zemindar Jagat Pal Singh, marched northwards from Ranchi. At Manka, ten miles from Palamau, he was joined on January 21st by Lieutenant Graham and his gallant little band of faithful followers. Against this combined force the fort at Palamau offered little resistance, and was finally stormed and taken with the loss of only one killed and two wounded, the rebels seeking safety in flight and leaving guns, ammunition, cattle, supplies and baggage behind them.

There only remained the Bogta country in the south. Marching rapidly across the hills, the Baghmara and Tungari ghats were taken with little opposition. As the troops drew near the latter pass, news was brought that the insurgents were plundering a village in the vicinity. Lieutenant Graham, with a party of Ramgarh cavalry, immediately hurried on in advance and caught them in the act as they were driving off the villagers as prisoners with their cattle. At Chemu, on the banks of the Koel river, the headquarters of Nilambar and Pitambar Sahi, there was a last determined stand, but as elsewhere, when once the British troops could be brought face to face with the ill-organised rebel levies, the decision was not long in doubt. The great difficulty here, as elsewhere in Chota Nagpore, was the nature of the country which afforded such impenetrable retreats for the armed gangs into which the insurgents broke up after each defeat, postponing their final subjugation to law and order until the latest possible moment. Pitambar and Nilambar Sahi were among those who escaped from the final encounter, but though they continued their depredations for a time at the head of small robber bands they were both eventually captured, and after full trial found guilty and hanged. The official note on the mutiny in Palamau closes with this well-deserved tribute to the young British subaltern who had so worthily upheld the traditions of his race. 'I must not quit the subject without recording my high admiration of the conduct of Lieutenant Graham, who, without another Englishman near him, surrounded by thousands of the enemy, never thought of retreat, and by maintaining his post prevented the district from falling entirely into the hands of the insurgents.'

The years that have followed have been years of unbroken peace and steadily increasing prosperity such as Palamau has never previously known. The development of its coal mines has given it an added importance, bringing wealth and employment to thousands of its people, while cultivation, undisturbed by raids and forays, has rapidly recovered. In 1859 the headquarters were transferred to Lesliegunj, but owing to the site being supposed to be unhealthy, the present station of Daltongunj, named after Colonel Dalton the Commissioner, was chosen four years later. In 1891 Palamau had made such rapid strides that it was considered no longer suitable that it should remain a sub-division of Lohardaga. The district as constituted was an extremely unwieldy one, consisting of the enormous area of 12,044 square miles. Daltongunj itself was 104 miles from its headquarters station at Ranchi, from which the farthest parts of the Palamau district were no less than 150 miles away. The differences in race, language, and custom were no less marked, and accordingly in January 1892

Palamau was formed into a separate district of Chota Nagpore. After its many vicissitudes it had at last fallen completely into line with British order and administration, the last of all the districts constituted in Bengal.

CHAPTER IX

A TRAMP ON THE GRAND TRUNK ROAD

THE Grand Trunk Road has lost much of its life and interest in the twentieth century. The days have gone for ever when it formed one of the great highways of northern India by which every traveller from Calcutta must pass who would reach on foot the up-country cities of Oude, the Punjaub, or the North-West. Threading its way, straight and white, like a measuring tape, it was trodden by a motley throng of traders with their merchandise from the far-away centres of the north, pilgrims wending their way to Parasnath or further on still to the great temple of Jagannath at Puri by the sea, troops marching to some new headquarters, or occasionally the camp army of the Viceroy or the Commander-in-chief slowly marching up country on a tour of peace or pushing on with greater speed to the scene of outbreak or revolt.

It was a busy stream of life, in those days, that poured along its route with its monopoly of ceaseless traffic. But the first line of rail that, once begun, crept with lightning speed over the land, robbed it for ever of its great position as the most important highway of Upper India. It was not for long that the native mind retained its first suspicion of the iron horse, and a journey in the train soon became an everyday occurrence to the crowd of travellers whom the Grand Trunk Road would know no more.

But, great as the decline has been, all traffic has not yet deserted it. For over a hundred miles the Grand Trunk runs through Chota Nagpore, and there it retains perhaps more of its old conditions than anywhere else along its route. Here, there is no train close at hand to tempt the wayfarer from the road, and all those who live near by must make their way along it before they can reach the railway or their destination. It is quiet and deserted now, compared with what it once was, but something of the charm of its ever-changing views of native life still remains and well repays a tramp along its length.

In the old days, the Barakar cut the Grand Trunk Road in two. Forming here the western boundary of Chota Nagpore, it was a serious obstacle in the way of traffic and even of the traveller on foot. There was no bridge then, and the fording of the river must often have proved a source of wearisome delay. It is a typical river of the district, nothing but a stretch of sand, until the rains, higher up among the hills, make of it a rushing torrent. Before the bridge was built, there was nothing to be done but to sit patiently on the bank till the flood had passed. It might be hours or it might be days, but the traveller was entirely at its mercy. He had need of all the patience he possessed, though time was of less value in those days. What, after all, was a day more or less in a journey from Calcutta to Delhi on foot? There is no hurry on the Grand Trunk Road. Haste is one of the things that have rarely come its way. Only very occasionally has its peace been disturbed by the rush of hurrying feet. Yet as one begins the tramp on the famous road, one's mind goes back irresistibly to those exciting moments in the great year of mutiny, from which the oldest of the natives still count the years that have followed. Then there was a sudden stir and haste as the troops rushed on in a race of life and death to reach the cities up country where the issues hung in the balance. There are still old men to be met with along the road who remember the time and can tell of the rapid march of the troops, waking the villagers long before the dawn with the noise of their passing, and leaving everywhere behind them a feeling of awe and wonder at their marvellous speed and endurance. And as they saw them pass, the old men say that they knew that the British Raj was safe.

But the days of such excitement on the Grand Trunk Road are gone for ever. The railway, crossing the Barakar, bears away with it many who would otherwise have had perforce to make the journey on foot. Only those to whom money is a consideration, and time is none, take to the road, unless trade or their destination lead them where no train runs.

A fine arched bridge spans the river, built just over thirty years ago when the railway first came as far as Barakar. There was a toll to be paid in its early days—four annas for every bullock cart—and the tollhouse still stands on the Chota Nagpore side. But, the toll abolished, travellers have since made of it a resting-place, and the broad verandah in front is filled now by a group of sharp-eyed, keen-faced merchants, who are resting awhile by the way, deep in conversation that hovers always round the fascinating subject of pice and profits. They are at the end of their journey by road here, having come a hundred miles from Hazaribagh on foot. At Barakar they will take the train to Calcutta, and finish the second stage of their journey in as many hours as the first stage has taken days. Lazily leaning against the wall and listening idly to the merchants' talk are a couple of constables from the *thana* (police station) just behind the toll-house. Puggarees and belts discarded, only the short blue coats, edged with red, distinguish

A BARBER AT WORK BY THE WAYSIDE.

THE POTTER'S WHEEL.

them from the white-clad group of merchants, who turn to them from time to time for local information or to pass a friendly pinch of betel-nut or *khaini* (native tobacco). Close by, in full public view, a barber busily plies his trade with typical Eastern unconcern, side by side with a sweetmeat seller, whose stall, in spite of the hosts of flies that hover round it, never fails to attract the passers-by. Further up the street the potter sits at his wheel, surrounded by his handiwork, which under his swift, sure touch grows rapidly out of the shapeless clay.

Across the bridge crawls a long line of bullock carts from Barakar, their wheels creaking hoarsely as they move slowly past. The bullocks, with their mild uncomplaining eyes, are of the smallest description and seem scarce able to bear the weight of the heavy yoke that presses on their necks. They are bound for Nirsha, eight miles off, and if they cover the distance in four hours it will be as much as they can do. But it is a straight road all the way, and though the drivers may at times belabour them with sticks and encourage them in no endearing terms, it will have little effect on the stolid complacency of the beasts, whose kind for countless generations have always failed to recognise the necessity of haste.

Leaving Chirkunda, the small village that clusters round the road on the banks of the Barakar, the journey along the Grand Trunk in

Chota Nagpore begins. The first stretch of the way lies through land black with coal. Close by are the oldest collieries in the Gobindpur Subdivision, working long before Jherria was opened out, and dating back to the days before the railway crossed the Barakar. It is a very different scene now from what the Grand Trunk Road must have witnessed in its earlier days. All along here was once an excellent shooting-ground for big game : now a few years have changed it into a scene of busy activity. But a little further on, where the Katras-Jherria line cuts across the road, the Grand Trunk parts company with the railway only to meet it once again in Chota Nagpore beyond Topechanchi, at the foot of Parasnath. Henceforward it resumes its old conditions, almost untouched, as they were in its earliest days.

There is nothing but a wide stretch of paddy field on either side now, studded here and there with mango topes and the never absent patches of sal tree jungle. Nirsha is the first halting-place, one of those established when the road was made. These stages in the old days were not only resting-places for travellers, but the headquarters of special police to guard the roads. With the rush of traffic that poured down the newly opened road, came a choice collection of the worst characters, *badmashes* drawn from every district far and near by the hope of plunder. Dacoity and murder had quickly become of almost daily occurrence, rendering the roads unsafe for any but the largest cavavans and threatening to put a stop to traffic altogether. Prompt measures were quickly taken. The ordinary police of the districts being entirely unable to cope with the disorder, mounted sowars were appointed to patrol the road and protect travellers and the mail. They were placed at each of the halting-stages, which thus afforded greater promise of safety for the night's rest, and from which they could guard the road on either side within their beat. It was only recently, when the traffic had grown small and the ordinary police of the district more efficient, that the sowars were abolished. Some of them are still to be found, living on a pension from Government, in the places they had so long guarded, and always eager to tell vague tales of the old times when there was something doing on the Grand Trunk Road.

Nirsha is only a small straggling village that grew up round the original halting-stage in the days when traffic was greater and the inhabitants did a good trade in supplying the necessaries of life to the travellers on the road. There is a two-roomed Dâk Bungalow that serves as a European rest-house, not in the best state of repair. But it serves as a temporary halting-place for an hour or two in the heat of the day or a rest at night, and the Europeans who pass this way are few.

Just entering the village from the Gobindpur

side is a long line of pack bullocks, half buried beneath the huge burdens that balance one another across their backs. Small as the bullocks are, not half the size of those up country, they will carry a load of two maunds [160 lbs.], but their ordinary march is not more than eight or ten miles a day. Often miserable little country *tats* serve the same purpose. Their owners seem to have little mercy on them, piling up their burdens till their feeble legs bend under them and they stagger beneath the weight. A little further on, the smallest of *tats* shambles on wearily, a native seated on its back with his legs encircling its diminutive body and his feet crossed underneath, a quaint position, apparently so safe and comfortable that the rider can fall asleep with impunity on the journey.

Two miles behind Nirsha off the Grand Trunk Road lies Pandra, with its fine large tank, known as the Rani Bandh. It was built by a lady famous in her day, who was created Maharani by the British Government for help given at the time of the Sepoy Mutiny. Her works of charity were known throughout the countryside, and most things in Pandra seem to owe their origin to her—the imposing building of the Raja's palace (now falling into decay), the dispensary, the schools, and a number of temples and shrines. Close by is an older temple, resembling those on the banks of the Barakar and the Damuda, the work of a people who have long since disappeared.

A TEMPLE AT PANDRA

The road begins to change somewhat after leaving Nirsha, becoming less flat and more characteristic of Chota Nagpore. Crossing the bridge over the Khudia, a long gradual ascent brings one to the little village of Kurkabad, perched on the top of the slope. Sheltered by its grand old banyan and pepul trees, it is a cool and welcome halting-place to a crowd of pedestrians. Here is a group of Kabulis in their picturesque costumes, with white baggy trousers and gay-coloured waistcoats and turbans. They are squatting by the side of the road, taking their rest and enjoying the inevitable *hookah* (native pipe), a subject of interest to the men, women, and children of the village, whose sole excitement in life centres round the passers-by on the Grand Trunk Road. The Kabulis are not unwilling to enter into conversation. They have found their way down from Afghanistan, sometimes by rail, sometimes on foot. They finally left the train two hundred miles away and have marched down the Grand Trunk as far as this, only branching off at Barhi to visit Hazaribagh and joining it again at Bagoda further on. About their business they are somewhat more reticent. They will join the train at Barakar, they say, and so reach Calcutta, returning this same road again a month hence. Their bundles, that lie around, slung through with sticks for greater convenience in carrying across their shoulders, contain all that they will need by the way. They can purchase what else they want along the road, and they are in no hurry. Twelve miles is all they hope to cover to-day, and to-morrow—that happy Eastern word—will bring them to Barakar.

Three miles out of Gobindpur, on the left of the road, still remain the pillars that mark the site of what was once the headquarters of the Sub-division. The name of the place, Baghshuma —'the smell of a tiger'—is reminiscent of the days when the traveller down the Grand Trunk Road went with his life in his hand, not only from dacoits but from the denizens of the jungle, who had their home on its very borders. Stories are still told of how numbers of the convicts who were employed in making the road were carried off by tigers as they worked, and many a traveller in those days met a similar fate. So badly infested were some of the original halting-places that it was found necessary to remove them to more open spots, thus accounting for the unequal distances apart at which the stages are found to-day. Baghshuma is deserted now. If there was once even the smallest of villages here, which one imagines must have grown up round the head-quarters of the Sub-division, all sign of it has disappeared. Only a few pillars and a heap of ruins are left, though the trees that once formed the avenue and grew about the compound still remain and flourish.

Hobbled under a wide-spreading banyan tree, right opposite the Jail on the outskirts of Gobindpur, are a group of horses on their way down country from the great Sonepur fair. But the fair has been over some time, and these horses are far from being the best of the show—those have been picked up long before they reached as far as this down the Grand Trunk Road, though occasionally even here a good animal is to be got that has somehow hitherto escaped notice. But most of them are a rough lot, and were it not for the fact that there are no limits to what a native will use in the way of a horse, one would wonder how they will ever be disposed of. The dealers themselves look a rougher lot still, as they sit round their gipsy-like encampment, half buried in the smoke from the fires they have lit to cook their food. They will be glad to crouch round them, too, later on, towards night, when the temperature falls to within three or four degrees of freezing-point, which the native, more accustomed to the heat, considers most unpleasantly cold.

For over a mile, Gobindpur borders on the Grand Trunk Road. The long irregular rows of houses on either side stand back fifty yards or more from the centre—the distance fixed by Government which none may encroach upon by so much as an inch of overhanging roof or awning. Halfway up the village a small crowd has gathered in the wake of a *tamasha wala* (showman). The bundle on each side of the *banghi* that he carries is surmounted by the smallest of infantile bears, while a third of larger growth shuffles along behind tied by a string. Bringing up the rear come the man's wife and three children of diminutive sizes, each carrying the inevitable bundle tied in a cloth, all except the youngest member of the party, who looks as if he needed to be carried himself. The man puts down his *banghi* at last, stopping to answer questions about the tiny bears that cannot fail to attract attention as they cling to the bundles, like balls of long black hair. They have come from the Midnapore district two hundred miles away, where the man has been to get them from the jungle for his troupe. The older bear is already half trained, and he exhibits her accomplishments with pride. She has made marvellous progress for her age, and at the sound of the drum and the monotonous droning voice of the man she goes hopping through her performances, dancing different steps to the changing tunes and ending up with a mock fight with her trainer, lying at last full length on the ground as if dead, comically stiff and stark. The smaller bears meanwhile crawl about, sniffing all round, too young as yet to take part in the entertainment, though their time, as the man says, will soon begin.

Further on, at the end of the village, stand

TRAVELLING ON THE GRAND TRUNK ROAD. RIDING A NATIVE TAT (PONY).

the tall white pillars that mark the military camping-ground, some three acres in extent. It is provided for troops on the march, and similar halting-places occur at intervals of ten or twelve miles all down the road. It is only in the winter months that the marching is done; ten miles a day, from one-camping ground to the next, is the usual programme *en route*. It is excellent training for the men, if a trifle monotonous when the march lengthens out into hundreds of miles. A start is made at daybreak, or before if there is a moon, with a halt for 'coffee shop' and a rest halfway. The next camping-ground is reached by eight or nine o'clock, and, though the camp equipment necessarily takes longer to come up, there is no time lost when once it arrives. In an hour the whole of the maidan is covered with regular rows of white tents, and the camping-ground that for ninety-nine days out of a hundred is devoid of life is for the time a busy scene of stir and activity. It is only a small detachment of sixty men there now from the 6th Cavalry on their way down to Calcutta to furnish an escort for the Lieutenant-Governor. They form a picturesque group as they start off down the road and an unusual object of interest to the villagers, who crowd round to see them pass.

From the camping-ground there is a splendid view of Parasnath, which for some way back has been a clear-cut landmark against the horizon.

All along to the north runs the Tundi range of hills, Domunda, with its two heads, being easily distinguishable among its peaks, its delicate blue haze thrown up by the brilliant flash of colours from the western sky as the sun sets behind the Sacred Hill. But the view must be seen in the rains to be seen at its best. Then the land far and near is clothed in its wonderful garment of green of every shade, and all nature is alive with a life that seems almost to justify the Eastern flight of imagination that makes the earth to 'laugh and sing for joy.' Then, too, the sun sets in all its splendour, clothed in a marvellous blaze of colour, right behind Parasnath, lighting it till the very last flicker of twilight has fallen, as if loth to leave the towering heights of the home of the gods.

Three miles further on is another memory of the old days on the Grand Trunk Road. It is a fine well-built house, standing back behind an avenue of trees, but bearing now the shut deserted look born of long disuse. Erected in times gone by, as a halting-place for Viceroy or Lieutenant-Governor on his way up country before the days of steam and rail, it must, if report speaks true, have seen something of livelier days. The oldest of the villagers at Rajgunj, a few miles further on —an old sowar, bent and withered, looking more than the seventy years he admits—could still tell seven years ago how the Bara Lat Saheb (Viceroy) passed this way. Vaguely and perhaps with a touch of imagination he was wont to describe the escort, the line of elephants and pack-horses and the crowd of camp-followers. It was possible that it might have been the Jangi Lat Saheb (Commander-in-Chief) and not the Bara Lat Saheb, and the date he had forgotten—it might have been twenty or it might have been forty years since. It was all so long ago, he pleaded, when you pressed him further, and he was an old man on whom the weight of years lay heavily. But he served Government well, he would hasten to add, until the sowars were abolished, and he still drew a pension of four rupees eight annas a month (six shillings). It is the same thing all along the Grand Trunk Road. The memory of the old days is fast dying out, and only vague stories of its past remain.

Through Barwa and Rajgunj, with its camping-ground, and Kotaldi, with its huge spreading trees almost spanning the whole width of the road, the traveller approaches Topechanchi. It is mostly undulating here, with a nearer view of the whole range of hills to the north and Parasnath dominating the scene more and more as one advances. There is a sleepy old-world charm about Topechanchi that one gradually begins to associate with Chota Nagpore as one passes up the Grand Trunk Road. The few houses that the village contains, most of them of mud and thatch, lie back on either side, half buried beneath great banyan and pepul trees, that act as second roofs against heat and rain to the frail buildings underneath. Halfway down the road is the Thana, the headquarters of the police and the visible symbol of the authority of the British Raj. Further on lies the dispensary, a boon to all the country round, where the prejudice against European medicine has almost entirely died out. Many a traveller, suddenly attacked with fever or cholera by the way, has owed his life to the timely help of these dispensaries placed at intervals along the road. In the old days, when no medical aid was to be obtained, pilgrims died in hundreds by the way. The Grand Trunk Road is one long cemetery of unrecorded graves. Many Europeans, too, have found their last resting-places beside it, but only a tombstone here and there preserves the memory of one more fortunate than the rest whose very names have been long since forgotten. In the Dâk Bungalow compound at Topechanchi, a well-preserved stone still records the virtues of a sergeant of the 98th Regiment who died here on the line of march in 1847. It was erected as a mark of esteem by the officers of his regiment, and the oldest inhabitant of the village can still remember the day of his death and the military funeral his comrades gave him.

Almost opposite is the *serai*—that most typical of Eastern resting-places. No carts are allowed to stop on the Grand Trunk Road at night, except in the *serais*, which at every halting-place offer them shelter by the way. The *serai* is nothing but an open enclosure within four square walls and a narrow strip roofed in, as better shelter for the cartmen. Every year at the *sudder* (headquarters) station the lease of the *serai* is put up to public auction. At Topechanchi the leaseholder will come out to meet you if you are on inspection bent. He is doubtless doing a good thing by it, but no native of his class would ever admit that he was making money. Sixty rupees (3*l.* 15*s.*), he says, he pays for the lease of it, and the cartmen pay but one pice (a farthing) per cart for the night, and he is losing money every year. If you ask him, in surprise, why he still takes it at a loss, he will only smile deprecatingly and tell you that though times are not what they used to be on the Grand Trunk Road and carts are fewer, someone must needs still take the lease.

It is worth while waiting a day at Topechanchi and beating the jungle on the smaller hills at the foot of Parasnath. There is always the chance of a bear or possibly a stray leopard or tiger, and a beat rarely fails to turn out cheetal or barking deer to provide one with a shot. There is an old shikari here, hopelessly lame, with one leg doubled up under him, but wonderfully energetic as he literally races along with the help of a stick and his one sound leg. He has shot with all the Sahebs from Gobindpur and remembers them all by name, delighting to recount their exploits in the days when the shooting at Topechanchi was worth coming for. Many an officer, too, passing down the road, has left his name behind in the memory of this old man, who can point out with pride the exact spot where the leopard or the bear fell to this or that Paltan Saheb's rifle.

One leaves Topechanchi with regret. It is the prettiest spot along the Grand Trunk Road while it runs through Chota Nagpore, and one misses, after passing, the great mass of hills and the grand summit of Parasnath that have dominated all the road for the last twenty miles. Crossing the bridge over the Jamoonia, one passes on through Rangamatti, where the Gobindpur Subdivision ends and the Hazaribagh district begins. Dumri, the next halting-stage, is the point where the Giridih road joins the Grand Trunk, and here one meets again the now familiar push-push on the way to Hazaribagh. From Dumri to Bagoda, fourteen miles, the Grand Trunk forms a portion of the road from Hazaribagh to Giridih, which was formerly its nearest railway station, seventy-three miles away. This is by far the busiest part of the road throughout its length in Chota Nagpore. The Grand Chord Line of the East Indian Railway now runs from Dhanbaid to Gaya, opening up new country and crossing the Grand Trunk Road close by. The Hazaribagh Road station, eight miles from Bagoda, has thus replaced Giridih as the station for Hazaribagh and all this portion of Chota Nagpore. But though traffic is heavier, modern conditions have as yet made no greater inroads here than elsewhere, except in the immediate vicinity of the railway. Everything is primitive and slow-moving, and nothing faster than the push-push, with its average rate of four miles an hour, passes along the road itself. Only very occasionally a cyclist from Hazaribagh flashes by, with a strange contrast of modern speed, intent on doing the run to Giridih in record time.

Further on, at Barkatta, are a group of mineral springs, famous through all the country round. There are four of them, not far from the side of the road, rising up in the midst of a rock and bricked roughly round like wells. The hottest of the springs, in which the temperature of the water stands at 190°, is known as Surajkund, the Well of the Sun. They are objects of great veneration among the natives, who, unable to explain their existence, regard them as supernatural and attribute to them special powers.

Once a year, on the first full moon in the month of January, a great mela is held here. Crowds of people come from all parts of the district, attracted by the fame of the wells and that curious mixture of worldliness and piety that makes up an Eastern pilgrimage. But there is a special object in coming to the mela here. It is the greatest desire of every Hindu woman to bear a son, and the gods at Surajkund are kind and seldom fail to bless a visit with the longed-for offspring. The Grand Trunk Road is thronged with a crowd of eager women, as the day of the full moon approaches and the time of the mela is at hand. Some of them have come long distances and are staking their all on this pilgrimage of faith. Half hopefully, yet half dreading to hear the worst, they approach the Brahmin who presides at the springs and can tell them the verdict of the gods. As each woman comes up in turn, he takes a small green berry pierced through by a tiny twig and drops it into the spring. The woman, leaning eagerly forward, looks down with straining eyes into the hot bubbling water, for on the fate of the berry the realisation of her hopes depends. If the berry sinks, the gods have spoken against her, and she will never be the happy mother of a son, and the unfortunate suppliant turns away in a passion of despair, to be looked at suspiciously for all time as one unfavoured of the gods. But if the berry floats, as in nearly every case it does, the happy woman goes on her way rejoicing, blessed of the gods, and confident that in due time a son will be hers.

There are other women, besides, who throng the approaches to the well—those to whom the fulfilment of the promise has come. These return with proud swinging step, bearing the infant of so much desire in their arms, the admiration and

TRAVELLING ON THE GRAND TRUNK ROAD ON FOOT.

envy of those who have not yet passed the springs and seen the berry float. They have come back to show their gratitude to the gods, and bring with them as offerings for the Brahmin and the little Hindu temple by the well the ever-welcome goat and rice and pice and gay garlands of *genda* blossom. They form a wonderful throng, these women, with their hopes and fears, giving one real glimpses of human nature with all the *abandon* of the East. The men who come with their womenfolk share their joy or sorrow, but more soberly. To them also it is a pilgrimage fraught with much moment. The lack of a son is almost as great a stigma to the husband as it is to the childless wife.

Not being able to explain the presence of the springs in any other way, the native has invented a story to account for them. If you ask the Brahmin in charge or any of the worshippers as to their origin, they will only shake their heads with a vague smile and pass on, wondering at the curiosity of the Saheb in wanting to know the reason of things and not being content to take them as they are. But here and there one will give you disjointed fragments of the mythical story that has grown up round them. In the olden days, so the tradition runs, when caravans were numerous along the road, one of them had halted here to bivouac for the night. As the travellers sat preparing their evening meal, an old woman passing along the road turned aside and wandered through their encampment, asking alms. She was poor and hungry and alone, but they one and all roughly ordered her away, refusing her food and pice and calling her a witch. Pursuing her way along the road, she stopped a short way off and cursed them for their want of charity and hospitality. While she spoke, the earth suddenly opened and swallowed them up as they sat. From the place where they disappeared underground the hot springs immediately rose up.

Surajkund left behind, there is little more of interest till one reaches Barhi. But there is more traffic here than in the earlier stages of the journey, and some new touch of life along the road, not met before, is continually presenting itself. A string of camels passes slowly by—a rare sight in Chota Nagpore—laden with packs, the huge ungainly beasts winding their way along in lazy desultory fashion, as if it were almost too much trouble to put one foot before the other. They are a poor, ill-fed lot, and they have travelled for days down the Grand Trunk Road at the same crawling pace in search of a purchaser. There is not much demand for them here, but these will doubtless go to swell the motley live-stock collection of some local Raja. Elephants are far more often seen, and no zemindar with any claim to importance would be without one at least. Not long since a splendid group of twenty Government elephants belonging to the Commissariat Department passed down from Jhansi to Calcutta to be sold, on the abolition of the elephant battery. They formed a fine array of giants as they stood chained on the camping-grounds or marching ponderously along the road.

At Barhi the end of the tramp is reached. It is the last big halting-stage in Chota Nagpore, and strikes one as a large place compared with the small *bastis* that are all the traveller has passed through hitherto. Whatever importance it has, is owing to the opium weighments that take place here every year. Then a crowd of cultivators fill the place, bringing in their yearly crops from all the north of the district where the opium is grown. The seed is sown in the beginning of the cold weather and the poppies are ripe at the end of March. In April and May the weighments take place, and Barhi for a time presents a busy scene.

A crowd has gathered at the further end of the village street, and even the fat Babu, lolling in his palki, which the coolies with their curious mechanical motion must find a heavy burden, stops as he approaches and gets out to look. It is a group of travelling conjurers and acrobats who are attracting attention, and the native, to whom sleight of hand and tricks of balance irresistibly appeal, presses round to watch. Some of the less ambitious tricks are excellent, but the famous mango and basket tricks are unconvincing and badly done. One sees a woman or a boy tied up in an extraordinarily small bundle and shut down inside a basket which looked incapable of containing a human being at all. But then the conjurer places the basket on one side and proceeds with another trick, so that, although when it is opened again the woman or the boy has disappeared, one's attention has been diverted in the meantime and the cleverness of the trick is still open to much doubt. The conjurer, with his monotonous sing-song intonation, soon grows wearisome, and one turns away, almost falling over a group of three fakirs seated cross-legged on the outskirts of the crowd. With their matted hair coiled on their heads and their bodies naked save for a strip of dirty cloth and a plentiful covering of ashes, they sit stolid, contemplative, and immovable, absolutely ignoring the conjurer and the crowd beside them—but another of the many sharp and varied contrasts that a tramp on the Grand Trunk Road presents.

CHAPTER X

THE GARDEN OF A THOUSAND TREES

IT is a picturesque title—The Garden of a Thousand Trees—and, if somewhat fanciful, yet given with a true touch of Oriental imagination and love of high-sounding words. A huge mango tope, containing a thousand trees, some of which still remain, was known as Hazari, and round these a village grew, spreading in time into the modern town of Hazaribagh, the Garden of a Thousand Trees. Such is the interpretation of the name the oldest of the inhabitants give, one of them adding, with pardonable pride in his native town, that this is the garden of Chota Nagpore, and that the motto over the old gateway of the Emperors at Delhi might well be written of Hazaribagh :

'If there is a paradise on earth, it is here, it is here.'

It is a charming approach along the Bagoda road, and the sight of the town, half hidden in its wealth of trees, is a welcome one. For if Hazaribagh be a Paradise, it is another matter getting there. It is the old story of the push-push again, from which a journey in Chota Nagpore so long seemed inseparable. Hazaribagh Road on the Grand Chord Line is now the nearest railway station, forty miles away. Until four years ago, however, the nearest station was at Giridih, thirty-three miles further still, and after crawling that distance in a push-push, with perhaps a delay at the Barakar if the river was in flood, one was in the mood to appreciate the first glimpse of Hazaribagh to the full.

The few miles just outside the town afford some of the best views along the whole stretch of road from Giridih. It is typical of Chota Nagpore, all undulating and well wooded, with hills scattered here and there, rising solitary and abrupt over the countryside. The colours of the landscape, rich with every shade, seem to blend one with another in a soft delicate haze that envelops all things in its marvellous light. Every passing season adds some fresh dominating colour to the scene—the brilliant yellow of the sirguja, the gorgeous red of the palas, or the rich bright greens that only the Indian rains can ever quite produce.

Drawing near to Hazaribagh the road runs straight towards Silwar Hill that blocks the way. It is popularly known to Europeans as Tower Hill, from the old survey tower that crowns the top, and the road bending sharply round at its foot comes suddenly on a fine open view of the land beyond. The number of little conical hills that rise up all over the plateau is a striking feature of the landscape. On the left is Kunhuri, called Gibraltar, because of its supposed resemblance to the famous rock; beyond lies Sitagarha, the highest of them all, with a tea garden on its slopes; behind Hazaribagh rises Bamunbeh on the Ramgarh road, with Rinadag and Tibat further off to the right, and Ranjeeta nearer at hand, completing the circle of hills that lie like watch-towers round Hazaribagh.

The town itself is almost hidden in its garden of trees. Every compound has its share of sal and nim, karanj and tamarind, and every road is an avenue. Only away to the left, high up, on the other side of the fine large lake, the Reformatory stands out, white and prominent. It is a long low building with wings projecting on either side, and round those who in days gone by have been immured within its walls strange traditions linger among the older inhabitants of Hazaribagh. Twenty years ago it was the European Penitentiary, only abolished in 1882, when the troops that had kept it under control were removed altogether from the station. From all the accounts that remain, the old building must have closed its gates on some curious characters in those days. When the Penitentiary was first started, the inmates seem to have been treated with great laxity, and to have had by no means a very bad time of it. But with the admission of some particularly desperate characters a more stringent application of discipline became necessary. Prisoners were constantly escaping, and many an exciting chase has taken place over the surrounding country. It is hard, however, for a European to hide himself in India, and few got clear away. The attempt to tighten the reins of authority only aggravated the existing spirit of insubordination and finally led to an open outbreak among the inmates. The officer in charge at the time was warned one morning, as he was about to start on his round of inspection, that an attack upon him had been planned. He was not to be deterred, however, from his usual round, and was only saved from a violent attack on the part of half a dozen of the most desperate convicts by the strength and address of the chief warder. This man's enormous physique and exceptional strength have left a great impression on the native imagination, who still talk of him as the 'largest Englishman' they have ever seen. He is said to have been at one time in the army and to have been a noted pugilist. It was well for him if he had been, for he too had many narrow escapes in the Penitentiary, if report speaks true.

One of the most notorious of the many convicts who have left strange rumours behind them was a certain captain in the army, well known at one time in Calcutta, and said to have been on the vice-regal staff. The story, as it is still told in Hazaribagh, is that he misappropriated some gymkhana funds and, when detection became inevitable, fled up country. Here some time later he was recognised by a private in his old regiment. Brought back to Calcutta and convicted, he was sent to serve his time in the Hazaribagh Penitentiary. But the strangest part of the rumour is yet to come. After his release, he is said to have gone south to Hyderabad in the Deccan, and taken service under the Nizam, but turning up again some time later in the Soudan he made his last appearance as the Mahdi himself. How such a wild story originated only those who know the ways of rumour in the East can at all understand. One can only wonder what atom of truth there is in the midst of such amazing improbability.

There are many more stories of doctors, lawyers, sergeants, and others, who must have proved a strange crew when brought together within the walls of the Penitentiary. What was once the chapel still retains the coloured representations of the four Evangelists covering all one wall of the room, painted by the convict who was known as the 'pirate,' and whom rumour designates as the most accomplished and at the same time one of the most desperate characters ever confined there.

After the Penitentiary had been closed, partly on account of the insubordination which had been rife there and partly on account of the removal of the troops without which it would have been impossible to maintain it, the building was opened again a short time later as a reformatory. There are now something like a hundred and eighty boys occupying it, varying in age from six to eighteen. They have all been sent there for some more or less serious offence that gave promise of the youthful offenders developing into habitual criminals in later life, if prompt measures were not taken while they were still at an impressionable age. In the Reformatory they lead a healthy life, working in the large adjoining garden or learning carpentering, tailoring, weaving, or boot-making, and always with the chance of being hired out as labourers or servants, if after two years their record is good. They are a bright-looking lot of boys, going about their work cheerfully and seemingly contented with their lot.

It is a striking contrast that they form, in bearing and demeanour, to the men in the Jail beyond. In the one, the buoyancy and hope of youth remain and a future: in the other, the convicts, ticketed and numbered, move slowly in an awful, never broken silence, as if they had lost the power for all save a dull mechanical round of labour. Never so much as raising their eyes, they plod on dully with their work, in a stillness that grows maddening and appalling, as the

PRISONERS AT WORK BEATING OUT ALOE FIBRE.

long-drawn minutes creep slowly by. Despair is as absent as hope on the faces of the workers: they move like men who have lost all interest, and listlessly walk through their parts. With typical Eastern resignation, each has uttered his 'kismet' and passed out of life beyond all possible feeling and emotion. The future, if there be one, is too remote to count.

There are convicts from all parts of Chota Nagpore here. It is the central Jail for the whole Province, and, standing just behind the Reformatory, it covers a large area of ground with its watch-tower in the centre and numerous wards opening out from it in a circle all round. In one, a number of prisoners are beating out aloe fibre to be made into rope. It is simple labour and work that the least intelligent can do. Outside the Jail a huge bed of aloes, trim and regular, has been planted for this purpose, extending all along one side of the lake and away beyond, a patch of grey-blue against the surrounding green. In another ward the men are busy at weaving, preparing the cloth for their own prison garb, and making *dhurries* and rough carpets. In one of the sheds, on the opposite side, is a printing press, managed entirely by convicts, many of whom are skilled workmen in their own trades.

Hazaribagh owes much to Sir George Campbell, a Lieutenant-Governor of thirty years ago. He visited the station twice, spending portions of the hot weather there and contemplating making it the Government resort, instead of Darjeeling, during the summer months and rains. For his use, the fine large circuit house was built near the lake, and the road from Bagoda made to save the long détour by Dumri from Calcutta to Hazaribagh. It was during Sir George Campbell's time in 1874 that Lord Northbrook, the only Viceroy who visited Chota Nagpore proper during last century, came to Hazaribagh, passing on thence to Ranchi. Lord Cromer, then Major Baring and Private Secretary, was among those who accompanied the Viceroy, and the journey was accomplished from Giridih, partly on horseback, partly by palki, and partly in carriages, Lord Northbrook, in his diary, voicing the complaint, which is not yet silent in Chota Nagpore, of the bad condition of the roads.

Under the trees, in a corner of the Katcherry compound and bordering the road, is a curious monument, without name or inscription, for an explanation of which, as of so many things in Chota Nagpore, one inquires in vain. There seems to be absolutely no authentic record of any kind concerning it. Carefully railed in and well preserved, it remains a mystery, only a strange tradition lingering round it among some of the older natives of the town. It is a simple monument, a tall stone pillar, raised on a flight of steps and surmounted by an urn roughly carved in stone.

During the Kol mutiny of 1831, so runs the native legend, Captain Taylor, commanding the 10th Ramgarh Light Infantry, was treacherously murdered in the Raja's house at Sambalpur, on the borders of the Central Provinces. The men of his regiment buried their dead commandant at Sambalpur, but, desirous of having some memorial of him at the headquarters of the Ramgarh Battalion, they sent his hair to Hazaribagh, erecting over it the monument in the Katcherry compound, similar to the one placed over his grave at Sambalpur. Another version of the story says that it was the commandant's coat that was sent to Hazaribagh, adding that his hat was sent to Purulia, a third monument of the same kind being erected there. It is a curious tradition, but it seems impossible now to discover whether it has any foundation at all, or if, like so many legends of the East, it has been invented to account for the otherwise unaccountable.

The old Lines at the other end of the town, with some of the cantonment buildings, still remain, recalling the days when Hazaribagh was the most important military centre of Chota Nagpore. Fifty years before the station became the civil headquarters of the district, the Ramgarh Local Force—famous in Chota Nagpore history—had been raised and quartered here. For just over a hundred years it remained a military centre, never, except for one or two brief periods, without at least some troops in cantonments. It was an excellent site, with its fine open parade ground and what once must have been extensive barracks. But, in spite of the healthiness of the town, there was much sickness latterly among the troops, and any urgent need for their presence having long since disappeared, Hazaribagh was finally given up as a military station some twenty-five years ago.

Some of the old cantonment buildings are now occupied by the Dublin University Mission. The main bungalow was once the military hospital with a splendid frontage of something like three hundred and fifty feet. It was on the point of being demolished when the Mission applied for it, receiving a grant of it from Government at the merely nominal rent of three rupees a year. This building now forms the residence of the Brotherhood, the schools and hospitals having separate premises close by in the same compound. Only making a beginning here within the last twenty years, the Mission has done a very large amount of work, starting outposts in various parts of the district, opening dispensaries and supplying services for the European population. It has been one of its chief objects to carry on medical work side by side with religious teaching, and to this it undoubtedly owes a large measure of its success. The fine church close by the Mission was built in 1842 for the British troops then stationed here, and for this the Brotherhood, in addition to its many other duties, supplies the services.

On the other side of Hazaribagh lies the Ramgarh road, running down to the Damuda valley and on to Ranchi, through some of the most charming bits of scenery, to which it is impossible for illustrations to do full justice. Hazaribagh is a land of jungle, with open stretches here and there, where the cultivator has reclaimed the land and cultivates his crop. So busy has he been in cutting down the timber that, although huge tracts of forest still remain, very few of the trees have attained the dignity of age or grown to their full size. Often the land for miles is covered with nothing but young sal jungle, small and stunted, probably growing on the site of some older forest that has entirely disappeared. So constant is the demand for timber that it would not be profitable to leave the trees until they reached maturity. Young sal saplings are particularly useful to the native in building his house, making his plough or fashioning his bullock-cart or *sagar*, and as soon as they grow to a useful size they are ruthlessly cut down. The native has no other instrument for felling the trees than the *tanga* (axe)—that weapon of so many uses that the young Munda or Santal rarely moves far afield without. The cutting of a full-grown tree would be a great undertaking, and few that can be made useful are allowed to grow to their full height.

But here and there in the jungle, or along the roads or clustering round a village, magnificent trees are to be found—the banyan, with its wonderful downward-growing roots and its multiplicity of trunks, spreading out its thick leafy branches live a patriarch among the trees; the pepul, escaping the hand of the destroyer by reason of its sanctity, with its flower-decked shrine at its feet, rising up tall and venerable above the village it protects; and the tamarind, with its delicate lace-like leaves showing every detail against the perfect blue of the sky, resembling some exquisite miniature for clearness and colouring. Only rarely where the hand of man is more apparent, the gold mohur is to be seen. It is a glorious tree when in full blossom, and the hot weather sees it at its best. It is the time for colour everywhere. Then the gold mohur is ablaze with red and yellow, vindicating its right to its place of honour among Eastern trees: the cotton, bare but for its wealth of crimson buds, that stand out clear against the sky, on the leafless branches: the palas, a thicker mass of salmon red: and the mango, heavy with its long shoots of tiny green-white blossoms—all add their touch of colour to the landscape. Though the glorious greens of the rains have long since passed and the grass and undergrowth in the jungles are withering at the first touch of the hot winds, it is yet the time of all others for colour and effect among the wealth of trees that seem to have chosen this fertile plateau, two thousand feet above the sea, as the spot where they can best revel in profusion.

To the people many of these jungle trees have a peculiar importance. In spite of the large clearings in the forest and extended cultivation, the improvident peasant still depends on Nature for a large portion of his means of subsistence. The hot weather is the time of famine ; and the paddy crop, gathered long since and lived upon through the winter months, grows scarce as the long dry season advances. Then it is that the cultivator turns to the jungle to supply the deficiency.

The poorest classes depend most of all upon the *mahua* crop. It bursts into blossom at the very beginning of the hot weather, at the time when the fortunes of the people are yearly approaching their lowest ebb. It is the slack season among the cultivators, and the gathering of the *mahua* forms a welcome task, the whole village often turning out to bring in the crop. The grass is sometimes burnt away beneath the *mahua* tree so that it may be easier to gather the blossoms and the risk of damage to them may be less. The women equip themselves with baskets, piling them one on the top of the other on their heads, and the children carry brooms to clear the ground, after all the blossoms have been gathered, in readiness for the next fall. During the short period —only about fifteen days—that the *mahua* falls, the villagers, in some parts, practically live in the jungle, the men finding plenty to do in carrying away the crop in *banghis*, as fast as the women and children can collect it.

The *mahua* is considered by the people by no means a luxury, but rather as a subsistence diet when nothing better is procurable. Yet often for weeks together during the hot weather it is their staple food. Laid out to dry on a smooth bare patch of ground that has been especially prepared and cleaned, the blossoms become quite dry and shrink to half their original size, changing from white to brown. The *mahua* is often eaten alone, but where it is possible sal seeds and rice are mixed with it to improve the flavour. The *mahua* is first boiled, and the sal seeds, previously dried in the sun and roasted, are then added with a small quantity of rice. In spite of its strong flavour when first gathered, the *mahua* becomes almost tasteless when boiled. From the distilled blossoms, however, is made the well-known country spirit on sale in every liquor shop. It is highly intoxicating and needs a large proportion of water to make it drinkable. The native as a rule likes quantity, and the liquor is sold with only one part spirit and twenty parts water. The price is the small sum of two pice (one halfpenny)

A BANGHI-WALA.

per quart for this quality, and the consumption is consequently large.

The population of Hazaribagh, occupied chiefly in the fields and jungles, is sparsely scattered all over the district. Large towns there are none. It is a land without manufactures, and causes to attract a rural population to large centres are almost entirely wanting The great exceptions are the coal mines on the border of the district in the Giridih Sub-division, and even these have been largely recruited by labour from outside.

The Giridih mines were the first to be worked in Chota Nagpore. As early as 1851 a start was made, some years before the railway entered the district, and when all the coal had to be carted to the Ganges by road. But with the completion of the branch line in 1865 the working of the mines rapidly developed, and Giridih is now one of the busiest coal-fields in Bengal. In 1908, the last year for which figures are available, the output was no less than 782,713 tons, and the daily average number of people employed 7615.

Mica, found in large quantities near Kodarma, in the extreme north-west of the district almost on the Gaya border, constitutes the only other important labour centre. The tea gardens that once flourished in the district and employed large numbers of local coolies, have most of them fallen victims to hard times and ceased to work. Lac cultivation, though engaging many hands, does not take the people from their homes. There are only two small factories, employing some one hundred and twenty-five workmen a day. Sugar cane is grown all over the district, and in the illustrations the villagers are seen extracting the juice in the most primitive of mills worked by hand.

Ichak and Chatra, two old native towns, once famous and important, are interesting and typical of Chota Nagpore, giving one a glimpse of what it must once have been and of the change that has befallen it. The one was famous as the home of a feudal Raja of the old days; the other owed its importance to its large annual fair. But the days of petty potentates and great yearly gatherings for trade and commerce are past, and Chatra and Ichak bear stamped upon them the impress of decay.

Ichak, picturesque in its fallen grandeur, is a city of ruins over which Ichabod is writ large. The palace of the Raja of Ramgarh, its chief glory, must have been a splendid building in its heyday, with its high dome-shaped gateway and courtyard with galleries and countless suites of rooms. It was three stories high, and a terrace on the roof looked down over the town and all the surrounding country far afield. It is a scene of utter desolation, with its rooms dismantled and even the woodwork roughly torn away to build a newer house at Padma. Building after building

A SUGAR MILL.

is nothing now but a heap of stones, and as one passes along the ruined corridors and through the deserted apartments one has to pick one's way among the débris. It is only a few years since the last Rani died here, but her successor has lost no time in completing the ruin that must have been in progress long before. The terrace on the roof, where, in the old days, the Raja idled with his courtiers, or the ladies of the harem took the air secure from observation and intrusion, affords a striking scene of Ichak in its desolation. Just below, across the road, lies an enclosure that was once the deer park, now all overgrown with rank grass and brambles, its picturesque stone gateway half hidden in a mass of jungle growth, while beyond is the long low building in which the Raja is said to have kept, at one time, as many as a dozen tigers caught in the forest near by. Away on the other side lies the Rani's tank, with its flight of steps all round, and the remains of the pillars that supported the roof, and the stone built *ghat* where the ladies of the house could enter unseen. The tank is fast becoming filled up and the water has almost disappeared save for a shallow pool, muddy and green-coated, that completes the look of ruin and neglect. Further off are many other tanks, built, as the native will still relate, by this Raja or that, in the palmy days of Ichak. There are temples, too, every-where, peeping out here and there among the trees. No less than twenty-five, it is said, can be counted from the roof of the palace, and, from the number that catch the eye at a casual glance, Ichak deserves the name of the city of temples. They are the only part of the handiwork of a past generation that has not shared in the general decay, and, numerous as they are, worshippers never fail to keep them in rough repair.

Further on, on the outskirts of the town, is an *akhara* or monastery, occupied by about forty Brahmins, who spend here a time of meditation and study during the intervals of their itineracies among the holy places of India. It is a remarkably well-kept building, with its clean white walls and verandah filled with geraniums, crotons, and nasturtiums—unusual flowers for native decoration. Inside, round the courtyard, are the lodgings for the priests and the temple with its curtained doorway on the further side. A long high-walled garden filled with fine trees adjoins the building and strikes one again with the care that has been bestowed upon it. Fresh and well kept, awake with the stir of coming and departing guests, it has survived the general ruin of Ichak.

Chatra is best remembered as the scene of the last stand of the mutineers in this part of Chota Nagpore. But the one eventful chapter in the history of the town was soon closed, and a stone monument, without name or inscription,

A GROUP OF TEMPLES AT ICHAK.

is all that remains to mark the site of the battle and preserve the memory of those who fell. The market here was once the largest and most important in the district, and the cattle fair, held annually during the Desara festival, attracted dealers from all parts of Bengal and the north-west. Close by the borders of Gaya and Palamau, and in touch with the tributary states, it was well situated in a country unapproached for miles by a line of rail. But the days of its importance are long since past, and, like all the big fairs of Chota Nagpore, it must eventually disappear before the opening out of the country and the steadily improving means of communication throughout the district.

CHAPTER XI

SOME MEMORIES OF THE MUTINY

WHILE Delhi and the cities of the north were held in the throes of the great Mutiny, Chota Nagpore was not without its own stirring events. News, travelling with wonderful rapidity through the native bazaars and passing on from village to village, reached at last the sepoys in the far-off cantonments of Ranchi, Chaibasa, Purulia, and Hazaribagh. But the troops here were few, and it was not till more than two months after the famous Tenth of May that their long-smouldering disloyalty, excited by rumours of success elsewhere, at length developed into open mutiny.

It was on the last day but one of July 1857 that the outbreak began among the small body of troops at Hazaribagh. All the four military stations of Chota Nagpore were occupied by detachments of the Ramgarh battalion, which consisted of a full company of infantry with cavalry and artillery attached, and, although a local force, was composed largely of Hindustanis, differing little from a regiment of the line.

Besides the Ramgarh detachment there were two companies of the 7th and 8th Native Infantry quartered at Hazaribagh, sent for station duty from Patna. These had been possessed by a spirit of unrest ever since the first news of revolt had reached them from the north. Only the smallness of their numbers had caused them to delay so long. But messengers had been rapidly passing backwards and forwards between them and another detachment of the Ramgarh battalion stationed fifty-six miles away at Doranda, and the latter were now only awaiting the signal to throw off their allegiance. Thus encouraged, the troops in Hazaribagh were at length ripe for revolt, and a day and hour were fixed for the outbreak. The Europeans in the station were to be murdered, the treasury looted, and a march at once made upon the headquarters of the Division at Ranchi.

There seem to have been only three Europeans in Hazaribagh at the time, Captain Simpson, Deputy Commissioner, Dr. Delpratt, and Mr. Liebert who lived at Sitagarha, some three miles outside the station. Captain Oakes, the Judicial Commissioner of Chota Nagpore, had been there up to the very eve of the outbreak, holding sessions. But seeing that it was only a question of days before the disaffection among the troops broke into actual mutiny, he had hurried off to give the alarm to Colonel Dalton and the small group of Europeans at Ranchi. Several stories are still current among the older generation of natives in the district as to the escape of the Europeans from Hazaribagh. The most authentic seems to be that Captain Simpson got news the day before from one of his servants of the actual hour fixed for the outbreak. There could be no question of remaining with the whole available force entirely disaffected, and the only safety lay in immediate flight. Starting out early the next morning, with their guns and a couple of servants, as they were often accustomed to do, Captain Simpson and Dr. Delpratt made their way over to Sitagarha and warned Mr. Liebert. Together that afternoon, the three hastily set out on foot across country towards Ichak, which they reached at nightfall. Here they were hospitably received by the Brahmins in the monastery there, and provided with horses to continue their journey. Starting off again the same night, after a few hours' rest, they made for Bagoda on the Grand Trunk Road, whence they could communicate with the Government at Calcutta and await the coming of troops to their assistance.

Meanwhile, Captain Oakes had covered the fifty-six miles between Hazaribagh and Ranchi and brought the news of the impending outbreak to the Commissioner on the morning of the 1st of August. It was the worst time of the year for the rapid transport of troops, and report says that it was raining in torrents when the news, hastily sent on by Colonel Dalton from Ranchi, reached the officer in command two miles off at Doranda. But the need was urgent and no consideration of weather could be heeded. That same day two companies of sepoys of the Ramgarh Local Force, with about twenty-five irregular cavalry, under Lieutenant Graham, started off for Hazaribagh at a moment's notice in the pouring rain. They took with them two six-pounder guns, and chose the Ramgarh road to Hazaribagh as the quicker of the two possible routes at that time of the year when the roads were certain to be heavy and the rivers flooded.

But on reaching Ramgarh they were met by unexpected news. The mutineers from Hazaribagh had already passed, hurrying on to Ranchi by the old Ranchi road that ran through Baddam and Pitoria. It was an unlooked-for check, and there was every reason to fear that the mutineers had by this time reached Ranchi unopposed, and found it almost defenceless.

The effect of the news on the troops under Lieutenant Graham was disastrous. Their loyalty had long been doubtful, and on learning that the mutineers had evaded them and were probably already marching on Doranda, panic seized them. It was an exciting moment as the small company of troops stopped at the branch roads, halting for a moment between two opinions.

But the prompt action of the Hazaribagh troops and their quick success had caught the imagination of the sepoys and turned the scale in favour of revolt. Led by Mahdab Singh, the Jemadar, they threw off their allegiance and hurried back to Ranchi to join the mutineers. Scarce fifty men remained with Lieutenant Graham, but to their credit it is to be recorded that the small band of cavalry stood loyal without a single desertion, not a man of them going back with Mahdab Singh.

That day—the first of August—was one of intense excitement in Ranchi. Rumour after rumour flashed through the bazaar with more than Eastern swiftness. All was panic and uncertainty. For once the everyday round of life was stopped: the *baniya* forgot to buy and sell, and the litigant to make his way to court, while the labourer left his work in the fields and straggled into the bazaar to discuss this wondrous news of the downfall of the British Raj. But there was no plan of action, no attempt among the natives to take part in the rebellion, only a great wonder and surprise as each man talked with his neighbour of the turn events were taking.

Away at Doranda the excitement was greater still, for here were the troops who had been left behind when their comrades had been hurried off to Hazaribagh, and in their hands lay the fate of the station. Their officers, hopeless of their remaining loyal, had gone into Ranchi to consult with the Commissioner. All duties were forgotten, and discipline relaxed as the men crowded together, eagerly passing from mouth to mouth the latest scrap of news. They threw off all restraint at last, as the excitement grew, fed by fresh rumours from the bazaar, and only awaited the arrival of the mutineers to join in the revolt. It was a judgment on the Sahebs, said Jai Mangal Singh, who was the leading spirit among them, because they had sanctioned widow remarriage, that abomination of the orthodox, and had ordered them to defile themselves by using greased cartridges. They were in the mood to be led, and Jai Mangal's eloquence swept away the last sentiment of loyalty, and the troops at Doranda pledged themselves to mutiny.

Meanwhile at the other end of the station their officers had come to a hasty decision in consultation with the Commissioner. It was one o'clock in the afternoon, and news had come that the mutineers were hurrying back from Ramgarh towards Ranchi, while vague rumours were afloat in the bazaar that a larger force of rebel sepoys from Hazaribagh was in the immediate neighbourhood. Their officers knew that the approach of the mutineers destroyed the last chance of the troops at Doranda remaining loyal, and, failing them, the small band of Europeans lay absolutely at the mercy of the force approaching from Ramgarh. There was no hope of saving the treasury or defending the station, and to remain would have been to throw themselves into the hands of the mutineers. Their only hope of safety lay in the direction of Hazaribagh and the Grand Trunk Road: there was no other quarter whence help might be expected. Consequently at two o'clock the few Europeans in the station, including the Commissioner, the Judicial Commissioner, the officer commanding at Doranda, and one lieutenant, set out for Hazaribagh, choosing the old Ranchi road in order to avoid the force which had been sent out under Lieutenant Graham the day before, and which was now known to have mutinied and to be hurrying back along the Ramgarh road. There were rumours that the old Ranchi road, too, was blocked, but nothing definite had been heard of the advance of the Hazaribagh troops, and the Europeans, well mounted, trusted to being able to cut across country in case of need.

The danger, however, was greater than they anticipated, and but for the loyalty of Parganait Jagdao Singh, a local zemindar, they would have had a hard task to evade the Hazaribagh troops. The latter, consisting of two full companies of the line besides the Ramgarh detachment, had been marching rapidly on Ranchi on the previous day when they met with a determined check at Pitoria. Parganait Jagdao Singh, whose name deserves to be remembered on the roll of those who stood firm in that year of great loyalty and disloyalty, had heard of the mutiny at Hazaribagh and of the coming of the mutineers. Summoning his people and the villagers for miles around, he hastily threw up earthworks across the road, cutting down trees and blocking the way far across the fields on either side. Armed with bows and arrows and *baluas* (axes), the only weapons they possessed, he and his men waited the coming of the troops, concealed behind the entrenchment. It was a plucky thing to do. There were two companies of the line advancing down the road, and behind in Ranchi all was uncertainty and doubtful loyalty. Hope of assistance there was none, but, in spite of the odds against him, Jagdao Singh's show of courage won the day. The mutineers stopped at sight of the unexpected barrier across the road, and, lost without their usual leaders, this first check hopelessly disorganised them. Ignorant of the fact that the Ramgarh Local Force from Doranda had already started for Hazaribagh, they imagined that it must, after all, have remained loyal and be now strongly entrenched behind the barricade. Huddled together on the road in sudden fear, they took hasty counsel, and, judging that Ranchi was well defended, they turned aside and under cover of night made off by another road through Chouriya and Lohardaga and on to join the rebels in the Tributary Mahals, taking no further share in the mutiny in Chota Nagpore. It was thus that the Europeans found the old Ranchi road clear, and succeeded in making their way to Hazaribagh unopposed.

They had left Ranchi, however, as it proved, only just in time. Two hours after they had gone the station was a scene of wild confusion. Down the Ramgarh road came the two companies of sepoys that had started out the previous day. The news, quickly gathered as they drew near the town, that the officials had left and that their comrades at Doranda were only waiting their arrival to revolt, threw them into a frenzy of excitement. Outside the Katcherries on the outskirts of the station, a motley crowd of natives had collected, drawn by a wondering curiosity to see the men who had dared to defy the British Raj. For hours they had waited in the rain, anxiously looking up the Hazaribagh road for the advent of the force that held Ranchi at its mercy. At last at four o'clock in the afternoon it came in sight—a shouting, hurrying crowd, elated by its unopposed entry and mad with the lust of plunder and destruction. It was a wild scene that followed. With a yell of triumph, the sepoys rushed upon the Katcherries, and in a pandemonium of cries and shouts and curses broke open the treasury, each man scrambling for his share and trampling his neighbour under foot. Everything of value looted, the Katcherries were fired and a move made to the Jail. Here the warders had all fled, and, led by Mahdab Singh, the Jemadar, the mutineers soon forced the gates. The prisoners were released and marched off in triumph towards Doranda, most of them throwing in their lot with their deliverers.

It was growing dark by this time, and the bazaar through which they passed promised little in the way of loot, with its shops closed and deserted by the *baniyas*, who had fled in fear, carrying with them what they could. But, half-way down the road, the tower of the German Mission Church stood out clear against the sky, and to the mutineers who had brought back their guns with them, the solid mass of masonry proved too tempting a target to be resisted. Pausing, with one of their six-pounder guns, they fired and struck the tower halfway up. But no great damage was done. The sepoys were anxious to get on to Doranda, and one shot sufficed, the mark of which is still to be seen in the tower—the only visible reminder of the mutiny left in Ranchi.

At Doranda, Mahdab Singh and Jai Mangal Singh joined forces and a night of orgy followed. Hazaribagh, where the nearest troops lay, was fifty-six miles away—and they, if report spoke true, had mutinied,—Chaibasa was still further off, and there was no white man left in Ranchi to cast over them the magic of the British name. Intoxicated with this first success, they threw off all restraint and passed the night in a wild scene of licence and debauchery.

But with the dawn came sobering reflection and unexpected news. The mutineers from Hazaribagh should have reached Ranchi before them, but their non-arrival had passed unnoticed in the general excitement of the night before. Now uneasiness turned to dismay as rumours, passed from mouth to mouth, confirmed the news of the check to the mutineers at Pitoria. It was an unlooked-for blow. The troops at Doranda still remained masters of the station, but there was now little hope of help from outside, and the Sahebs might return at any moment with a loyal force. They were already thoroughly disorganised, and the Jemadars realised that without assistance they could not hope to stand against the first show of opposition. Hitherto the local zemindars had shown a distinct reluctance to throw in their lot with the mutineers, but towards them the sepoys now turned. Pressure must be brought to bear upon them to swell the ranks and coffers of the rebel force. At Hatia, seven miles from Ranchi, lived Thakur Bishnath Sahai and Thakur Jhitnath Sahai, zemindars, with no mean following, and their help the sepoys determined to enlist. A capable and persuasive envoy was needed to bring them in. Gunpat Rai Panre, once a mohurrir under the Maharaja of Chota Nagpore, but dismissed eight or nine years previously, offered to undertake the *rôle.* He had been one of the leading spirits of the mutiny among the troops at Doranda, and if any man could induce the zemindars to join their ranks, it would be he. But at Hatia he met with small success. Jhitnath Sahai refused point-blank and Bishnath hung back, until at last, after much persuasion, he consented, with unconcealed reluctance, to return to Doranda with Gunput Rai to meet and consult with the mutineers. But the state of chaos in cantonments held out little promise of success, and Bishnath Sahai slunk back to Hatia, uncommitted to the cause.

There was consternation at Doranda when this became known, and the sepoys, their cause desperate, resolved on a show of force to bring Bishnath and his cousin to their side. With their two guns, the troops marched out along the Hatia road. The Thakur's fort, marked now only by a line of ruined wall, could offer no resistance against guns and an armed force, and Bishnath Sahai gave in without a blow, joining the sepoys with all his men. Jhitnath Sahai lived two miles further on, in his fort at Basargarh, still standing with its picturesque half-ruined gateway and its wide deep moat and trenches, but, distrusting its capacity for defence, he had wisely fled at the approach of the mutineers, so escaping his cousin's ultimate fate.

In the camp of Doranda, dissension soon proved fatal. With no recognised and capable leader, everything was confusion and disorder. The first spirit of enthusiasm had quickly passed, leaving doubt and distrust in its place, and only the news that a European force was advancing against them from the north was needed to complete their discomfiture. A hasty evacuation of Ranchi was decided upon. Their only hope was to escape to the north-west, giving Hazaribagh a wide berth on the way, and this they attempted to do. They made first for Chouriya, where their flagging spirits were raised for the moment by the accession of Bhola Singh, the zemindar, and thence through Kuru and Chandwa to Chatra. But here, at last, the long arm of the British Raj overtook them and brought their short career of mutiny to an abrupt end.

In the meantime, however, the European officials of Ranchi and Hazaribagh had spent anxious days of waiting. Colonel Dalton on reaching Hazaribagh had found it practically free of mutineers, but the cantonment was deserted and effective military aid had to be sought from outside. It could only come down the Grand Trunk Road, and thither Colonel Dalton followed the Hazaribagh officials, who had already reached Bagoda and communicated the news of the mutiny to Government. It must have been a weary time of inaction and uncertainty at Bagoda. There was nothing to be done but to wait till help came. Meanwhile they knew little, except by rumour, of what was going on in Ranchi, and they were absolutely at the mercy of the mutineers had they followed them up and cut off their retreat.

But at last, after many days of waiting, help came. The five hundred Madrassis and the detachment of Her Majesty's 53rd Foot must have been a welcome sight as they came up the Grand Trunk Road. Three English officers accompanied the troops, and a start was made at once for Hazaribagh. Finding all quiet there, the Commissioner, with the larger part of the relieving force, pressed on to Ranchi, which they reached on September 23rd. But here, too, the same unexpected quiet reigned. The sepoys had left for Chouriya and the north-west twelve days before, and not a single mutineer remained. Only the ruined Jail, Katcherries, and cantonments, which the men had destroyed on leaving, told of the mutiny that had come and gone.

Determined to bring the mutineers to justice, one hundred and fifty men of Her Majesty's 53rd Foot and one hundred and fifty of Rattray's Sikhs were sent back to Hazaribagh in pursuit under Major English, one of the officers of the relieving force. Joined there by Captain Simpson, the Deputy Commissioner, they hurried after the sepoys, who were moving rapidly towards the north-west, coming up with them at Chatra. Here the only action with the mutineers in this part of Chota Nagpore took place. A hill commanding the town had been strongly posted by the rebels, with their four guns overlooking the open country at its foot. But there was no withstanding the disciplined attack of the English troops and loyal Sikhs, and the sepoys were cut down with terrible slaughter, few of them escaping. There were two Victoria crosses won that day for 'conspicuous gallantry in capturing two guns by pistolling the gunners who were mowing down the detachment with grape.' The recipients were Lieutenant Daunt of the 70th Bengal N.I. and Sergeant Dynon of Her Majesty's 53rd Foot.

The villagers of Chatra aided the British troops, and catching Bhola Singh of Chouriya put an end to a long-standing feud by cruelly shutting him up and starving him to death. Bishnath Singh and Gunpat Panre fled, and it was not till some time later that they were caught at Kakraj in Lohardaga by Major Nation, commandant of the 9th Bengal Police Battalion. They were brought to Ranchi and tried. Speedy punishment was meted out to them, and they were hanged on one of the trees to the north of the Commissioner's compound, Bishnath Sahai on a Friday and Gunpat Panre on the following

Wednesday, as the few natives of Ranchi still alive, who saw these summary and impressive acts of justice, are wont to relate with the curious Oriental memory for detail. Over two hundred sepoys were also hanged, and the trees that served as gallows are still pointed out. But Mahdab Singh, the Jemadar, escaped, and, although a price of one thousand rupees was placed upon his head, he was never caught. Nothing more was ever heard of him, and even tradition for once fails to supply an appropriate end.

But away in the south-east corner of Chota Nagpore, the mutiny was not so easily quelled. There were two companies of Ramgarh Light Infantry at Chaibasa, but at the first news of the outbreak in Ranchi the Assistant Commissioner in charge of the station had fled to Calcutta. It was a hasty step, and from the inquiry held afterwards it appeared that the troops might almost certainly have been kept loyal had their commandant taken prompt measures, and the Assistant Commissioner paid for his desertion by dismissal from the service. Chaibasa was thus left without a head before mutiny had actually broken out. Mewa Lal, the Sarishtadar, with exemplary promptitude, took charge on his own responsibility and tried to stem the rising tide of disaffection. The sepoys urged their Subadar and Jemadar to break open the treasury and join the mutineers at Ranchi, but they hesitated, waiting further news from headquarters. The Sarishtadar took prompt advantage of their hesitation, and, borrowing over a thousand rupees from the neighbouring Raja of Seraikela, he paid the sepoys and burkandazes (Government peons) their wages in full for August. So, for a time, mutiny was averted by the courage and address of Mewa Lal.

But in September there was no more money forthcoming, and it was impossible longer to put off the outbreak. The sepoys looted the treasury and wrecked the Katcherries, marching off immediately afterwards along the Ranchi road with the intention of joining the mutineers at headquarters. But the Sanjai river, in full flood, blocked their way. The rains had been heavy, and the stream had become a rushing torrent, forcing the troops to camp upon its banks until the full flood was past. Mewa Lal took prompt action. Marching after them with fifteen hundred men and three native cannon, he moved further up the stream to the west, encamping over against the sepoys to be even with them when the river should subside and a crossing become possible.

At this juncture Urjun Singh, the neighbouring Maharaja of Porohat, who played so confusing a part in the struggle just begun, appeared on the scene. Weak and vacillating, he was at one moment acting the part of a loyal feudatory and

THE PRESENT RAJA OF SERAIKELA.

doing good work for Government and the next in rebellion, leagued with the sepoys he had just been opposing. The key to his conduct, however, is to be found in his long-standing feud with the Raja of Seraikela. The latter was loyal, and had just given proof of his loyalty by lending the money for the payment of the sepoys before they revolted. The Maharaja of Porohat, seeing the district apparently at the mercy of the mutineers and anxious to score over his rival, determined to throw in his lot with the rebel force. Sending messengers down to the camp on the banks of the river, he offered them his help and invited them to Porohat. The sepoys gladly welcomed his assistance and, crossing the river by night in relays on the Maharaja's elephants, marched on to accept his hospitality.

But Mewa Lal, on learning his intention, sent out urgent remonstrances to Porohat, and the Maharaja grew suddenly frightened at the course he had adopted. The sepoys with their guns had already arrived at his gates and were being entertained as his guests. It seemed impossible to draw back now, yet the remonstrances, promises, and threats of Mewa Lal grew more insistent, and rumours of the failure of the mutiny in Ranchi were being circulated. The Maharaja wavered as to what course he should pursue, then, by taking a half measure, tried to keep in with both parties. It was October, the time of the Desara festival, and Urjun Singh asked the mutineers for their guns, saying that he needed them to take part in the ceremonial acts of worship. Having got the reluctant sepoys to part with them, on a solemn promise to restore them as soon as the festival was over, he sent off a messenger to Mewa Lal to say that he was loyal and had deprived the rebels of their guns. It was a weak attempt to run with the hare and hunt with the hounds.

But meanwhile Mewa Lal had been superseded at headquarters. Captain Birch had arrived to take over charge of the station, and he at once adopted strong measures. A sum of one thousand rupees was placed upon the head of Urjun Singh, and a move with every available loyalist was made to Seraikela to enlist further help. Here Mewa Lal came up with the news that Urjun Singh had disarmed the sepoys by depriving them of their guns. In consideration of this the reward on his head was withdrawn, but unfortunately not before it had terrified the Maharaja into further acts of rebellion. Captain Birch with Mewa Lal and about four hundred men hurried on to Porohat in the hope of finding the mutineers unarmed. But as they came in sight Urjun Singh was seized with sudden panic. He was already deep in rebellion, and a price had been set upon his head. Moreover, the hated Raja of Seraikela was in the camp of the advancing force. The sepoys were clamouring at his gates for the return of their guns, and, in a moment of weakness and alarm, he gave them back and bade the rebels turn them on the Government troops. The sepoys, in possession of their guns, were more than a match for the small hastily levied contingent with Captain Birch, who was forced to beat a hasty retreat towards Chaibasa.

It was obvious that the sepoys could not be beaten without outside help, and urgent messages were despatched to Calcutta for troops. One hundred Sikhs were sent with as little delay as possible, but before they could reach Chaibasa fresh developments had taken place. Urjun Singh was now almost beside himself with terror at his temerity in so openly defying the British Raj. His only hope of making his peace at headquarters was a conspicuous act of loyalty. The mutineers lay at his gates, and by a bold stroke it might be possible to render them powerless. Gathering a vast crowd of his personal followers together by night, he fell upon the sepoy camp, and in the darkness and confusion robbed them of their guns and ammunition. Recognising that his case with the authorities at Chaibasa was desperate, he determined to take the mutineers prisoners to Ranchi, hoping to find there forgiveness for past offences by such an act of merit.

The news reached Chaibasa that Urjun Singh with the mutineers was on his way to Ranchi, and, suspecting his intentions, Captain Birch sent off one company of Sikhs to intercept him. But Urjun Singh had made all speed and had been in Ranchi some days before his pursuers came up. His loyal action in bringing in the mutineers had favourably impressed the authorities at headquarters, but the arrival of the Sikhs bringing the latest news from Chaibasa threw a fresh light upon his conduct. He was at once ordered to return home and report himself to Captain Birch. Of the hundred sepoys he had taken prisoners, forty-three were hanged, and the remainder sentenced to transportation and imprisonment for various terms.

But while matters were going more or less in Urjun Singh's favour at Ranchi, misfortune had occurred in his own home at Porohat. By a strange coincidence that appealed to his Oriental imagination, his only son of eight or nine years of age died suddenly at the very time that the mutineers were being hanged at Ranchi. It was at three o'clock in the afternoon on the last Thursday in November 1857, so tradition relates, that these events in Ranchi and Porohat took place simultaneously. Native superstition at once connected them with one another, and Urjun Singh hurried back to Porohat, convinced that the death of his son was a judgment on him for the betrayal of his guests, the mutineers, and half suspecting his enemy of Seraikela of having been the instrument of fate and the murderer of his son. Once more, in a paroxysm of rage and excitement, he rebelled, and, collecting all his followers, established outposts round Chaibasa. Breaking through the line, Captain Birch and his companies of Sikhs met the main body of the mutineers at Kudaikela. The fight was short and the undisciplined levies broke and fled. Kudaikela was burnt to the ground and Chakradharpur met a like fate, both having been rebel strongholds and a menace to Chaibasa. Jagoo, Dewan of Porohat, advancing with five hundred men to support the mutineers at Charkadharpur, arrived too late, and, falling into the hands of the British troops, he and many of his followers were hanged.

Urjun Singh, meanwhile, had kept continuously in the background, but Captain Birch, determined to bring the insurrection to a close, hurried on to meet him. Outside Porohat he encountered the rebel forces, but again they fell back, unable to face the Government troops. Urjun Singh fled with a few of his followers before the battle was over, leaving his immense stores of silver and all his belongings to fall into the enemy's hands.

In spite of their leader's desertion, however, the rebellion lingered on among the fighting Kols who had joined his standard. The character of the mutiny, however, had entirely changed. The sepoy element had disappeared, and there seems to have been no reason for the Kols to continue the struggle, except the fact that Urjun Singh had called them out against the hereditary foe of Seraikela and that they had an innate love of fighting for its own sake. They kept alive the revolt with wonderful tenacity. Several small skirmishes were fought with varying success, the mutineers at times, with their rapid irregular movements, gaining unexpected victories. At Serimerah Ghat, Raghu Dao, a relative of Urjun Singh, who had taken up the chief command, suddenly appeared with ten thousand men armed with bows and arrows. Sweeping down upon a company of Sikhs that lay encamped there, they took them entirely by surprise. Scarcely a man escaped. Their captain, mortally wounded, only got away from the camp alive owing to the devotion of his orderly, who, supporting him on his horse, ran beside him the whole way into Chaibasa, covering the thirty miles within five hours.

On another occasion Colonel Dalton, who had come down to Chaibasa as soon as quiet was restored in Ranchi and Hazaribagh, was the victim of a similar surprise and barely escaped capture by the mutineers. He was in camp at Chakradharpur with a small company of troops when Raghu Dao suddenly appeared with one of those huge crowds of native levies that seem to have been as easily raised as dispersed. But they overwhelmingly outnumbered the British troops, who with difficulty threw up defences and escaped total annihilation. For four days Colonel Dalton and his small force held out, until at last a messenger got through and help came from Chaibasa. In the presence of a larger body of Government troops the native levies melted away. Raghu Dao was forced to retire, and, pursued into the jungle, his following rapidly diminished. For the future he had to confine himself to midnight raids upon Seraikela or an occasional attack upon the regular forces. Until his death three years later he managed to evade pursuit, but the last flicker of actual rebellion had by that time long since disappeared.

To Mewa Lal fell the credit of the arrest of the Maharaja of Porohat in 1859. For two years he had lived the life of an outlaw in the jungle, and it was only on venturing too near Chakradharpur that he was caught. He was brought into Chaibasa and tried by Colonel Dalton, his case being under consideration for several months. His conduct throughout had been weak and headstrong, but it was evident that his repeated risings had been more against the Raja of Seraikela than against the British Government. There was, moreover, to his credit the great service he had done in bringing the sepoy mutineers unarmed to Ranchi. The final judgment against him was that his estates should be confiscated and himself banished to Benares on a pension of four hundred rupees a month. His lifelong enemy, the Raja of Seraikela, got the pargana of Kudaikela rent free in consideration of his services and consistent loyalty.

Only recently the old Maharaja of Porohat died, and his estates, except Kudaikela, were restored to his son. The reason for this act of clemency on the part of the Government was that, after the fullest inquiry, it was evident that some excuses might be made for the conduct of Urjun Singh, and that the premature placing of a price upon his head had driven him against his better judgment into the arms of the mutineers.

CHAPTER XII

THE CROWNING OF A RAJA

THE cry of 'The King is dead' quickly merges in the acclamations of 'Long live the King' in the Raja's palace. The same company that assembles for the funeral rites remains to feast at the board of the new chief and see him, with due pomp and solemnity, seated on the *gaddi*. For eleven days the mourning lasts, then the scene rapidly changes and the festivities of the installation begin.

It is the smallest of villages right away in the jungle, where stir and excitement rarely come. But to-day, it is evident, events of unusual importance are taking place. The sun has barely risen over the neighbouring line of hills, but every soul in the village seems to be up and about. Some have not retired to rest all night, others have risen even earlier than usual before the dawn. Groups gather here and there along the village street, moving off one by one towards the Raja's palace to join a larger crowd that has already collected outside its gates. Within, the old Raja, who has long since passed the allotted span of life, and who for sixty years has been their chief, lies dying.

It is the most unpalatial of palaces. Built like all the other houses of the village, mostly of wattle and mud, larger and on a more extensive scale but with few added comforts or conveniences, it is only distinguishable by its slightly more pretentious air. A high wall shuts out all view of the house from the village road, save an irregular cluster of roofs, that rise above, fitting into one another and overlapping in curious confusion, giving no idea of what manner of rooms there may be within. Round the broad entrance in the mud-built wall, with its rickety wooden gates, a crowd of the poorer villagers waits, peering into the courtyard or seated on the ground in silent groups, stolid and expectant only of the inevitable. Meanwhile, they make themselves as comfortable as may be, chewing betel nut or taking long whiffs from the *hookahs* they have brought to while away the time. Further off, half a dozen youths, more eager for excitement, anticipate in subdued, half-muttered whispers the doings of the installation ceremonies soon to come.

Inside the gateway there is a large courtyard. The low straggling house itself forms two sides, while the high mud wall that faces the road is continued on the fourth side, completing the

THE THAKUR BARI, WHERE THE FAMILY GOD RESIDES.

square. In one corner stands the Thakur Bari with its double circular roof, where the family god resides. All around there is a look of absolute neglect. The hard sun-baked floor, generally well swept and clean, lies thick with dust and odds and ends of rubbish, a heap of ashes and evil-smelling refuse thrown carelessly in a corner close against the house. The door that leads through the wall into the wilderness of a garden beyond has lost both lock and latch, and swings back creaking in the wind, a huge stone beside it having long since done service as the easiest and least troublesome method of keeping it shut at night. The house, only boasting of two stories for a portion of its length, shows every evidence of the same neglect. The broad verandah is as unswept as the courtyard, and the torn strips of matting, and two cane-bottom chairs that look unsafe and uninviting, are all that is visible in the way of furniture. Over the wooden balustrade of the verandah that runs along the upper story hangs a bright-looking *sarhi*, adding its one vivid patch of colour as it flaps in the early morning breeze that stirs with the dawn. Behind, crouching in the shadow, is a group of women peeping down curiously between the rails at the crowd below, ever and anon shrinking back timidly and drawing their face cloths closer. A flock of pigeons, circling in the air above, alight fearlessly on balustrade and balcony, their soft cooing and flutter of wings the only sound that breaks the stillness outside the house.

In the courtyard below there are fewer people, mostly of the better sort, Brahmins many of them, seated cross-legged and reading diligently from their sacred books—long strips of paper closely printed with the heavy Sanskrit type. They form a striking picture. Every thought and passion portrayed on human features are there. The old priest, sitting wrapt in contemplation close beside the verandah steps, bears on his ascetic face, clear cut, immovable, every mark of the mystic, of meditation on things unseen and aloofness from the world. His deep fathomless eyes gaze straight before him into space, as if they looked beyond into the unknown, where the spirit of the dying man is passing, and communed with the Lord of Creation, Preservation, and Destruction. Beside him, craft and greed look out of a sharp pinched face and shifty eyes that even now pay no attention to the sacred book before them, but rove round the courtyard, with their calculating gaze, as if summing up the cunning of the others seated there and weighing it against his own. Further off, fat and old, sprawls the needy cousin and hanger-on of the family, moodily counting up his chance under the new rule and wondering if the crumbs that fall from the new Raja's table will be as plentiful as of yore. In a corner near the gateway, the village *baniya* (shopkeeper) and *mahajan* (money-lender) have thrust themselves into better company, busily comparing the Raja's indebtedness in their accounts and consulting as to what means to take to ensure prompt payment by his successor. The *mahajan* shakes his head. He has lent no less than 'rupees three hundred'—at least he lent 'rupees seventy-five,' but with interest in a few months it has amounted to 'rupees three hundred'—he doubts if he will ever see it all again. It will be a question of a compromise, he fears. Still, fortunately he refused to advance a loan of 'rupees one hundred' that the Raja besought him for, scarcely ten days ago. The *baniya* is in better plight. The debt to him is larger, but he is also a tenant of the Raja's, and he can withhold his rent until his claim is satisfied. The *mahajan*, however, shakes his head again. 'A debt,' he mutters pessimistically, quoting an Eastern proverb as he moves away, 'is like an ugly daughter: both hang heavy on one's hands.'

It is the same all through the throng, with only an exception here and there. Everywhere greed and self-seeking are uppermost: nothing but considerations of possible gain or loss has brought the majority of the crowd to await the Raja's end. Life to them is only of momentous interest so far as it touches their pockets. They will score, it is true, in the feastings and enforced liberality of the Raja that must accompany the *shrâddh* and installation ceremonies, but most of them are tenants of the estate, and the *salaami* will be a grievous burden—half a year's rent at least. Only in one small group can any genuine regret for the Raja's death be traced. They are some of the chief tenants of the estate sitting in a group in the middle of the courtyard, old men all of them who knew the Raja in his youth, who have grown up with him side by side and waited at his father's deathbed as they now wait at his, paying their last tribute of genuine respect for one whose passing away cuts another link with the past, to which in thought and spirit they belong.

From within comes the low droning sound of the Brahmins' voices as they chant their *mantras* (incantations) for the passing of the Raja's soul. Beside the bed stand the *guru* (spiritual adviser), dignified, refined, ascetic, with a powerful clear-cut face and tall stooping figure that might have graced a pope or cardinal, and the *purohit* (priest), a strange contrast, short, fat, unctuous, with sensuous mouth and keen ferret-like eyes behind which lies a whole volume of the lust of the flesh. Unceasingly in apparently endless repetitions the low monotonous rhythm of their formulas goes on—the only sound that breaks the long silence of the crowd without.

Then suddenly they cease. A hush of breathless expectation holds the throng in the courtyard and in the road beyond the gates. Each man stands spellbound, the sharp cessation of all noise within, typical of the rending veil of life, more impressive than the droning *mantras*. But a moment later, the long drawn wail of the women bursts from the inner apartments, and the sing-song intonations of the Brahmins, now pitched in a louder, shriller key, begin again, telling that all is over. The momentary tension relieved, there is a quick movement among the crowd. The Raja is dead, and a stir of excitement at last breaks through the calm apathy of the waiting groups, those near at hand pressing round the door of the inner room to catch a glimpse of the scene within and salute the new Raja as he issues forth. Inside, the priests, having led the dead man's son and successor to another apartment, request permission to carry out the funeral obsequies, in phrases long fixed by time-honoured custom. 'A stranger,' they say, 'has come into thy country: he is poor, and the journey that he pursues is long: all that thou seest is thine: give him, we pray thee, what he needs.'

The first and essential part of the funeral ceremony is performed that same day. The Raja's body, covered with a snow-white cloth, is brought out on a litter and carried to the banks of the river that flows near by. There the funeral pyre has been erected and the last rites over the body of the dead are performed. The new Raja, directed always by the *guru* and the *purohit* and guided by many fixed rules and formulas, sets light to the pyre. The noise of the drums and the plaintive soft-toned notes of the flutes, mingling with the swinging recitatives of the Brahmins and the deep vibrating voice of the *guru* that dominates them all, make a weird and solemn funeral march, while the flames leaping round the bier add their touch of strangeness to the scene. As they finally flicker and die out, the ashes of the Raja are reverently collected and carefully preserved, to be taken later to the Ganges, the sacred river where every orthodox Hindu hopes to find his way at last.

Ten days of mourning follow. Most of the observances that fill up the time are meaningless to those of another creed. Even the mourners themselves seem to know little of what should be done, prompted from first to last by the priests. Everything is in the hands of the *guru* and *purohit*, and the people, ignorant and superstitious, obey implicitly all that they direct. On the day following the funeral an earthen vessel filled with water is hung on the branch of a banyan tree just outside the village. It is a libation to the departed spirit, and round it collect the Brahmins, seating themselves on the ground with their sacred books, Gita and Bhagabat, reading passages aloud or reciting long *mantras*.

Observances such as these fill up the time until the tenth day. During all this period the son and successor of the dead Raja must go unshaved. No razor is allowed to touch his head until the tenth day, and then its work must be complete, leaving no single hair on head or chin. Washed and shaven, he is ready to perform the final rites—the *shráddh* ceremony in honour of the dead.

Round a magnificent banyan tree that grows beyond the Raja's house, close on the edge of the jungle, the ceremony takes place. An enormous crowd has gathered. Many Rajas from the neighbourhood have come to pay a last tribute of respect to their brother chief and to assist at the installation of his son. Representatives from every village on the estate have not failed to put in an appearance as their last act of service ; while no less than six hundred Brahmins, attracted from far and near, have assembled, and, next to the local Rajas, have the place of honour, beneath the banyan tree, at the rites about to be performed. It is a vast concourse of white-robed mourners, in which the new Raja is the central figure. Barefooted and bareheaded, like the rest of the throng, he is clothed in a single sheetlike garment of spotless white, thrown round his shoulders and reaching almost to the ground. Beside him are the never absent *guru* and *purohit*, always at hand to guide and prompt. Bound to the tree is the finest bull that can be procured, to be released before the other ceremonies begin with much formality and many blessings from the Brahmins. Henceforward he is sacred and may roam about at will, damaging the crops if he pleases, without fear of any serious retaliation. The Brahmini bull is safe from molestation.

Then begin again the long intoning of *mantras* and reading of the sacred books, all the mourners seated on the ground with eyes downcast, impassive, muttering prayers and invocations or doing *puja* silently. It swells to a perfect babel of sound at times, the low monotonous singsong voices, each intent on its own repetition, rendering everything unintelligible. Among the Brahmins pass the Raja's servants, distributing to them clothes, blankets, and even cooking utensils. The priests continue their devotions, never so much as once raising their eyes to look at the gifts, and apparently supremely unmindful of their presence, though none will forget to take them carefully away when the ceremonies cease.

Meanwhile a pot of rice is being prepared in the centre of the group. When cooked it is placed in an earthen vessel and carried by the Raja, who leads the way. The whole company, to the music of drums, kettle-drums, and flutes, forms a procession to the river. Arrived there, the food is committed to the water, the Brahmins crying appropriate *mantras*, in loud long-drawn wails of supplication and lamentation. 'O River, on whose breast is peace, thou knowest whither the soul of the departed hath fled. Bear, then, on thy swift-flowing stream, this vessel, that in the place where he hath gone the dead may not feel the pangs of hunger, or, thinking that his name is forgotten, brood in eternal grief and sorrow.' So ends the *shráddh* ceremony.

At once all sign of mourning is cast aside. Hasty preparations are set in train for the installation of the new Raja. For the following day, the first great feast is fixed. The Brahmins' duties during the past days have been no light task—long hours of prayer and fasting. Consequently they rise on the eleventh day with pleasurable anticipations of the Raja's hospitality. But unfortunately a hitch occurs. The news quickly spreads that the provisions, which have been sent for from the next district, and which have many miles to come from the nearest railway station, have not yet arrived. It is an awkward predicament. Never before has the tiny village of the Raja been so full of guests. They crowd in every house, sleeping ten or twelve in a verandah eight feet square, and occupying every quarter of the palace courtyard, garden, and temporary sheds beyond. The supply of food available has been already strained to its utmost limits during the period of mourning and is utterly inadequate to cope with the demands of feasting and revelry. The failure of the huge quantities of grain and rice, flour and ghee, that should have arrived in good time on the eleventh day, is serious news. Including the poor, who have also to be fed, a company of something like eight hundred guests sits waiting the arrival of the expected feast. Anxiously they look down the main road for the return of the line of bullock carts that have gone to meet it.

But the twelfth day passes and there is no sign. Only with great difficulty can sufficient food be provided to stay the pangs of hunger, and the unfortunate Brahmins who should have spent the day in feasting perforce go supperless to bed. But they hug the consolation that on the morrow the carts must arrive and the feast will be all the more enjoyed, because delayed.

The dawn of the following day, however, brings no sign or news of the provisions, and throughout the long hours the guests sit waiting as before, murmuring now at times and some quietly disappearing towards evening, perhaps remembering an engagement at another *shráddh* ceremony where things are likely to be more plentiful. The Raja meanwhile bears the delay with typical Eastern equanimity, contrasting strangely with what would be the state of mind and feelings of a Western host under like conditions. Only a dignified apology is forthcoming to the expectant guests and a confident assurance that 'to-morrow' the feast must come.

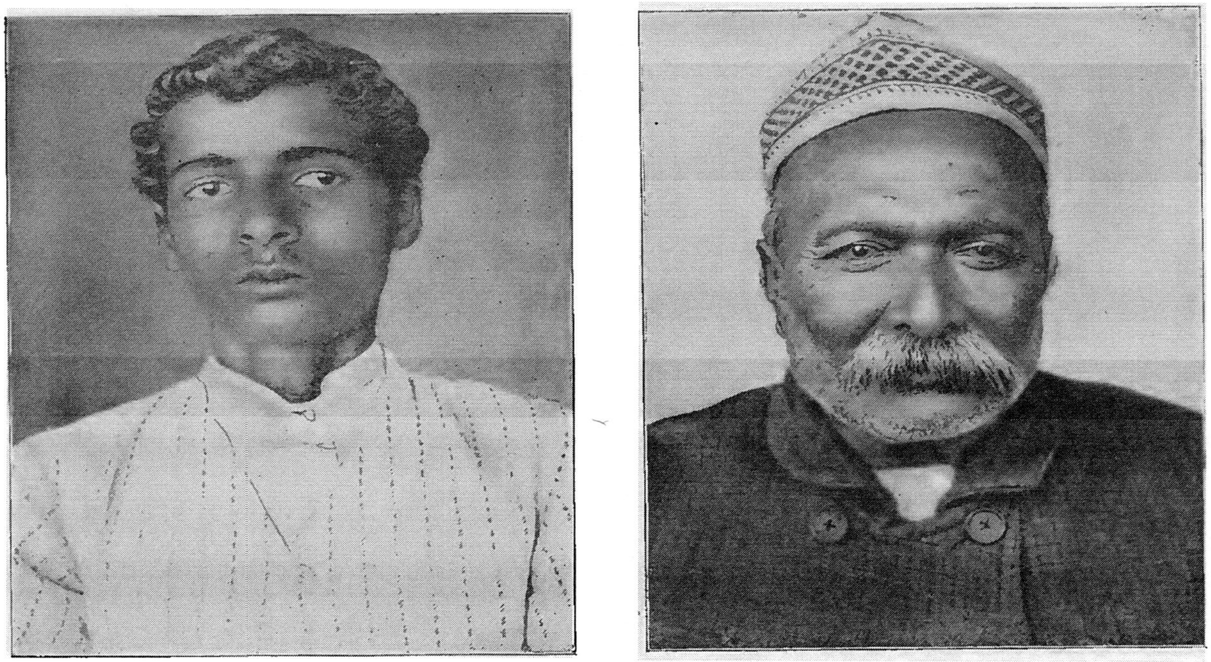

TWO OF THE RAJA'S GUESTS.

It is a sadly diminished company of Brahmins that hails the arrival of the feast on the afternoon of the third day. Many had taken their departure under cover of night, impatient of the delay and doubtful if the provisions would ever actually arrive. But those who remained are rewarded, for the provisions, when they arrive, are ample, every bullock cart on the estate seeming to have been pressed into the service.

It is still a large company, covering the whole of the Raja's courtyard and verandah and overflowing through the gateway into the road beyond, that sits down to the feast when all is ready. In the temporary kitchens outside, superintended by Brahmins alone so that no defilement may creep into the food to affect the caste prejudices of the guests, there is tremendous activity. Huge earthenware vessels hold the rice and *dal*, and each man provides his own plate or manufactures one of leaves for the occasion. It is long before the last one gets his share, and the whole day has passed before the feast is ended.

The Raja is poor and his estate encumbered, and he hurries on the installation ceremonies so as to shorten the stay of his huge assemblage of guests and save undue expense. But the preparations necessarily take some time, and it is not till the tenth day after the *shráddh* that all is ready. Great changes have taken place, meanwhile, in the outside aspect of his palace.

Neglected in the last days of the old Raja, it now takes on a gay and festive appearance. Much sweeping and many applications of whitewash work wonders. Garlands of flowers and coloured tinsel, hung on every available space, make the exterior bright with colour. A huge shamiana, borrowed from a neighbouring and wealthier Raja, has been erected in the courtyard, and here the installation on the *gaddi* finally takes place.

For this occasion important fresh relays of guests have been arriving. Those who could not get here in time for the *shráddh* ceremony have not failed to put in an appearance for the festivities that follow. To provide food for them all becomes an increasingly difficult task, yet each must be liberally entertained or the Raja's much-prized reputation for hospitality will be tarnished. But, in spite of all that he can do, a contretemps occurs on the day before the installation. One of the most important Rajas, twenty miles away, arrives unexpectedly with a huge following. Now gossip whispers that this Raja had come with the secret intention of humiliating and embarrassing his host. Ten years ago, when he himself was crowned, the people of this estate had gone with their Raja in enormous numbers to be his guests. Being wealthy, food at his installation was plentiful, and these guests seized all they could get, even carrying off home with them cartloads of what they could not eat on the spot. Their host could do nothing to stop them then, because of the traditions of hospitality, but now he, in turn, was the guest, and his time for revenge had come. The Raja about to be installed was poor, and a large and unexpected increase in the number of his guests on the day before the ceremony would be, at the least, a great inconvenience. Consequently, in gorgeous apparel, and amidst every possible sign of wealth, the Raja arrived. Never before had the country road that led to the village beheld such a display. A carriage and pair, preceded by outriders and followed by over a hundred mounted sowars, besides an innumerable army of servants and retainers of all sorts, suddenly looming on the astonished gaze of the unfortunate Raja and his already distracted attendants, were viewed with as much dismay as if they had been a swarm of locusts. Smilingly, however, the Raja welcomed his guests, outwardly calm and dignified, though inwardly his mind must have been making rapid calculations of ways and means. The presence of such a gorgeous Raja and his following was doubtless a great honour, but unhappily the burden fell on his already exhausted treasury.

Installed in a quarter of the village hastily prepared for his reception, the newly arrived guest sent his servants to the palace with a demand for a hundred maunds [8000 lbs.] of rice and a corresponding quantity of grain, flour, and ghee to feed his hungry retainers. Even the imperturbable dignity of the Raja was shaken at last. His reputation for hospitality, sacred among his caste, was at stake. To provide so much was an absolute impossibility. Forty maunds of rice was all that he could contrive to muster, and that meant that some of his own men must go short. With courtly apologies for the small quantity available, it was sent to his guest. The hour of the wealthy Raja's revenge had struck. Contemptuously refusing it, he sent back to repeat his original demand. When the same answer came again that there was no more to be had, his simulated wrath and offended pride knew no bounds. He would take nothing from his host, he declared, if that was all his idea of hospitality. He would find his own provisions for that night and shake the dust of the place off his feet with the dawn. All night the village was astir with his preparations for departure. At cockcrow the carriage and pair, with its attendant horsemen, swept out of the village, leaving the sacks full of provisions sent by the Raja untouched on the ground. No sooner had he gone than the guests that remained made a rush for them and a scramble ensued, each man looting all he could. It was a strange scene of almost incredible greed and selfishness, but typical of the self-seeking and squabbling that often unfortunately occur at the ceremonies in connection with a Raja's installation.

The departure of these undesirable guests may have been an insult, but it was undoubtedly a great relief and soon forgotten in the interest of the events of the day. The time for the installation had been fixed by the pundits, who had taken endless precautions to ensure that the day and hour chosen were auspicious. Everything, as at the *shráddh* ceremony, is in their hands. Few in the village were alive when the old Raja was installed sixty years ago, and, though some doubtless had been present when neighbouring Rajas ascended the *gaddi*, tradition handed down among the priests is deemed the only safe guide. In different places different rites hold. There are at least eighty-four *gaddis* in Chota Nagpore, each with its own particular customs, similar in kind but varying in detail.

At five o'clock in the afternoon the ceremony begins. An enormous concourse of spectators crowds under the shamiana, in the courtyard and verandahs and pressing round the doors. It is a wonderful gathering, full of life and interest, with its patches of colour here and there, a group of gorgeous Rajas, or still more brilliant chaprassies swinging huge tinse -covered punkahs, contrasting strikingly with the throng of white-robed priests, all close-packed, seemingly unmindful of the awful heat and unaffected by the overpowering scent of attar of roses or the indescribable atmosphere that hovers round a native crowd.

On a raised shrine in the centre under the shamiana stands the family idol. It is nothing more than a rough unhewn stone, as Nature made it, shapeless and uncarved, but the prized possession of the Raja's family from time immemorial. Known as Damuda Chandri, it represents Krishna, the Lord of Creation, Preservation, and Destruction. Strings of flowers and lighted candles surround it on the shrine, and, with much bowing and muttering of formulas, offerings of ghee, rice, and sandal-wood are placed before it. Close by sits the Raja, dressed in the gayest costume his wardrobe can furnish, blue velvet and much gold braid with a wonderful puggaree of violet shot with gold. Beside him stands his brother, scarcely less magnificently attired, and holding over him a large umbrella with a curiously wrought massive silver handle. Near at hand, as ever, are the *guru* and *purohit*, and behind, in a semicircle, the relatives of the family and the Rajas, a blazing line of colour with their puggarees of red, blue, violet, and yellow. Further back, unoccupied as yet, is the *gaddi*, a carpet covering a raised platform a foot from the ground. It is capable of seating about a dozen people, Eastern fashion, and there, later, the final crowning takes place.

During the first part of the ceremony the

Raja remains close beside the family idol, while the offerings are made and the *puja* continues. Mantras, calling down blessings on the Raja, are recited—long, pauseless phrases, swinging and grandiloquent, rolled out with breathless monotony for hours together.

But at last the idol has been sufficiently worshipped and the offerings and prayers completed. Music, that has been absent hitherto, suddenly, at some unseen signal, breaks forth. Drums and kettledrums clash, and the sound of pipes and flutes mingles with the twanging of the *sitars* and *bahalas*. The Raja rises, and, led by the *guru* and *purohit*, walks towards the *gaddi*. All the guests rise simultaneously, and the Brahmins acclaim the new chief in verses ascribing to him all the virtues and wishing him happiness and prosperity. The Raja mounts the step, and, turning, faces the people, until the babel of sound suddenly ceases. Then bowing once more to the idol he takes his seat on the *gaddi*. The *guru* sits on his right and the *purohit* on his left, while the relatives and Rajas form again in a semicircle close behind. As soon as the vast company settles down again—no light task, so close are they packed—bards posted in various parts of the shamiana sing long stanzas composed by themselves in the Raja's honour. To understand what they are saying is impossible for any but a native born, yet one cannot but admire their inexhaustible energy and ringing voices. Verse after verse they shout at their loudest pitch, never breathless or hoarse, like machines wound up and guaranteed to run through their performance, a string of words with no full-stops till the end is reached. Suddenly, without a lowering of the voice or the slightest inflection, each one brings his verse to an end, only to be succeeded by another equally monotonous and apparently equally endless.

During the self-satisfied performance of the bards, one has time to take in the curious scene in detail. In the centre, the candles still burn on the shrine, throwing the family idol into relief in the uncertain light of the shamiana. Filling half the space on either side of the *gaddi* are the Brahmins, wedged in without an inch of room to spare. In front of them pass the Raja's servants distributing more cloth and money. The priests score heavily, be the ceremony one of mourning or rejoicing. A mixed crowd fills the other half of the available space in the shamiana. In the first rows is a group almost as gorgeous as the Rajas. They are doubtless relatives who have come in attendance on the neighbouring chiefs. Behind them, evidently their followers, sit a number of up-country men, distinguishable at once by their bearing and appearance. Some tall, black-bearded, with high spotless puggarees, are unmistakably Sikhs, others no less tall and striking are Pathans or Rajputs. But these are few. The majority of the guests are drawn from the immediate neighbourhood. Bhuiyas or Chetris and every cast of Hindu, they sit, stolid and silent, absorbed in the declamations of the bards, or half dazzled by the brilliant unaccustomed spectacle. Further back round the doorway, with a sense of detachment as if they looked on something in which they had no part, stands a group of Santals, their blacker skins and broad thick faces marking them out at once as men of another race.

Behind the *gaddi*, long purdahs hang to the ground, hiding one of the entrances to the inner apartments of the house, and behind these peep cautiously the female members of the Raja's family. There is not much to be seen of them as they glance between the curtains timidly, with their veils drawn close against their faces. They are strictly purdah-nashin, and no man but their own immediate relatives has ever seen them. The old Rani is there, looking on at the installation of her son which deprives her of her former authority in the house, and doubtless not unmindful of the old Eastern proverb that applies to her change of fortune: 'When my husband lived, I was under a benevolent ruler: when my son succeeds to the throne, I am under the rule of a boor.' The new Rani is rejoicing in her freedom from her mother-in-law's control. 'The best of mothers-in-law is like a large boil,' but henceforward she is no one in the house, and her daughter-in-law's rule is supreme in the zenana. The wife of the Raja's younger brother pulls aside the curtain with the extreme of caution, for the Raja, being her husband's elder brother, must never look upon her face. She catches a glimpse of him now as he sits on the *gaddi* ; but though he has never seen her, she has probably often seen him before from the women's apartments, through the bars of which the ladies of the house get many a sight of the outside world into which they may not enter.

At length the last of the bards has declaimed his ode and the most curious part of the ceremony begins. Before the Raja is placed a bowl of sandal-wood mixed with water, while on either side in front of the *gaddi* two mohurrirs (clerks) take up their position, a large brass tray in front of each. Then the *guru* rises, and, taking a new white puggaree, proceeds to tie it on the Raja's head over the gorgeous one of shot gold and violet he is already wearing. At the same time he offers his congratulations, and dipping the third finger of his right hand into the bowl of sandal-wood makes a mark on the Raja's forehead. The *purohit* and the Brahmins, following him, repeat the ceremony, each tying another puggaree on the top of the last, until the Raja's head and face are almost smothered

THE CROWNING OF A RAJA.

beneath the weight of the huge head-dress. When at length it grows too big for another puggaree to reach round, an attendant lifts the whole edifice off his head and a fresh start is made. Ten or twelve times during the ceremony, the mass of turbans has to be removed, as guest after guest comes forward to 'crown' him and add to the huge ungainly head-dress.

The Rajas, as they perform the ceremony, in addition to the puggaree, give the newly installed Raja *salaami*—a present on accession. This is placed on the trays on either side of the Raja, the mohurrirs writing down the name of the giver and the amount of the gift as each one passes. The guests give what they like, but for the ryots—tenants of the estate—there is a fixed *salaami*, and the installation means a serious drain on their perennially low exchequers. The trays are soon full of rupees, and one of the mohurrirs empties them from time to time into a huge red bag placed behind the Raja on the *gaddi*. It is the last, and, from the newly crowned Raja's point of view, perhaps the most important ceremony of the installation.

The air has grown heavier and more stifling with the sickly scent of attar of roses, sandal-wood, and the strong-smelling flowers on the shrine. Not a breath stirs inside, and the heat under the shamiana grows intolerable, and even a native here and there in the crowd nods, half asleep. There is nothing more of interest to take place, and one is glad at length to escape outside from the heavy atmosphere within. The last puggaree has been tied but the Raja still sits on the *gaddi*, beneath his huge shapeless head-dress, tired and listless, but duly and with ceremony crowned.

APPENDIX

AGENTS TO THE GOVERNOR-GENERAL OF THE SOUTH-WEST FRONTIER PROVINCE AND COMMISSIONERS OF CHOTA NAGPORE

	Date of Assumption of Office
Major E. R. Roughsedge, Commanding Ramgarh Battalion and Agent to Governor-General	1817
Lieut.-Col. W. R. Gilbert, Commanding Ramgarh Battalion and Agent to Governor-General	1822
Major W. G. Mackenzie, Commanding Ramgarh Battalion and Agent to Governor-General	1828
Sir Thomas Wilkinson, Agent to Governor-General	1830
Lieut.-Colonel J. R. Ouseley, Agent to Governor-General	1839
Capt. J. Hannynton, Agent to Governor-General	1849
Mr. J. H. Crawford, Agent to Governor-General	1849
Mr. W. J. Allen, Commissioner	1853
Colonel E. T. Dalton, Commissioner	1857
Mr. W. L. Robinson (offg.) ,,	1875
Mr. V. T. Taylor (offg.) ,,	1877
Mr. A. C. Mangles (offg.) ,,	1878
Mr. J. F. K. Hewitt, C.S. ,,	1878
Sir John Edgar, K.C.S.I. (offg.), Commissioner	1882

		Date of Assumption of Office
Mr. J. F. K. Hewitt, C.S., Commissioner	. .	1882
Sir Cecil Stevens, K.C.S.I.	,, . . .	1888
Mr. W. H. Grimley, C.I.E.	,, . . .	1889
Mr C. R. Marindin (offg.)	,, . . .	1896
Mr. A. Forbes, C.S.I.	,, . . .	1896
Mr F A. Slacke, C.S.I.	,, . . .	1902
Mr. E. A. Gait, C.I.E.	,, . . .	1905
Mr. L. P. Shirres, C.S.	,, . . .	1907
Mr. H. J. McIntosh, C.S.	,, . . .	1907

INDEX

AGENTS to the Governor-General, 23–5; list of, 321–2
Allen, Mr. W. J., 321
Asansol, 203

BAGHSHUMA, 238
Bagoda, on Grand Trunk Road, 246; road to Hazaribagh from, 253, 260; flight of officials to, 284; Colonel Dalton at, 284–5
Bamunbeh, 255
Barabhum, 16
Barakar river, 59, 189; Jain remains near, 180–2; cuts across Grand Trunk Road, 230–4
Barhi, 237, 250–1
Baring, Major (Lord Cromer), 260
Barkatta, 247–250
Barwa, 243
Basargarh, 283
Bengal-Nagpur railway, 189, 198–9, 203–4
Bengal Police Battalion, 9th, 286
Bhagmundi hills, 167
Bhola Singh, zemindar, 284, 286
Bhuiyas, 27, 86
Bhumij Kols, settlement in Manbhum, 27; characteristics of, 159, 177–80
Birch, Captain, 290–4
Birhors, 28, 45–6
Birsa, 78–9
Bishnath Sahai, Thakur, 282–4, 286–87
Boojoodih, 189
Boram, 180
Brahmins, 13, 15, 45, 300–320
Brijas, 28
British occupation, 16–20
Broughton, Colonel, 73
Bundu, 82
Burdwan, 194, 200

CAMAC, Captain, 17
Campbell, Sir George, 259–60
Chaibasa, headquarters station of Singbhum, 96–9; during the Mutiny, 287–96
Chakradharpur, burned during Mutiny, 293; Colonel Dalton's force surrounded at, 294–5; Urjun Singh captured near, 295
Chandor, the Moon, 35–6
Chandwa, 284
Chatra, former importance of, 268, 270–1; mutineers arrive at, 284; last stand of mutineers at, 286
Cheros, the, 27, 44–5, 206–222
Chirkunda, 233
Chouriya, 279, 284
Churuk Puja, 54–5
Chutia, 57–63
Commissioner of Circuit, 21
Commissioners of Chota Nagpore, 25; list of, 321–2

Cotter, Major, 225
Crawford, Mr. J. H., 321

Dalton, Colonel, in Palamau, 225–7; in Ranchi at time of Mutiny, 273–8; at Bagoda, 284–5; surrounded by mutineers, 294–5; trial of Maharajah Urjun Singh, 295–6
Daltongunj, headquarters station of Palamau, 83, 227
Damuda, sacred river of Santals and Kherrias, 51, 160; remains of Jain temples near, 181–2; difficulty of crossing in rains, 189
Daud Khan, 215–18
Daunt, Lieut., won V.C. at Chatra, 286
Dawson Falls, 81–2
Delpratt, Dr., 273–4
Desara festival, 271, 290
Deswali, 35, 43
Dhalbhum, 96, 109, 180
Dhanbaid, 182–204
Digambaras, 143, 153
Doisa, 64–5, 211
Domunda, 242
Doranda, military cantonment, 73–4; mutiny of troops at, 275–84
Dripnath Sahai, Maharaja, 17, 90
Dublin University Mission, 262-263
Dumri, 246
Durga Rai, 213–14
Durgan Sal, Maharaja, 11-12
Dynon, Sergt., won V.C. at Chatra, 286

East Indian railway, 195
Edgar, Sir John, K.C.S.I., 321
Emigration, 44, 175–8
Encumbered Estates Act, 200-3
English, Major, 285
Execution Hill, 166–7

Famine, 1866..15; 1897..77–8
Forbes, Mr. A., C.S.I., 322
Funeral ceremonies, among Mundas and Oraons, 51–2; among the Hos, 103–4; of a local raja, 303–7

Geological survey, 1866..194
German mission, in Ranchi, 74; a Moravian survival, 76–7; in Chaibasa, 107; church fired upon during Mutiny, 281
Ghasis, 13–14
Ghulam Husain Khan, 219
Gilbert, Lieut.-Colonel, 321
Giridih, 62, 139, 254, 260, 267
Gobindpur, 182–5, 199, 238–242
Gossner, Pastor, 74
Graham, Lieut., 224–7, 275–8
Grand Trunk Road, opening of, 5–6; desertion of, 7–8; chap. ix.; 74, 278, 284–5
Grimley, Mr. W. H., C.I.E., 322
Gulgulias, 52–4
Gunpat Rai Panre, 283, 286–7
Gwalior Mandir, 146–7

Hannynton, Capt., 321
Hatia, 282–3
Hazaribagh district: included in Ramgarh Hill Tract, 18; formed into separate district, 23; Birhors of, 45–6; description of, 263; Giridih mines, 267; few industries, 267–8; Ichak, 268–70; Chatra, 270–1
Hazaribagh, supposed origin of name, 229; description of, 254–9; Lord Northbrook and Sir George Campbell, 259–60; monument in Katcherry compound, 260–1; old cantonments, 261–2; Dublin University Mission, 262–3

Her Majesty's 53rd Foot, 285–286
Hewitt, Mr. J. F. K., 322
Hindus, influx of, 5–6, 19–23; Churuk Puja, 54–5; claim of local zemindars to be, 15–16, 44–5
Hos, Larka or Fighting Kols, fable of their origin, 13; join in Kol mutiny, 21–3, 94–95; occupation of Singbhum, 27, 87–90; funeral ceremonies, 51; exclusiveness of, 86–8, 103–4; quarrels with Rajas of Singbhum, 89–90; fighting powers of, 90–5; under British rule, 95–6; physique, 99; Ho women, 99–103; Magh festival, 104–5; characteristics of, 105–9; national hunt, 109–12; *see* chap. iv
Hundru Gagh, 81

Ichak, 268–270
Ikir Bonga, 34–5

Jagannath, temple of, 66–9
Jagdao Singh, Parganait, 278–79
Jagoo, Dewan of Porohat, 293
Jai Mangal Singh, 277, 281
Jail, Purulia, 171; Ranchi, broken open by mutineers, 281; Hazaribagh, 258–89
Jains, in Singbhum, 86; their temple of Parasnath, 138–158; in Manbhum, 180–2
Jharkhand, 10
Jherria, 3, 183; centre of coal-field, 189–204
Jhitnath Sahai, Thakur, 282–4
Jhitpur, 186
Jom Sim, 133

Kakraj, 286
Kali, 179–80
Kharwars, 208–11, 223–7
Kolhan, chap. iv
Kols, 26–40
Kunhuri, 255
Kunti, 78–9
Kurkabad, 236
Kuru, 284

Lac, 170, 267–8
Laikdih, 189
Larka or Fighting Kols. *See* under Hos
Lesliegunj, 227
Liebert, Mr., 273–4
Lohardaga, 23–4, 227

Mackenzie, Major, 321
Madhuban temples, 142–7
Magh festival, 104–5
Maharajas of Chota Nagpore (Nagbansis), legend of their origin, 9–11; Durgan Sal, 45th Maharaja, 11–12; earliest home, 57–8; ruined palaces of, 64–6; Dripnath Sahai in Singbhum, 90
Mahdab Singh, jemadar, 281–282, 287
Majhli Mandir, 145
Malin Budhi, 120–1
Manbhum, opening up of, 5–6; included in Ramgarh Hill Tract, 18; separate district, 23; Bhumij Kols, Santals, and Kherrias, 27–8; cultivation of, 160–5; Pachete, 166; Raghunathpur, 169; Purulia, 170–5; emigration, 175–7; Bhumij Kols, 177–9; Jain remains, 180–2; *see* chap. vii.
Mangles, Mr. A. C., 321
Manjhi, 118–19
Marang Buru, the Great Spirit, 14–15; his importance, 34–35; creation of human beings, 119–24
Marindin, Mr. C. R., 322

Marriage customs, among Kherrias, 47–50; Mundas, 50–1; Hos, 102–3; Santals, 127–9
Mewa Lal, Sarishtadar, 287–290, 295
Mica, 267
Milman, Bishop, 75
Missions, in Ranchi, 74–7; in Singbhum, 107–8; at Pokhuria, 186–7
Mohurrum, 55–65
Moravian custom, 76–7
Mundas, legend of their origin, 12–14; settlement in Chota Nagpore, 26–7; characteristics of, 27–33; mythology, 33–40; Munda and Pahn, 40–4; marriage customs, 50–51; funeral rites, 51; graveyards and memorial stones, 52
Musulmans, conquer Chota Nagpore, 11–12; figure in Santal legend, 14; influx of, 19–21; the Mohurrum, 55–56
Mutiny, of the Kols, 19–23; of sepoys, *see* chap. xi., 78–79, 94–5

NAGBANSIS. *See* Maharajas of Chota Nagpore
Nation, Major, 286
Native Infantry, 7th and 8th, 273
Nichli Mandir, 144–5
Nirsha, 234–5
Northbrook, Lord, 260
Nowagarh, 198

OAKES, Captain, 273–5
Ojha, 38–9, 132–3
Oraons, mutiny of, 6; settlement of, 27; Sarhul festival, 42–4; characteristics of, 44; funeral ceremonies, 51; boast of, 85
Ouseley, Colonel, 72, 321

PACHETE, 166–7
Padma, 268
Pahn, 40–4
Pak Don, 129
Pakhira, 180
Palamau, included in Ramgarh Hill Tract, 18; Parheyas and Brijias, 28; separate district, 83; chap. viii.
Palandu, 81
Palkot, 65–6
Palma, 180
Pandra, 236
Parasnath, the Home of the Gods, 3, 181; chap. vi.
Parheyas, 28
Parvati, 9–10
Penitentiary, Hazaribagh, 255–257
Pilchu Budhi, 122–4
Pilchu Haram, 122–4
'Pimple,' the, 68
Pitoria, 66, 275, 282
Pokhuria, 186–8
Pratap Rai, 211–15
Pundarika Nag, 9–11
Purulia, headquarters station of Manbhum, 170–3, 203–4

RAGHU DAO, 294–5
Raghunath Sahi, Raja, 65
Raghunathpur, 169, 188
Rajgunj, 243
Rajputs, 15, 45
Ramgarh, light infantry, 18, 73, 24, 272–3, 287–95; ruined palace of Rajas of, 268–9
Ramgarh Hill Tract, 17–18
Ramtollya, 79
Ranchi, headquarters station of Chota Nagpore, 24; situation of, 69; description of, 70–4; cathedral, 75; Moravian custom, 76; during Mutiny, 272–87
Rigunjan, 194, 203
Rath-jatra festival, 67–8
Rattray's Sikhs, 285–6
Reformatory, Hazaribagh, 257–258

Rinadag, 255
Robinson, Mr. W. L., 321
Rohtasgarh, 208–11
Roughsedge, Major, 18, 191–2, 222, 321

Sangai river, 288–9
Santals, legends of their origin, 14–15; antipathy to Brahmins, 15; funeral rites, 51; Santal village, 113–18; manjhi, 118–19; legend of creation of the world, 119–24; marriage ceremonies, 127–9; Sohrae festivals, 131–132; ojha, 132–33; national hunt, 134–7 at; Pokhuria, 186–7
Saranda of the Seven Hundred Hills, 88, 109–10
Sarhul festival, 42–3, 133
Sarna, the Sacred Grove, 35, 41–4
Sealy, Mr. C. T., 18
Semi-Hinduised races, 16, 44–45
Seraikela, 91, 289–96
Serimerah Ghat, 294
Shaista Khan, 211–13
Sherghati, 17
Shráddh ceremony, 302–7
Sijua, 192
Silli, 58
Silwar Hill, 254
Simpson, Captain, 273–4
Sing Bonga, the Sun, 13, 33–9, 82
Singbhum, included in Ramgarh Hill Tract, 23; settled by the Hos, 27; account of, chap. iv.
Sirdar, 37
Sitagarha, 255, 273
Slacke, Mr. F. A., 322
Sohrae festival, 120
Sole Hako, 120
South-west Frontier Agency, 23–4; agents to Governor-General in, 321
Stevens, Sir Cecil, K.C.S.I., 322
Subarnarekha river, 27, 59, 167
Surajkund, 247–50
Svetambaras, 143, 145, 149–53

Taimara, 82
Tamar, 20, 78
Tapkara, 77–8
Taylor, Captain, 261
Taylor, Mr. V. T., 321
Tea-gardens, Assam, 44, 175–7; on Parasnath, 149; in Hazaribagh, 267
Tej Rai, 213–14
Telkupi, 181–2
Thakur Bari, 299
Thakur, the Supreme Being, 119–22
Tibat, 255
Tirthankaras, 157, 181
Topechanchi, 243–6
Tulin, 175
Tundi, 3, 113, 185, 186
Tussor silk, 188

Urjun Singh, Maharaja of Porohat, 288–96

Vikramaditaya, 16

Wellesley, Marquis, 91
Wilkinson, Sir Thomas, 94, 321

Zabardast Khan, 213–4

THE END